Information Highways and Byways

Information Highways and Byways

From the Telegraph to the 21st Century

Irwin Lebow

IEEE PRESS

The Institute of Electrical and Electronics Engineers, Inc., New York

This book may be purchased at a discount from the publisher when ordered in bulk quantities. For more information, contact:

IEEE PRESS Marketing
Attn: Special Sales
P.O. Box 1331
445 Hoes Lane
Piscataway, NJ 08855-1331
Fax: (908) 981-8062

Printed in the United States of America

10 9 8 7 6 5 4 3 2 1

ISBN 0-7803-1073-X

IEEE Order Number: PP4275

Library of Congress Cataloging-in-Publication Data

Lebow, Irwin.
  Information highways and byways : from the telegraph to the twenty
-first century / by Irwin Lebow.
      p. cm.
  Includes bibliographical references (p.) and index.
  ISBN 0-7803-1073-X
  1. Communication--History--19th century. 2. Communication-
-History--20th century. I. Title.
P90.L365 1995
302.2'09034--dc20   94-45457
                                                               CIP

To my children and theirs

Judy and Andy
Sam and Sonia
Bill and Laura
David and Coletta
Jeremy

Contents

Preface

Communications is in the midst of a revolution. It is one of those revolutions where you know something important is happening even though you cannot tell exactly what it is. Hardly a day goes by without the appearance of a news item touching on some aspect of the subject. It may be about some new technical development, or about a merger or acquisition, or, perhaps, a court decision or some activity on Capitol Hill. Some of the items have national politics as their source—terms such as *information superhighway* and *National Information Infrastructure* figured prominently in the Clinton/Gore campaign in 1992 and later in their administration. Many of these items are considered significant enough to merit a headline in the business section of the newspaper. Every once in a while, an event makes the front page. Some are even newsworthy enough to be boiled down to sound bites for the television evening news. However, it is in the nature of journalism that each item is written independently of all others, and so the story of the revolution reaches to you in bits and pieces. Thus, while today's story may be quite clear in its own right, its relationship to yesterday's story is anything but.

Of course, most of us do not need the press to tell us that something revolutionary is happening. We can sense it from the way in which our own businesses and professions have become increasingly dependent on computers and communications. Yet even with this hands-on experience, it is hard for anyone, information professional or not, to make sense out of these disconnected press reports.

As I tried to decipher the significance of the day-by-day events, I asked myself how a layperson might gain such an understanding. I soon came to the not unreasonable conclusion that to understand where we are and where we are going, it is necessary to understand where we have been. Or, to use the transportation metaphor that appears so often in the press, the information superhighway can only be understood by traversing the byways and highways that have led up to it.

While there are obviously many differences between the communications world of today and that of the last century, there are trends that began in the days of Samuel F. B. Morse that are still current. The dominant trend has been the steady stream of inventions and technology. If we are dazzled by the new technology that has appeared in our lifetimes, just imagine how our nineteenth-century forebears were affected by the telegraph, the telephone, and the wireless. Not only did the new gadgets captivate the public, but their inventors became national heroes.

However, to ascribe everything that has happened in communications in the 150 years since Morse to technology is a vast oversimplification, because, typically, as soon as the technology appeared, entrepreneurs—the inventor and others—rushed in to exploit it. And almost as soon as that happened, the courts began to play a role by adjudicating the suits and countersuits, first over patent rights and later over antitrust issues. (For example, the biggest story of them all in recent years was the breakup of the Bell system, a legal action precipitated by entrepreneurship that had technology at its roots.) Thus the story of communications is as much about entrepreneurship and litigation as it is about inventions and technology. To obtain a coherent picture of what is happening today and what might happen as we move into the next century, it is essential to have a view of the three-stranded fabric out of which this history has been woven.

Trying to clarify the historical path to today's communications revolution is what motivated me to start writing this book. But it did not take too long before I became fascinated by the story itself, not only by the inventions, entrepreneurship, and litigation, but also by the inventors, entrepreneurs and lawyers, a parade of colorful people, many of them with extraordinary vision whose exploits have influenced our history and our culture. This has made the book into one that chronicles not only events but also the people responsible for them and the cultural changes that have resulted from them.

The book is for anyone interested in the information revolution regardless of technical background. Its thrust is to describe a history driven by technology not the technology itself, and, to this end, I have seen to it that anyone, regardless of background, can understand enough of the technology to appreciate the historical developments.

Acknowledgments

I owe debts of gratitude to many people who helped me in many ways.

Andy Oram read an early draft of the manuscript and made many helpful suggestions about how to bring out long term trends. Conversations with Lee Paschall gave me insight into the history of military communications. He also read the almost final manuscript and made helpful suggestions from his own background as both a general officer and a historian. Similarly, conversations with Robert Kahn over many years time gave me his unique insight into the beginnings of computer communications and into today's trends. He also made many helpful comments on the almost final manuscript.

Jonathan Coopersmith, A. Michael Noll, and Brian Evans reviewed the manuscript at different stages of its progress and I am grateful to all of them for their comments and suggestions. Any deficiencies that remain are, of course, attributable to me and not to them.

I am grateful to many others for information in specific areas. Lucien Capone, Nick Frankhouser, Bill Harding, and Stuart Starr gave me the benefit of their experience in specific aspects of military communications. I talked to Howard Blank early in the process and obtained his view of the communications industry. An interview with Ross Glatzer of Prodigy gave me insight into the workings of information service companies. Discussions with Michael Marcus of the FCC helped me with the regulatory environment. I spoke at length with John Seazholtz and Jay Grossman of Bell Atlantic to gain insight into the views of today's Bell companies. David Lebow located research papers describing the economic impact of the early telegraph. William and Laura Lebow were helpful in finding information about the origins of electrical engineering as an academic discipline. Judy Lebow made some excellent suggestions on the layout and artistic design of the book. I would also like to thank Lynn Schafer Gross who kindly made available the proofs of Chapter 4 of her book "The International World of Electronic Media," McGraw Hill, 1995.

Many of the photographs came from the Center for the History of Electrical Engineering, a joint project of the IEEE and Rutgers University. Andrew Goldstein, Curator of the Center was very helpful, cooperative and patient in guiding me through his archives, making available the ones I selected, and pointing me to other sources. I am grateful to Tom Lewis, the author of Empire of the Air, for sending me his personal copy of the New York Herald-Tribune article describing Howard Armstrong's suicide and to Frank Heart for sending his personal copy of a photograph of the original ARPANET team. I am also grateful for Norma MacCormack's help in finding suitable photographs in the AT&T archives.

My thanks also goes to Ann Westerlin of Texas Instruments, Jean Stitt of Western Union, and Phyllis Smith of the David Sarnoff Research Center for making photographs available. My thanks also go to the people at the IEEE Press for their help. I am especially grateful to Dudley Kay, Director of Book Publishing, and Deborah Graffox, in Production, who so carefully and cheerfully carried out the laborious process of converting my manuscript into a book.

The final word of thanks goes to my wife, Grace, who was always there to offer encouragement in this endeavor as she has in so many other ways for so many years.

Irwin Lebow
Washington, DC

Introduction

Ours is the Information Age. Just as previous ages were named after the technology that dominated their civilizations, so ours is designated as it is because of the central role played by information in the way we live and do business.

When did the Information Age begin? It is not the kind of thing that one can date very precisely. The term began to be used in the 1960s when it was becoming apparent that the computer was affecting more and more aspects of our lives and that its marriage to communications would accelerate its influence. The computer was becoming the repository of information of all kinds, and communication systems were making it available far and wide.

But, in a very real sense, society has always depended on information. The problem was that, until the advent of electrical technology, it took so long to obtain information that people lived their lives and made their decisions more in its absence than its presence. A case can be made for the invention of the printing press as the milestone that started the age of information, but a better case can be made for the invention of the device that first liberated the transfer of information from physical transportation. This device was, of course, the telegraph. The transmission of those famous words "What hath God wrought!" from Washington to Baltimore took place 150 years ago, and the world has never been the same since.

Books and articles keep telling us how this Information Age in which we live is going to change our lives at a rapid rate as we move into the future. The world will be wired up with optical cable, these writers tell us, and this cable will bring us multimedia information that will allow us to do all manner of things that are impossible today. Instead of going out to the video store to rent a film for an evening's entertainment, we will simply select any one of hundreds of offerings from a menu on our computer, and we will have the movie in short order. With another menu we may call up the catalog of our local public library and even the Library of Congress and request electronic transmission of all kinds of information. If we do not know where the information we want resides, a Knowbot will search all the libraries and other sources of information in the country to find it for us.

Yes, the Information Age is going to provide all these and still more wondrous things in the future. Yet many of those predicting the future write as if this rapid change brought about by advances in information technology is something unique to our times. But this is only so if we date "our times" from the inception of electrical communication in the days of Morse.

When facsimile first became common a few years ago, the average office worker was astounded that a little box could actually reproduce a document thousands of miles away. Is this more remarkable than the telephone that did the same for the human voice well over a century ago? We marvel at how television brings world events into our homes and how its graphic portrayals contributed to the fall of the Soviet empire. But is this feat more earthshaking in our day than was the emergence of newspapers that carried timely news of the Mexican War as a result of the new telegraph, or the way radio broadcasting took the nation by storm in the 1920s?

We think that our generation is unique because of the wondrous modern inventions of things like desktop computers, fax machines, VCRs, and compact discs. The fact is that a parade of inventions has been the rule in every generation ever since Morse's time. The details have changed with the march of technology, but people's attitudes have not. As revolutionary as we imagine today's information technology to be, the succession of new devices that began with Morse's telegraph were at least as revolutionary in their time both in the way people reacted to them and in the way they affected the lives of our forebears.

There is indeed a world of difference between the crude inventions of the last century and the sophisticated technology of this one. There is similarly a large gulf separating Morse and the other early inventor-heroes with little scientific training working in their home workshops and today's teams of anonymous, highly trained scientists and engineers working in sophisticated industrial laboratories.

But these differences notwithstanding, the result of the advances in communication from the 1840s to the present and beyond has been to replace transportation by electricity as the vehicle for transferring information from one place to another. The overall effect has been to bring people and events together without requiring their physical presence. It was as true for the early telegraph and telephone as it is for today's automatic teller machines, fax machines, and cable television systems. And just as the societal effects of the new technologies were essentially unpredictable in their day, so no one can predict with any accuracy what new technologies the future will bring and how they will affect the way we live and work. The history of communications has been filled with surprise, and there is no reason to expect this to change as we move into the future.

We are essentially no different from generations past in our craving for information and in our eagerness to take advantage of the technology that brings information closer to us. Even modern technology itself did not spring up out of nowhere. It is, rather, the latest in a long sequences of steps. And what the future will bring is nothing more than the next steps in the sequence. "There is nothing new under the sun," wrote the author of Ecclesiastes more than 2000 years ago. This bit of wisdom surely does not apply to technology, but it certainly does to the way we react to the technology.

Indeed, it all started with Morse. What has happened since is his legacy.

. . . it would not be long ere the whole surface of this country would be channelled for those nerves which are to diffuse, with the speed of thought, a knowledge of all that is occurring throughout the land; making, in fact, one neighborhood of the whole country.

Samuel F. B. Morse

Part

I

Wiring up the World

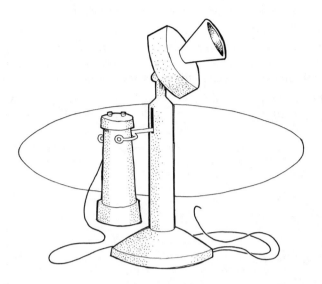

In the days before World War II, the Western Union boy delivering telegrams on his bicycle was a familiar sight in every American city. Today, the telegram is pretty much out of style, having been replaced by overnight mail delivery, facsimile, and electronic mail. This situation is not surprising since the telegraph is now 150 years old. On the contrary, the fact that people still send telegrams at all is a remarkable tribute to the staying power of this venerable medium of information exchange.

The telegraph was the *first kid on the block*, the first in a long sequence of inventions and technologies designed to exchange information electrically. Before it, information exchange was tied to transportation. Just before the telegraph hit the scene, transportation, and, with it, communication, was being transformed by the steam engine. But this transformation pales in comparison to the revolution in communication caused by replacing transportation by electricity.

All the telegraph did was to reduce the time to send messages from one place to another from days, weeks, or months to a few hours, and it was this time compression that produced unpredictable societal changes. While the telegraph itself has all but faded away, replaced by other communication techniques, most of the social and economic patterns developed in its wake have nevertheless persisted to our day.

The telegraph changed the world in many surprising and unexpected ways. But then, at the very pinnacle of its success, came the biggest surprise of all: a competing system that was to eclipse it in popularity in just a few years. The telephone provided even faster means of communication than the telegraph. But it was not speed alone that made the telephone the irreplaceable device that it has become. Rather it was its *user friendliness* in an age long before that term was coined. Nothing could be more natural than a telephone conversation. The telegraph required an intermediary in the form of a Morse code operator. The telephone required only the human voice and the human ear.

The telegraph started the process of wiring up the world; the telephone continued the process, and the world has never been the same.

Chapter

1

"The American Leonardo"

The idea of the telegraph came to Samuel Finley Breeze Morse in what he called a "flash of genius".[1] He was returning home across the Atlantic in 1832, after three years of study and work in Europe as a portrait artist, and became engaged in a conversation with fellow passengers on the experiments of the famous French physicist André Marie Ampère in electricity and magnetism. How did it happen that a group of people, educated, to be sure, but not especially in physical science, would occupy their time on board ship in discussing the experiments of a physicist? On the face of it, it seems comparable to a group of artists, physicians, and businesspeople today discussing the big-bang theory of the origin of the universe while on a Caribbean cruise. But the fact is that the cleavage between physical science and other branches of knowledge pointed out by C. P. Snow in this century was not nearly so evident early in the nineteenth century. Today it is more likely that the conversation between people in such circumstances would have to do with politics, finance, perhaps the theater or the arts, anything but science. To be sure, *A Brief History of Time*, Stephen Hawking's book on cosmology, was an unexpected best-seller, but I wonder how many of its readers derived enough understanding from it to make it part of their social conversation. But in the early part of the nineteenth century the notions of electricity and magnetism being studied by the likes of Ampère and Michael Faraday captivated their contemporaries and were widely reported in the press of the day.

Someone in Morse's group raised the question as to whether the speed of electricity through a wire was retarded by the length of the wire. The answer given by Dr. Charles Jackson, a Boston physician, later to be celebrated as the discoverer of anesthesia, was that electricity passed instantly over any length of wire. Of course, Jackson was not quite accurate. We know today that nothing can move instantaneously; the limiting speed is that of light. But to the early nineteenth-century person, the frame of reference for speed was that of a transportation system, whether it was the newly invented railroad train or the stage coach that it was replacing, or a sailing ship such as the one on which they were traveling. Without quibbling about the relative speeds of any of these, they were all far from instantaneous. The speed of light, even if they had some conception of what it was, was so fast that it was instantaneous as far as anyone was concerned.

The notion of using the speed of electrical propagation to send information captivated the middle-aged artist. By the time the ship reached New York, Morse had sketched out the broad outlines of the telegraph system—the transmitter, receiver, and, above all, the code that came to bear his name.

It is interesting to speculate as to what impelled Morse to do this. He was one of those people who in his youth did not appear to have a burning ambition to achieve in a particular field. He seems to have been motivated largely by an ambition to succeed in something, no matter what, perhaps as a way of keeping up with his father, Jedidiah Morse, a Massachusetts clergyman who had attained fame as an outstanding geographer. Young Finley attended Yale, graduating in 1810 without particular distinction. While there, he showed some aptitude for science, taking courses in chemistry and electricity. But even if he had had a burning ambition in science, there was little calling for such talents. He had a more obvious artistic talent, for which there was some market. Thus, upon graduation, he turned his attention to painting. He was ultimately to become a highly respected artist, a professor of art at New York University, and founder of the National Academy of Fine Arts. His later success with the telegraph was to earn him the name "the American Leonardo."

But then, as today, the road to success as an artist was long and difficult. Morse studied abroad and, on his return, plunged into the local art milieu, gradually building his reputation. At the same time, he continued to maintain some connection with the scientific world, particularly with the experiments in electricity that were going on at the time. Thus, when he embarked from France in 1832 to return home after his second tour in Europe, he was apparently as current as any layperson on the latest developments in the world of electricity and magnetism. We have no clue as to what specifically prompted his self-proclaimed "flash of genius." He probably just put two and two together. If, indeed, electricity traveled instantaneously, and, if this electricity could be made to represent information in some way, then information could be sent to distant places instantaneously. What remained to be done was to determine the representation and build transmitting and receiving devices. And, with his smattering of technical knowledge, that was what he set out to do. He certainly had no particular application in mind. He simply had the intuition that the ability to communicate electrically was so revolutionary that humankind could not help but benefit from it in some way.

Morse was not the first to work on the idea of telegraphy. Several before him on both sides of the Atlantic had tried their luck with varying degrees of success, although he was unaware of their efforts. One of his American predecessors was the celebrated physicist, Joseph Henry, who, along with the Europeans, was seeking an understanding of the basic properties of electricity. Henry was a scientist who appreciated the role of the engineer. His philosophy is exemplified by his words in 1858 at the celebration in New York of the completion of the first Atlantic cable: "The distinctive feature of the history of the nineteenth century is the application of abstract science to the useful arts, and the subjection of the innate powers of the intellect as the obedient slave of civilized man."[2] But, in the end, he was more personally attuned to abstract science than to its application, and he was quick to encourage and assist Morse. Later some friction developed between the two men, resulting from Henry's feeling that Morse denigrated the role played by pure science and by Morse's resentment of the prevalent feeling among scientists that the intellectual foundations of invention were somehow less significant than those of the science that spawned them.

The physicists such as Ampère and Henry who, during the seventeenth and eighteenth centuries, were deriving an empirical understanding of the properties of electricity and magnetism, knew little about the fundamental nature of what electricity is. We know today that some of the fundamental atomic particles out of which all matter is composed carry elementary electric charges, and that the phenomenon we call electric current is the result of the flow of these charges through materials such as metallic wires. In the early decades of the nineteenth century, electrons and the other constituents of the atom were not known.

Of course, electricity itself had been known about since the days of ancient Greece. Certain substances when rubbed with the right kind of material had the ability to attract lightweight objects such as feathers and bits of straw. The word itself is derived from *elektron*, the Greek word for amber, the most notable of these substances. Until late in the eighteenth century, scientists investigating the properties of electricity had to use frictional effects hardly more sophisticated than rubbing an amber rod to obtain the electric charges with which to carry out their experiments. The discovery by the Italian scientists, Luigi Galvani and Count Alessandro Volta, that electric charges could be generated chemically led to the development of the device we now know as the battery. Its great appeal to the researchers of the day was its ability to function as a controlled reproducible source of electricity. Using these primitive storage batteries, they were able to observe how the amount of electrical current flowing through a wire depended on the material out of which the wire was made. They knew, for example, that metals conducted electricity well and that, as a result, a metallic wire connected between the two terminals of a battery drew a large current flow.

These early researchers also discovered that the Earth itself was a moderately good conductor. This meant that if both terminals of a battery were connected to the ground, a current would flow from one terminal of the battery to the other through the path or circuit formed by the connecting wires and the ground. As soon as one of the wires was disconnected from the battery, the flow of current was interrupted. Moreover, this same effect was observed even when one of the wires was long and connected to the ground some distance away from the battery.

Morse was also not the first to recognize that information could be transferred by the flow of electric current through a single long wire connecting two distant locations with the return path through the ground. Where Morse differed from the others was in the relative simplicity and reliability of his sending and receiving devices and his technique of sending a unique combination of short and long bursts of electricity—dots and dashes—to represent each letter and number. For example, some of his predecessors used more than one wire; one of them used twenty-six wires, one for each letter of the alphabet. Morse's success in developing a successful sender and receiver combined with his ingenious code is an example of what modern engineers call sound systems engineering.

The sending device is very simple in principle. All that is necessary is to be able to start and stop the flow of current in a convenient way. Morse came up with a device called a *key* to do this. The circuit was normally *open* with no current flowing. Depressing the key *closed* the circuit allowing current to flow as long as the key was depressed. A skilled hand on the key could tap out the pattern of dots and dashes with some facility. Actually, Morse's first sending device was a little more complicated than this, but he soon replaced it with the simple key.

To receive the coded information, one needs a way of telling whether the current is flowing or not and of estimating the duration of the burst of current in order to distinguish between the short dots and long dashes. Morse's technique made use of another then recently discovered principle, the fact that electricity and magnetism are closely related, and it was for this reason that his invention was known as the magnetic telegraph. This relationship is fundamental: Whenever an electric current flows through a wire, the wire becomes temporarily magnetized. No one in Morse's time understood the nature of magnetism any more than they understood electricity. They knew, for example, the empirical fact that some materials were naturally magnetic with the property of attracting iron objects. Other materials, such as soft iron, while not permanently magnetic, became temporarily magnetized when wrapped about with wires carrying electric current and then demagnetized when the current was interrupted. Such a device is called an *electromagnet*, and this was the basis for Morse's telegraph receiver. When electric current flowed through the electromagnet, it deflected a piece of iron connected to a pencil or pen drawn across a roll of paper. The result was a trace that showed the start and stop of each burst of current. Interestingly enough, the American Leonardo built this first receiver on an artist's canvas stretcher.

On his return to the United States, Morse plunged into the telegraph with as much energy as he could muster while simultaneously attempting to earn a living as an artist. With the help of several others, he developed the individual components of the system to the point where he could begin seeking backing for a full-scale demonstration. One of his most important advisors was a chemistry professor named Leonard Gale who would later become a partial owner of the telegraph patent. Gale was also instrumental in introducing Morse to Professor Henry. But the most influential was an eager young man with a technical bent named Alfred Vail. Vail not only refined Morse's crude instruments, but enthusiastically convinced members of his family to help finance the venture. For these efforts, Vail became a trusted friend and partner of Morse. In fact, when Morse applied for a patent in 1837, both Vail and Gale were listed as partners.

Morse looked to the government to support a full-scale demonstration. In 1837, Congress was being urged to support the construction of a telegraph between New York and New Orleans and submitted a request to the secretary of the treasury to report on the feasibility of the project. This circumstance turned out to be Morse's opportunity.

The Treasury Department's request in no way anticipated the electrical telegraph that Morse invented. From ancient times, people, frustrated by the speed limitations of communicating by physical transportation, sought various acoustical and optical schemes for overcoming this barrier as best they could. One such scheme made famous by Henry Wadsworth Longfellow was the lantern system in Boston's Old North church in 1775—"one if by land, two if by sea"—that gave Paul Revere advance warning of the route taken by the British army to quell the rebellious farmers of Massachusetts. By the early part of the nineteenth century, various examples of optical *telegraph* schemes were being constructed on both sides of the Atlantic. These schemes were what is called *semaphore* systems in which information would be transferred from one place to another by a kind of visual code. Two towers would be erected, and letters or other signals would be coded into the positions of a system of movable levers on each tower visible to an observer on the other. In this way information could be sent from one tower to the other as the operators manipulated the levers. Longer distances could be traversed by a series of such towers with the information being relayed from tower to tower. Various European countries had used schemes of this kind, and, in the United States, there was such a system in operation from Boston to Cape Cod near the turn of the century. These systems were hardly ideal. They had many drawbacks, the most obvious of which was their dependence on good weather conditions and the need for multiple relays to achieve even modest ranges.

Morse responded to the Treasury with a letter on the virtues of electrical telegraphy and applied to Congress for $30,000 to conduct a demonstration. But it was not until some five years later in 1842 that the appropriation was finally approved after an agonizing debate. Today we are familiar with the *humor* that sometimes goes on in Congressional debates. Well, that is not a modern phenomenon. Here was a man seeking money for an experiment that most of the lawmakers could not understand, that some thought was dishonest, and some thought was mystical. In fact, the debate was marked by references to the *sciences* of mesmerism and Millerism, named after a sect predicting the Second Coming later that year.

Morse's demonstration is one of those remarkable success stories that one finds more often in fiction than in fact. By 1844 a wire had been strung between Baltimore and Washington using the Baltimore and Ohio railroad right of way. It was over this forty-mile long wire that Morse transmitted the immortal words, "What hath God wrought!" from his telegraph key located in the Supreme Court chamber in Washington to Alfred Vail at the Baltimore railroad depot. Its role three days later in the Democratic National Convention then underway in Baltimore presaged the primary role that the early telegraph would ultimately play. The convention declined to nominate former President Martin Van Buren for a second term, choosing instead James K. Polk. In the attempt to placate the Van Buren forces, the convention nominated his friend, Senator Silas Wright of New York, as vice president. Since Wright was not in Baltimore at the convention, but in Washington, Vail *wired* this news to Morse who relayed it to Wright. Shortly thereafter a return message from Morse informed the convention of Wright's rejection of the nomination. The "lightning line," had made its appearance with a bang.[3]

The term *lightning line* was derived from the verse in the Book of Job, "Canst thou send lightnings, that they may go, and say unto thee, Here we are?" which had become a frequent preface to writings on the telegraph. If the world press reported with enthusiasm on the discoveries in fundamental science, it greeted practical inventions such as the telegraph, and later the telephone and radio, with hysterical enthusiasm and made their inventors national heroes. Along with this enthusiasm was a liberal mixture of mystery and awe. The notion of sending signals electrically was something on the borderline of magic to many. Hundreds of people flocked to see Morse's instruments in Washington and Baltimore. This kind of reception was to characterize the public reaction all during the early years of the telegraph. Even fourteen years after this first success, spontaneous street demonstrations greeted the completion of the first Atlantic cable. This kind of reaction was to continue throughout the century as amazing invention succeeded amazing invention.

Morse apparently did not view the resounding success of his demonstration line as simply a personal one. His vision of the telegraph was appropriately grand. When he first testified before Congress seeking funding for the demonstration, he predicted that "it would not be long ere the whole surface of this country would be channelled for those nerves which are to diffuse, with the speed of thought, a knowledge of all that is occurring throughout the land; making, in fact, one neighborhood of the whole country."[4] Morse's "neighborhood" clearly anticipated Marshall McLuhan's "global village" by well over a century. A neighborhood is, by definition, a community small enough for its inhabitants to be physically close enough to interact freely and easily. While it is still somewhat of an exaggeration to call today's world one neighborhood, nevertheless some of the attributes that Morse had in mind are readily apparent over much of the globe.

It was because of this grand vision that Morse held the conviction that the telegraph should be exploited for the public good to achieve this end, he offered to sell all rights to the government. The postmaster general, fearing the impact of private sector exploitation on his revenue stream, was inclined to accept the offer, but once the demonstration was over, Congress lost its interest, so prevalent was the strict constructionist view of the constitution in which the role of the federal government was severely limited. Because of this attitude, the telegraph was to be exploited in the private sector in the United States, setting the pattern for the telephone, radio, television, and all the other communications devices and systems that were to follow in the years to come. Interestingly enough, everywhere else in the world the telegraph was exploited in the public sector together with the mails,[5] and later with the telephone in a so-called *postal-telegraph-telephone* organization called familiarly the PTT. Only in very recent years has this worldwide pattern been in the public sector together with the mails,[5] and later with the telephone in a so-called *postal-telegraph-telephone* organization called familiarly the PTT. Only in very recent years has this worldwide pattern been modified in a few countries to allow private-sector competition to the established government-controlled systems. Of course, as we now know from 150 years of experience, exploitation in the private sector can mean either monopoly or competition and, over the years, we have seen now one and now the other. And a government such as that of the United States, which has sought to remain aloof from the doings of the private sector, has been forced to take regulatory action to protect the public from the excesses of monopoly in communication as well as elsewhere.

Once the government made its position clear, Morse and his partners proceeded on their own. If the coincidence between the demonstration of the telegraph and the Democratic National Convention was Morse's first bit of fortune, the second was the outbreak of the Mexican War in 1846, shortly before the opening of the first commercial wire in the country. The nation was thirsty for the war news coming from the Southwest. The press had jury-rigged all kinds of special trains, clipper ships, pony express circuits, and the like to speed the news reports to the urban dailies. And they were quick to take advantage of the telegraph lines coming into existence under private ownership. The first of these was a New York to Washington circuit that would make use of the demonstration link for its Baltimore to Washington leg. Its completion in June 1846 was announced in the *New York Herald* as the "first flash of the lightning line from Washington to New York." And it marked the start of a process of wiring the nation into something approximating Morse's "one neighborhood."

Chapter

2

Expanding the Neighborhood

The story of how the telegraph proliferated throughout the entire country in scarcely more than twenty years is a fascinating case study of economic Darwinism in which rampant competition among many entrepreneurs ultimately led to the domination of the industry by a single company. Morse himself was only an indirect participant in the competition. He continued to straddle the technological and artistic worlds by retaining his position as an art professor while allowing his interest in the telegraph to be pursued by others in this entrepreneurial contest. At various times there were companies that used telegraph equipment patented by others in competition with the Morse interests, sometimes covering the same geographic areas with their competing lines. While some of these competing technologies were more sophisticated than Morse's, they were also more complex and less reliable. The virtues of Morse's almost foolproof scheme led to its ultimate triumph in those early years in the face of this competition.

The lines proliferated rapidly and chaotically all over the world. Soon a web of wires covered the entire populated United States. It followed along as the pioneers moved to the west, reaching the Pacific as early as 1861. Three years before this there was a first attempt to cross the Atlantic, an exciting venture that finally failed after four weeks of shaky service when the company was unable to repair an apparent break in the cable.[6] But the fact that an attempt at such a formidable task was made so early in the game is remarkable in its own right. Morse may have invented a way of impressing information on a wire and then retrieving that information at a distant location, but before the telegraph could become a practical communications vehicle, there were numerous problems associated with the wires themselves that had to be overcome. One of the most formidable of these was crossing water. If the body of water was narrow enough, a wire could be strung between poles on either bank. But if the waterway were too wide for that method, there was no choice but to run the wires under the water, not over it, and to do so required the development of waterproof insulation. For want of such insulation, the last leg of the path from Washington to New York had to be traversed initially in the old fashioned way by a messenger who crossed the Hudson River by boat. This hurdle was overcome in short order, and within a few years cable was laid routinely under rivers. Thus, it was only a matter of time before that audacious first attempt to cross the Atlantic. The second attempt was successful, but had to wait for the Civil War to end. There were even plans being made to reach Europe through its back door by laying a cable up to Alaska and across the Bering Strait. But these plans were dropped once it became clear that the second Atlantic cable was going to be a success. Finally, in 1866 there was regular telegraph service between Europe and the United States over this cable. Morse's neighborhood was becoming global.

The year 1866 was also noteworthy because it was then that Western Union finally prevailed in the struggle to dominate the industry in the United States by merging with its chief rival, the American Telegraph Company, the descendent of the original Morse interests. Prior to this merger, one after another of the other competing companies had been bought out or put out of business until it became clear that Western Union was going to win the telegraph war. Even Morse observed naively at the time that the telegraph system was "...becoming, doubtless, a *monopoly*, but no more so than the Post Office system, and its unity is, in reality, a public advantage if properly and uprightly managed, and this of course will depend upon the character of the managers."[7]

The fact that Western Union won the contest is less significant than the fact that the prize was so large. By 1880, there were more than 100,000 miles of telegraph wire in the nation, more than 80 percent of which were controlled by Western Union, which had by then achieved the distinction of being the largest corporation in the nation. The corporation had also achieved the less appealing distinction of being the most hated by the public, a characteristic often brought about by the excesses in which a monopoly is likely to indulge. There were numerous attempts during the latter part of the century to introduce competition through a government-owned or -supported service, but, in the end, all failed. After the turn of the century, there were no more such attempts because Western Union was no longer considered a threat. The telephone was encroaching upon its turf.

What applications justified this enormous growth? In 1854, Henry David Thoreau was dubious about the whole thing when he wrote in *Walden*:

> We are in great haste to construct a magnetic telegraph from Maine to Texas; but Maine and Texas, it may be, have nothing important to communicate. . . . We are eager to tunnel under the Atlantic and bring the old world some weeks nearer to the new; but perchance the first news that will leak through to the broad, flapping American ear will be that Princess Adelaide has the whooping cough.[8]

One would expect, of course, that a person such as Thoreau who glorified the virtues of solitude would not be impressed by the proliferation of a system that increased communicability. Considering this, it is perhaps fortunate for Thoreau that he did not live long enough to witness the arrival of the telephone, the device that, more than any other, constituted an invasion of privacy. For while the telegraph had a major effect on the reporting of news, some of which was undoubtedly trivial by his standards, its other uses were what might be called legitimate business applications. Telegrams might have been used to some minor extent for personal gossip, but the telegraph was too expensive and not sufficiently *user friendly* to be used for too much of this. It was extensively used for sending information of importance to people in carrying out their business affairs expeditiously. It was not the telegraph but the telephone that became the universal instrument of human discourse, the instrument that people have continued to use both to exchange necessary information and for the closeness and intimacy that only the human voice can impart.

What the telegraph accomplished was to expand the boundaries of the region within which information could be exchanged before it became stale, because information, like other kinds of goods, is perishable. Stale information may have some value in some circumstances, but it is certainly different from its value when fresh. As a case in point, it is important that a person speculating in stocks know the going market price; an outdated price is as useless to the speculator as a head of lettuce that has sat on the shelf too long is to a chef. The kind of information that we call *news* affects us completely differently when it is reported so long after the event that it takes on the characteristics of history. As long as information had to travel at the speed of transportation vehicles, the distance over which it held its freshness was small. Once the telegraph liberated information transfer from transportation, the world became a very different place in which to live and do business.

There are many examples of this change, running from the dramatic to the mundane. Perhaps the most dramatic of all is the effect of the telegraph on the British empire. Early in the nineteenth century a person sending a letter from London to Calcutta could not expect a reply until some two years had passed.[9] The reason for this almost unbelievable delay was both the length of the path and effect of monsoons on sailing ships in the Indian Ocean. Beginning in the 1840s, wires were strung along pieces of the path allowing the transit time to be reduced commensurately. By 1870, telegraph wires spanned the whole distance and the turnaround was reduced to one day. This dramatic reduction of time was of incalculable value to the British in helping it cement together its worldwide empire, although I imagine that many of those British officials stationed in India looked back with some nostalgia upon their former autonomy.

Less dramatic but no less important was the way in which the railroad and the telegraph together helped forge the rapidly spreading population of the United States into a coherent nation within its broad boundaries.[10] The telegraph made its appearance so soon after the railroad— The Baltimore and Ohio Railroad had begun a small line from Baltimore to the West just four years before Morse's "flash of genius"—that the two were essentially concurrent in the way they spread through the country and the world. Robert Luther Thompson, the author of the definitive history of the early telegraph, put it well when he wrote:

> Perhaps the greatest value of the telegraph to the country was the part it played in breaking down isolation throughout the length and breadth of the land, and in fostering the feeling of nationality. Upon the completion of the transcontinental telegraph in 1861, for example, California was no longer a distant province only nominally associated with the government in Washington; it became an integral part of the nation . . . . A stronger and more unified nation—a people possessed of a self-assurance based upon a new sense of security—emerged with the development of the telegraph and the railroad.[11]

Of course, the telegraph and railroad interests did not plan this out as a joint project. The two spread cooperatively because it was in the self interest of each to do so, as a result of each being important to the other in the furtherance of its own peculiar interest. As the railroads were being rapidly expanded, the traffic level could not justify the expense of laying dual tracks between locations. But with single-track lines, the trains had to be scheduled very carefully and operated very conservatively to avoid accidents. A train would be run from, say, east to west on a route if the schedule did not call for a west-to-east train during its expected transit time. If one was expected, then the east-to-west train would wait until the other train had passed. But what if the latter were late? The prudent course of action would be to wait. But it was often tempting to take a chance, sometimes with disastrous results. Introduction of the telegraph to assist in scheduling permitted many railroad companies to double the capacity of these single-track lines at a cost that was far less than that of doubling the track.[12]

To the telegraph companies, the railroads constituted more than just another customer. Railroad beds were ideal locations over which to run wires. (This is of still more significance to the communications companies of today when so little real estate is available for such purposes and values are so high.) Consequently, a telegraph company that entered into an agreement with a railroad had an essential advantage over another company that had to find an alternate right-of-way to attempt to compete over the same route. In England the two industries worked hand-in-glove from the start. But in America the railroads' natural conservatism made them reluctant partners at first, especially since the early telegraph was not particularly reliable. By the 1850s when it had become apparent to the railroads that there was a tangible benefit to be gained from cooperation, they began to overcome this reluctance.

This cooperation between the railroads and telegraph companies paid further dividends of benefit to the many industries that used the railroads to transport their goods. With the development of the refrigerator car late in the nineteenth century, fresh produce was being shipped all over the country by rail. Indeed, the importance of such transportation innovations have been widely studied by economic historians. Much less attention has been paid to the importance of communication innovations. The refrigerator cars would have been much less effective had not the telegraph been there to assist in the transport process. Because just as the telegraph was used for scheduling the trains themselves, it could also be used to coordinate the distribution of the cars to the appropriate locations and to the delivery of ice to the stations along the route. The speed of telegraph communication also allowed the distributors to modify the destination of cars while they were en route to respond to last-minute changes in demand. The refrigerator car also changed the character of the meat-packing industry radically, allowing the animals to be slaughtered in the West rather than being shipped on the hoof to the eastern markets at far greater cost. The scheduling and management of these shipments would have been inefficient without the telegraph to assist in managing the logistics.[13]

The perishability of financial information has made the communication of market-related information a high-priority item among financial speculators, and they were among the earliest beneficiaries of the rapid communication offered by the telegraph. Before the telegraph arrived, individuals in the financial community would spare no effort to improvise fast communications to derive an edge over their competitors. There is the now-famous story of such an improvisation in which the Rothschild banking family turned their early information about the outcome of the

Battle of Waterloo to financial advantage. A Rothschild agent jumped into a boat at Ostend, Belgium late in the afternoon of June 19, 1815 with a newly printed *Dutch Gazette* describing the battle, reaching Nathan Rothschild at Folkstone harbor in England the next morning. Rothschild sped to London with the information, informing the government of the news hours before the arrival of Wellington's official envoy. He thereupon proceeded to his customary position on the stock exchange floor and began to sell his government bonds, driving the price down. Other traders attributed his action to inside knowledge that Wellington had been defeated and, in the panic that ensued, drove the prices through the floor. Whereupon Rothschild changed his sell orders to buy.

Of course, most financial dealings are more humdrum. In the absence of rapid information from great distances, traders would do the best they could. During the nineteenth century, U.S. government bonds were widely held in Europe and traded on a London market. In the days before the Atlantic cable was installed, the turn-around time for information exchange was about six weeks. Because this time was so long, the London and New York markets were essentially decoupled; any rapid price fluctuations in either location would not be felt in the other. In fact, the prices on the two exchanges differed significantly until 1866 when the Atlantic cable was put into operation. This same phenomenon was also noted in domestic markets that were far enough away from one another to make communication by transportation take so long that prices could change substantially in the interim. It is understandable, then, that investors have always been among the first to take advantage of new technologies that would increase their speed of access to information about the markets.[14]

Clearly, anyone with large sums of money at stake is an important consumer of news of relevance to his or her business dealings. Most people are not in that position. But, despite the sarcastic fulminations of the Thoreaus of the world, it appears to be a universal human trait to seek information about the comings and goings of both famous and ordinary people and about current events. It is because of this thirst for such news that the most important application of the early telegraph was in helping to create the press in the form in which we know it today.

Chapter

3

The Telegraph and the News

The outbreak of the Mexican War in 1846, only two years after Morse's first public demonstration, caused the nation to focus on what was to become the most important use of the early telegraph, an application that became so closely associated with the telegraph that the growth of the one could not readily be distinguished from the growth of the other. This application was the reporting of news. The telegraph completely transformed the business of news in ways that could not have been dreamed of before the invention. In the process, it established new institutions that have remained with us to this day. The story of how this happened is a wonderful example of the unpredictability of the paths on which new technology can lead us.

News is a very perishable commodity. A news event is, by definition, a piece of information that is something you hear for the first time and can therefore be called *new*. In today's world, we also expect that news is *new* in the sense that it happened very recently. But this expectation is strictly a modern phenomenon. Before the modern age, that criterion was applicable only to things that happened close by. Information about things that happened far away was reported long after the events occurred, usually so long after that the recipients of the news could do little but sit back passively and treat the events as history.

The whole notion of a written journal of current events is a relatively modern phenomenon.[15] Three things were necessary for the success of such a journal. The first ingredient was technical: There had to be an inexpensive way of reproducing a substantial number of copies of the pages. The second ingredient was political: Those responsible for reporting on events had to be free to write with minimal interference so that the recipients of the reports would find them to be believable and not simply government propaganda. In this regard, we have only to note that the so-called newspapers of the former Soviet Union were not taken seriously by average Russians. They obtained believable reports, if they dared, from the shortwave radio broadcasts of the the Voice of America and the British Broadcasting Company. The third requirement was again technological: There must be a way of gathering the information in a reasonably expeditious way wherever it happens.

The invention of the movable type printing press in the fifteenth century satisfied the first requirement, freeing the reproduction process from laborious manual operations. Until this invention, books were precious commodities and newspapers were inconceivable. But it was not until some two centuries later that the second requirement was met sufficiently well to permit newspapers to appear on the scene. The event that made this possible in England was the abolition of the Star Chamber (a court with arbitrary powers operating outside the regular system of justice) in 1641. It was only then that the first more or less free weekly appeared with the outside title, *The Head of Severall Proceedings in the Present Parliament* and the inside title, *Diurnal Occurrences*. Even then, we have to be careful in referring to concepts such as free speech and a free press in the context of the seventeenth century. That they did not exist in the modern sense is evidenced by the fact that the first paper in the colonies was published in Boston in 1690 by Benjamin Harris, once a bookseller and publisher in London, who fled from England after having been imprisoned for printing a seditious pamphlet. This paper, with the impressive title, *1690 Publick Occurrences both Forreign and Domestick*, was suppressed after its first issue. But even with these freedom limitations, it was still possible for newspapers to be published throughout the colonies and all over Europe in the eighteenth century.

The ability to gather news rapidly from anywhere in the world was not satisfied until the middle of the nineteenth century. It is, therefore, easy to see why the newspapers that predated that capability were far different from their successors. The only news that they could gather directly was local, and they did this in ways that are quite haphazard by today's standards. There was no such thing as a news reporter; the publisher would print news that he heard about or that was brought to him by interested citizens. Out-of-town news was obtained by an informal arrangement in which the newspapers in various cities in the country were exchanged by mail. Foreign news was obtained in a similar way. The publishers would meet the ships as they came from England carrying British newspapers. At the same time they would pick up whatever gossip they could from the passengers. Because of the paucity of news, it is understandable that these papers were published only weekly or semi-weekly.

It was the telegraph that provided the third ingredient and, in so doing, led the way to the creation of the newspaper as we know it today. But the telegraph had some help. Almost as if the press knew what was coming, the transformation began in the 1830s with the emergence of what came to be called the Penny Press. The name came from the price of the new papers: one cent instead of the six-cent price tag on the current papers. These papers were, in fact, smaller in size to help make the lower price viable. But more significant was the fact the new papers were aimed at the lower social and economic levels of the population with the hope of expanding their circulation. In so doing, their editors changed the tone of their papers from a primarily partisan political orientation that appealed to the upper classes to one that featured local news with emphasis on human interest material. As such, they became what we today call sensationalist. In later years these papers would become highly politicized like their predecessors, but they tended to retain their sensationalist orientation. Many of today's newspapers are the direct descendants of the Penny Press. And the modern media, whether print or broadcast, have continued the tradition of paying primary attention to those aspects of the news most calculated to capture the imagination of their customers, stories of war, murder, rape, incest, and the private lives of celebrities.

The pioneer newspaper was the *New York Sun*, founded in 1833 by Benjamin Day. It was soon followed by a succession of newspapers: James Gordon Bennett's *New York Herald* in 1835; the *Philadelphia Public Ledger* in 1836; *The Baltimore Sun* in 1837; Horace Greeley's *New York Tribune* in 1841; and *The New York Times* in 1851. The name *Penny Press* remained to characterize the genre for quite a while, even though all but the *Baltimore Sun* soon raised their prices to two cents and increased their size.

In their handling of the news, the new journals placed great emphasis on timeliness. They sought out the news rather than waiting for news to come to them. Of course, there was little they could do about remote events, because communication depended on the slow transportation vehicles available. The best that can be said is that they tried to do the best with what they had. For example, zealous publishers would rush to meet the clipper ships as they pulled into port to catch the news from Europe at the first possible moment. It is no wonder, then, that the press eagerly latched on to the new lightning lines.

When the Mexican War broke out in May, 1846, there were only 130 miles of telegraph wire in the country. Construction of a New York to Washington wire using the demonstration line between Baltimore and Washington was underway but not complete. There had been much talk of a connection between Washington and New Orleans, but, at the onset of the war, this link remained as talk. Thus, at the beginning of the war, communication from the war zone depended entirely on transportation. The normal method of communicating, the mail, required seven days to deliver information to New York. I noted earlier how the newspapers, exasperated by the slowness of the mails, were spending huge sums of money on special communication mechanisms—combinations of pony expresses, special trains, rowboats, and clipper ships—to beat the mails if only by a few hours or a day. The impetus of the war was the spur needed to accelerate some of the efforts at expanding telegraph service. From its very beginnings the telegraph made its presence felt. The "first flash of the lightning line between New York and Washington" created a stir by bringing news from Texas a day earlier than usual. And at about the same time, Horace Greeley introduced his *Tribune* readers to a new column entitled "Latest Intelligence by Magnetic Telegraph."

The expense of all the special efforts by individual newspapers was convincing evidence that some form of cooperative effort was desirable. Even before the telegraph became much of a factor, the *New York Sun* and the *Charleston Courier* joined forces on a joint pony express venture that could benefit both and save some money in the bargain. When more telegraph wire was installed and the newspapers began to take real advantage of it to report the war, the need for cooperation became even more desirable.

The modern profession of the newspaper reporter did not exist. Here was the telegraph that could carry information rapidly, but who would obtain the information to begin with? As long as the method of communication was by shipping local newspapers from place to place nothing special was necessary on the part of the recipients. But now that a rapid method of delivery was becoming available, it was no longer sufficient to rely on the delivery of local newspapers. Somebody had to get the news at its source and bring it to the telegraph office. Was this the role of the newspapers themselves, the telegraph operators, or perhaps a third party? In some instances, the operators tried to fill the role but in a less than satisfactory way. It turned out to be difficult for the same person to fill both roles. It was just as unsatisfactory for different reasons when the newspapers began to use their own reporters. They would get in the way of one another and often jam the telegraph line with more traffic reporting on the same events than it could reasonably handle. The solution adopted by six major dailies in New York was a unique form of cooperation in the establishment of two associations: the Harbor News for collection of foreign news from ships entering New York harbor and the New York Associated Press for news from other sources.

It was the function of the Associated Press to provide the reportorial function collectively for all its members. When founded, there was no thought that the organization would expand its membership beyond the original six, but events were to prove otherwise. Other associations were formed in other cities and intense competition broke out among the rivals. Especially intense was the competition in reporting news from Europe. The first port in a transatlantic crossing was usually Boston, where representatives of the American newspapers would receive the London newspapers and speed them on to New York as best they could. So cutthroat was the competition that the ships began to stop first in Halifax, Nova Scotia, simply to unload London newspapers. One method employed in the 1840s was to use a special fast boat to speed the news southward from Halifax to Boston. Later, as the telegraph appeared over portions of the route, various ad hoc combinations of media—telegraph, pony express, boats—were used at different times to cover the route. It is no wonder, then, that establishing end-to-end telegraph service between Halifax and the major American cities was such a high priority to both the telegraph entrepreneurs and the New York Associated Press, as well as the other press associations in the major population centers of the country. In the end, the New York AP dropped its *New York* specification as it beat out its rival press associations, in part because of its monopolistic agreements with the telegraph companies. As its power increased, its monopolistic status was the object of the same criticism that confronted the Western Union monopoly.

Sometime later other rival press associations would appear both in the United States and abroad to temper the stranglehold of the Associated Press. And, of course, the coming of the broadcast media in the twentieth century led to a redistribution of power in the entire news industry that keeps changing as new technology enters the picture. And nothing has happened in the last 150 years to indicate that this change begun by the telegraph is slowing down.

While the thirst for news of the Mexican War had much to do with giving the new telegraph the impetus to begin its period of rapid growth, the effect of the telegraph on wars turned out to be much deeper than simply affecting the way in which they were reported. Because electrical communication has also had much to do with changing the ways in which wars are fought, and, as in so many other areas, it was the telegraph that started things off.

Chapter

4

The Telegraph Goes to War

A military commander leads his troops by first obtaining all the information he can about the way in which the enemy is deployed and by determining his enemy's strengths and weaknesses, and then ordering his own forces to take appropriate actions. The military term for this process is called *command and control*. I suspect that the nineteenth-century lettuce shippers, meat packers, and financial speculators would have been surprised to see their daily activities described with such a military term, but that is precisely what they were doing, commanding and controlling. It is only natural then, that if the telegraph was to influence these areas in commerce and finance, then it would do the same on the field of battle. The telegraph was not too many years old when armies first found it useful. By the time the Civil War came along it was able to play a major role.

Until the telegraph decoupled information transfer from transportation, the military commander, of necessity, had to be located with his forces. Typically, kings, emperors and other ruling potentates would lead their troops into battle themselves. They did this not only because it was part of the royal job description, but also because once they delegated such important responsibilities as making war, they lost the ability to control the action. More trusting kings would stay home and send their generals to command the troops in battle, but in recognition of the fact that the battle was fully in the hands of the battlefield commander. So it was with George III when he sent his armies to the American colonies to stamp out the rebellion knowing that once they left home, he could maintain no control over them whatsoever, given the six to eight weeks required for an Atlantic crossing. Similarly, Lord Nelson would make elaborate battle plans that he would give to his ship commanders in a prebattle conference. But if the progress of the battle deviated from his plans, he knew that his subordinates had to take the necessary compensatory actions by themselves. Thus, when American and British officials signed the Treaty of Ghent in 1814 officially ending the War of 1812, they were well aware of the fact that it would take many weeks for the news to reach the direct participants in the war. In fact, the battle of New Orleans took place two weeks after the signing. Men were still dying, victims of the fact that the site of the battle was too far from the site of the diplomacy for the field commanders to get the word—an extreme example of the perishability of information.

The telegraph pioneered in changing the importance of the physical location of the commander. It left a lasting impression on the command and control of military forces that has been reinforced over and over again by the succession of inventions that have followed it. Just as it liberated many commercial undertakings from the bonds of geography, so it freed military commanders from the same geographical constraints. As an Army historian, Captain E. D. Peek, put it in 1911:

> In the old days a commander-in-chief placed himself, if he could, on a hill where he could see the whole battle-field. Now, with battles extending for miles both in width and depth, he can himself see but a small portion of the battle-field; he is best placed in some quiet, sheltered spot, where he can calmly digest and act on the information sent him by others. This spot will be the nerve center of the battle, to which all information comes and from which all directing orders issue, and should, if possible, remain constant throughout the battle.[16]

If this guideline were true near the beginning of the century, how much more so today with the existence of highly sophisticated communications that allow heads of government to stay in their offices at home and generals to be far removed from the field of battle.

The Civil War was not the first time that the telegraph was used for military purposes. The British, who had been so quick to apply the telegraph to worldwide communication to hold together their empire, were also quick to apply it in battle, the occasion being the Crimean War in 1857. They also took advantage of it within India itself in putting down a mutiny one year later. In that campaign, General Sir Colin Campbell Clyde's forces laid wire as they advanced from Calcutta to maintain communication with their headquarters. At about the same time, the armed forces of most of the other western European countries also began using the telegraph. Just before the Civil War, the Italian forces under Victor Emmanuel demonstrated the ability of rapid communication to coordinate widely dispersed forces in taking the city of Verona from the

Papal States in a two-pronged attack using forces that maintained contact with each other by telegraph.

The Civil War found the American Telegraph Company with assets divided between the North and South. The U.S. government, recognizing their wartime potential, took over those facilities in the areas through which its armies were operating. In addition, it established a so-called Military Telegraph service within the army under the direction of a Western Union official named Anson Stager, who ultimately received the rank of colonel. The Military Telegraph operated these commercial circuits. Most important, it outfitted telegraph trains that would carry all the equipment and personnel necessary to laying additional wire wherever necessary.

The telegraph was used rarely for tactical command and control on the battlefield itself. The equipment was still excessively bulky for that purpose. Rather it was used for strategic purposes. Thus both Generals George McClellan and Ulysses S. Grant, the successive Union commanders, made important use of the telegraph in coordinating the activities of their widely dispersed armies. The telegraph also provided the major connection between the War Department in Washington and the commanders in the field. Stories are told of how President Abraham Lincoln would spend many hours each day going over the telegrams received from the field.[17] From his headquarters with General George Meade's Army in Virginia in May 1864, Grant gave daily orders to all his forces operating over a territory of 800,000 square miles. He was able to prevent the reenforcement of General Robert E. Lee's Army and thereby shortened the war. Perhaps the most publicized application of the telegraph was in enabling General William Tecumseh Sherman to coordinate his march through Georgia and South Carolina with other Union activities. As Sherman said:

> The value of the magnetic telegraph in war cannot be exaggerated, as was illustrated by the perfect concert of action between our armies in Virginia and in Georgia in all of 1864. Hardly a day intervened when General Grant did not know the exact facts from me, more than 1500 miles off as the wires ran.[18]

It is also interesting to note that the role of the telegraph during the war had a significant impact on the companies contending for dominance. In contrast to the American Telegraph Company, the Western Union Company with assets primarily in the West continued to operate its entire system. It was free to continue its expansion unimpeded by the turmoil. This circumstance in itself probably contributed significantly to the ultimate domination of Western Union.

The two names most closely associated with the army's management of the Civil War telegraph are General Albert Myer and Edwin Stanton, who became Lincoln's Secretary of War in 1862. Myer, as a young army physician, developed a flag-based semaphore signaling scheme as a by-product of working with deaf patients, in a sense a predecessor of Alexander Graham Bell in deriving his interest in communication from working with the deaf. While Myer is virtually unknown outside of military circles, his interest in communication led to the establishment of the army's Signal Corps in 1860, just before the outbreak of the war.[19]

While Myer's primary interest in communication was through the application of his semaphore system, he recognized the potential of the new telegraph to military communication. So avidly did he promote the use of the telegraph within the Signal Corps that he and Stanton got into a power struggle that ended with Myer's removal from his position. The source of the friction between them was the issue of whether the Military Telegraph would remain attached to the Quartermaster Corps where it was directly under Stanton's control or be subsumed within the Signal Corps. With the exception of a few men such as Stager at the top, the service was entirely civilian. In 1863 Myer recommended to the Congress that in the name of efficiency and coordination this service be folded into the Signal Corps, and it was this recommendation that led to his dismissal by Stanton, who insisted on preserving the essential civilian character of the service. It is interesting to note that in 1867 when the war was over, Myer's organizational recommendation was approved, and Myer was restored to his old job, now with the rank of major general.

It did not take many years following the Civil War for the telegraph to become firmly established as a military tool. By 1870 the famous Prussian general, Count Helmuth Karl Bernhard von Moltke, was able to credit the telegraph with a critical role in his success in taking Paris in the Franco-Prussian war. To those of us accustomed to the use of radio to control mobile forces, it seems a bit surprising that so much use should be made of communication by wire in the days before radio existed, even when we remember that mobility in the nineteenth century was measured in terms of the speed of feet and horses and not mobile vehicles and jet aircraft.

By 1876, the telegraph had become so ingrained in the war-fighting capabilities of all nations that the British military tactician, Major C. F. C. Beresford could write:

> It has now been clearly established in every way that no extended operations can be carried on without the telegraph, and before long it will be equally recognized that its presence is as necessary to every part of an army as nerves are to a living body.[20]

But any effect as dramatic as that of the telegraph in expanding the information boundaries of the battlefield could not help but affect the viewpoint of those who remained within the physical boundaries. Wars have been so much a part of human culture, and the traditional ways of fighting wars had become so ingrained in this culture, that those on the battlefield did not always appreciate the fact that people far from the battlefield were able to participate in the battle strategy and tactics as a result of the new communications technology. Listen to this traditional point of view as stated by the British tactician, Colonel Lonsdale A. Hale, in a paper delivered in 1887:

> Telegraphic communication in the minds of soldiers is interference from without. . . . It will be argued that any tactical operation is made up of a number of smaller, almost minute tactical operations, and that these can only be controlled and carried out successfully by a leader present on the spot, untrammeled by interference from a distance.[21]

Colonel Hale goes on to calm the wary by making the case for centralized strategy and decentralized tactics as follows:

> It is hardly too much to say that in a tactical operation of any size in modern warfare, every man does what is right in his own eyes, anarchy, disorder, confusion, and chaos reign supreme. The reason for this state of things is, mainly, that owing to the difficulties of communication between the supreme leader and his subordinates, and to the fact that the decisions to be come to in tactical operations do not admit of delay, control of almost any kind, even the mildest, by the supreme leader is impracticable; and therefore subordinate leaders must act independently, whether they like it or not. . . . In a tactical operation of any size it would be an arrant absurdity for a supreme commander to interfere by telegram with the details of the attack to be carried out by an infantry battalion, or with the number of rounds to be fired by a battery of artillery, but as the records of battles tell us, it is frequently only that commander who can rightly determine whether that infantry attack shall be made at all; whether by the discharge of one single shot the presence of guns at some particular spot shall be made known to the enemy.

Hale alludes to the fact that military commands are typically arranged in a hierarchical fashion, each with its own command-and-control capability. The traditional military way has been to decentralize the decision making, that is, to permit the commander at each level to control his forces with only broad instructions from the next level above his. Under this philosophy, an army lieutenant would direct his platoon with broad guidance from his company commander, the company commander from the battalion commander, and so on up the chain of command to the topmost echelon. This traditional modus operandi evolved naturally from the fact that communication was good at the low levels of command involving small numbers of people in the same vicinity and poor at the higher, more dispersed levels. By virtue of this communication, the lieutenant was in close touch with his troops and was able to control them closely. In contrast, the higher-echelon did not have sufficiently close coupling to do more than provide broad guidance to his dispersed forces.

With modern communication, this traditional command structure is no longer mandatory. Higher-level commanders, no longer constrained to be in the immediate vicinity of the forces they control, can now be coupled into actions at any level. And they may choose to interpose themselves into what previously were lower-level decisions, despite the assurances of Colonel Hale. Because of this ability, the course of military strategy and tactics has been altered irreversibly.

It does not necessarily follow that a high-level commander will interpose himself into low-level decision making just because he has the technical capability to do so. It all depends on the nature of the situation and the propensities of the commander. Professional soldiers, brought up in the military system to respect the command hierarchy, are less likely to disrupt that hierarchy than political leaders with political as well as military agendas. President Lyndon Johnson tried to run the Vietnam War from the White House situation room. In contrast, President George Bush with even more responsive communications let his theater commander run the Gulf War, reserving to himself only the highest-level decisions. The two presidents had different styles, and the way they chose to exercise command reflected this fact. George III had no choice but to leave his revolutionary war generals full autonomy in trying to stamp out the rebellion.

It is also not clear that high-level officials are better or worse at making low-level decisions than lower-level commanders. Would Johnson and Bush have been more effective in the other's circumstances? It does appear that when a high-level commander interposes himself into low-level affairs too often, then the lower levels lose the incentive to go through the decision processes themselves. In the old days, football quarterbacks used to call plays. Today that job is done by the coach from the sidelines. I suspect that very few quarterbacks even make the attempt to second-guess their coaches. If too many generals play lieutenant, then the lieutenants become robotlike and lose the ability to command when it is their turn to become generals.

This same tendency to deviate from the normal chain of command applies to nonmilitary as well as military governmental affairs. Until the advent of the telegraph, diplomatic correspondence was necessarily linked to transportation, and the diplomatic pouch was the vehicle of communication. The slowness of this communication meant that diplomatic officials in foreign countries could operate on their own without interference from higher-ups, just as military commanders could conduct their affairs in conformity with the chain of command. In particular, it was the ambassador living and working in the foreign capital who was involved in all affairs between his country and the country of his post. Certainly, important treaties would call for visits of high-level diplomats to foreign capitals, but these were relatively rare. The ambassador, as the representative of his country in the foreign capital, represented it, in fact, in almost all affairs between the two countries.

First the telegraph and then the telephone began the same process of erosion of strict adherence to the chain of command in diplomacy just as they did in military affairs. During World War II, Franklin Roosevelt and Winston Churchill built up mutual trust through constant communication by telegraph and telephone, bypassing all the officials of high and low rank in between. And that trend has continued. Personal diplomacy by presidents and prime ministers is an inherent part of today's world order. As with everyone else, they take the extra time and make the personal trip for *summit* meetings more often than in the past because of the relative ease and speed of travel. Most of the time even very gregarious heads of government stay home but spend hours on the telephone with their counterparts throughout the world to conduct their foreign affairs. No longer are the ambassadors involved in almost all issues. Their new positions, redefined by modern communication, tend to focus on lower-level and ceremonial issues.

Paradoxically, a leader's new flexibility can itself be constraining. While he or she may have a choice as to whether or not to use the available capabilities, it is difficult to convince others that he or she has a power that is not used. For people are quick to believe that anyone will use a capability if he or she has it. Thus, there are occasions in which modern U.S. presidents may have to bear the consequences of embarrassing actions taken by subordinates that would have escaped earlier presidents without the power to act from a distance. For example, when President James Madison wanted to end the menace of the Barbary pirates operating out of Tripoli, his only choice was to send a naval squadron with the most general orders to do something about the situation. If the officers used excessive force, how could the president be blamed? No modern president has that luxury. When President Ronald Reagan wanted to warn the modern successors of the Barbary pirates in Libya to modify their policy of supporting terrorism, he attacked the terrorists from the air in full knowledge that he had to withstand any criticism from world opinion. The ability to command from afar is, therefore, a mixed blessing: It gives a commander more flexibility and power to do the job, but, at the same time, it creates hazards where none existed before.

It is nothing short of amazing that a such a simple device as the telegraph had such a profound effect on so much of nineteenth-century society. Perhaps even more amazing is the fact that the telegraph, which produced such change in just a few years' time was rapidly eclipsed by another device, the telephone, and that one monopolistic communications company was eclipsed by another. Such is the power of technology.

Chapter

5

Transmitting the Human Voice

"What use could this company make of an electrical toy?" With these words William Orton, the president of the Western Union Telegraph Company, rejected the offer of Gardiner Greene Hubbard, the business partner and later the father-in-law of Alexander Graham Bell, to sell the telegraph giant the rights to the Bell telephone patent at the price of $100 thousand.[22] It is not clear whether Orton did not truly appreciate the potential of the telephone, whether he thought he could get around the patent and save the money, or whether he did not want to do anything that might benefit his old adversary Hubbard. Whatever the reason, subsequent events were to demonstrate that passing up this offer was the biggest mistake Western Union ever made.

This offer was made shortly after Bell obtained his patent in 1876. Within three years Western Union was to contest the Bell people in the marketplace. But it was too late. Even though Thomas Alva Edison succeeded in developing an improved telephone instrument for Western Union, it was ruled by the courts to be in violation of Bell's ironclad patent, and Western Union was forever out of the telephone business.

By the time the telephone arrived in 1876, the telegraph was a mature capability proliferated throughout the world. In that year there were some 8,500 offices connected by 214,000 miles of wire in the United States alone supporting the transmission of 31 million telegrams. Its technology had advanced significantly since the first crude Morse instruments. New developments, such as the printing telegraph that converted the Morse signals directly into letters, were beginning to increase its *user-friendliness*. There was even talk about development of an *automatic telegraph* that would remove the requirement for a skilled

Morse operator. Other automatic features were also being used. The telegraph connections between brokerage houses of the day were the direct predecessors of the ticker tape made famous in Wall Street. There were direct lines between fire alarm boxes and the fire stations, and there was even a device that would be triggered automatically by the heat from a fire.

This was the communications environment in which the telephone appeared. It is no wonder, then, that the early history of the telephone, its invention, its public reception, and its first applications were dominated by the presence and influence of the telegraph. For a number of years, people conjectured that such a thing as speech communication might be possible. But there was something personal about the human voice as compared to Morse code that gave speech communication a special mystique of its own. As John Brooks wrote:

> Human speech, as opposed to dot-and-dash code, was considered sacred, a gift of God beyond man's contrivance through science. Public reactions to the very idea of telephony in the 1860s and 1870s wavered between fear of the supernatural and ridicule of the impractical. People were made uneasy by the very notion. Hearing voices when there was no one there was looked upon as a manifestation of either mystical communion or insanity. Perhaps reacting to this climate, most physicists and electricians took it as an axiom that electricity could not carry the human voice. To have the freedom of mind to take the last step, there was needed a man whose thought was centered not on electricity but on the human voice, and the man was Alexander Graham Bell.[23]

Bell's fixation on the human voice came from his father, Alexander Melville Bell, a distinguished Scottish phonetician who had developed a system of "visible speech," in which he laboriously characterized the physiology of the human speech-producing mechanism for each speech sound. Melville's failure to achieve due recognition for his work in England was one of the main factors in his decision to leave England and settle in Canada in 1870. The younger Bell directed his inherited interest in phonetics toward teaching speech to the deaf, originally in England and later in Boston after the family's move to Canada. Even after he had achieved fame for his invention, Bell continued to think of himself as a teacher of the deaf.

But Bell was a man with broad intellectual interests. He had a highly inquisitive mind and a flair for invention, similar in many ways to Morse and Edison. Like them, he had no formal technical training. But he made up for this lack, in part, by avid curiosity and intense motivation. While still a boy in England he had been fascinated by experiments to transmit electrical representations of tones over wires, and he revived these interests in Boston, a major center of science and invention, the place where Edison had gotten his start. It was the confluence of his scientific and phonetic interests that led to his friendship with Hubbard, a noted Boston lawyer, whose deaf daughter brought him to a passionate interest in the deaf and whose practice was intimately associated with telegraph interests often in conflict with Western Union.

Bell became fascinated with the notion of sending a number of individual tones over a wire simultaneously and came to the conclusion that if one could really do this, then each of these tones could carry its own telegraph signal. This achievement would then enable a single telegraph wire to carry a large number of telegraph messages at the same time. It was the forerunner of an important technique now called multiplexing that permits thousands of voice conversations to be sent between cities on a single electrical cable. Cognizant of the economic impact of such a capability, Bell set up shop to see if he could invent a practical way of building such a *harmonic* telegraph. It was in the process of this work that he made the conceptual leap to the idea of the telephone: If these multiple tones could be derived from the multiple frequencies in speech signals, then one could transmit the human voice electrically. Should one call this process of conceiving the idea of telephony accidental? After all, Bell did not set out to invent a way of transmitting the human voice the way Morse set out to transmit letters and numbers. The conceptual leap from the harmonic telegraph to the telephone required such a level of ingenuity that I would prefer to call it a serendipitous leap of understanding.

Bell made this conceptual leap in 1874 when he was twenty-seven years old. During the next two years, he worked feverishly now on the one invention and now on the other, all the while maintaining a full teaching schedule and giving lectures on his father's phonetic theories. Hubbard and another Bostonian, Thomas Sanders, greeted his telegraphic invention with great enthusiasm and contributed financial support in return for equal partnership in this endeavor. Initially they regarded his flirtations with the telephone as a frivolous diversion from the more serious telegraph improvement. It was only later that they realized the potential of the telephone. Finally, in 1875 Bell's experiments paid off to the point that he applied for several patents in connection with the telegraphic device. About a year later in February 1876 he filed a patent application for the telephone. The patent he subsequently received, number 174465, was to become probably the most valuable ever issued by the U.S. Patent Office.

In addition to Bell's conceptual leap in arriving at the idea of the telephone, the principal of telephony requires a level of implementation sophistication a step beyond that of the telegraph. All the telegraph required was a way of interrupting the flow of current through a wire and a way of detecting these interruptions. But to send the human voice over a wire, some way had to be found to convert the acoustic signals that we call speech into electrical replicas and back again—a task considerably more sophisticated than simply starting and stopping the flow of current. The invention of the telephone was, in effect, the invention of the devices that we now call the microphone and loudspeaker. Sound propagates through the air in the form of waves of alternating high and low pressure regions. A microphone converts these pressure variations into variations of the electrical current flowing through a wire, and a loudspeaker converts electrical variations back to pressure variations in the air.

The amount of current that flows in an electric circuit depends, in part, on a quantity called the *resistance* in the circuit: the lower the resistance, the greater the current. When a steel wire is connected between the two terminals of a battery, the current flow is less than when a copper wire of the same size is used because the copper has lower resistance: in other words, it is a better conductor of electricity. The principle of the carbon microphone, until recently the most commonly used in telephones, is the fact that the resistance of granular carbon depends on the pressure to which it is subjected: the greater the pressure, the lower the resistance. Such a carbon microphone consists of a small chamber filled with carbon granules, connected between the terminals of a battery. One side of the chamber is a flexible diaphragm. The pressure of the sound coming from the talker's mouth causes the diaphragm to vibrate, and these vibrations compress and decompress the carbon granules varying their electrical resistance. As a result, the current flowing through the microphone is proportional to the sound intensity.

The telephone loudspeaker works magnetically as did Morse's telegraph receiver. In the telegraph, switching the current flowing through an electromagnet on and off provides a mechanism for deflecting a stylus. In the telephone, the current variations due to speech intensity fluctuations produce a proportional variation of the strength of the electromagnet. The speech is reproduced by a diaphragm connected to the magnet that vibrates in proportion to the strength of the magnetization. Bell's original patent used the principle of the electromagnet for the telephone microphone as well as the loudspeaker, a kind of loudspeaker in reverse, but he recognized early that the electromagnetic effect was too weak to work satisfactorily as a microphone. He therefore included the principle of variable resistance in the patent application even though he did not successfully build such a microphone until a month or so after the application. This first variable-resistance microphone used liquid rather than carbon granules, and his famous first telephone sentence, "Mr. Watson, come here; I want you," was supposedly prompted by his spilling some of the liquid on his clothing, although the accuracy of this explanation is subject to question.[24]

Like Morse, Bell was not the only person approaching the problem of telephony. It is interesting that his rival inventor, Elisha Gray, followed the same path from the harmonic telegraph to the telephone. Gray beat Bell in the quest for the harmonic telegraph patent; much of Bell's 1875 application was ruled in interference with Gray's prior application. But not so in the case of the telephone where Bell beat Gray to the patent office by a matter of hours. American patent law decides precedence on the basis of conception not patent application. Even so, Bell's prior filing allowed him to start exploiting his invention without interference; the Bell Telephone Company was established a year later.

Subsequently, the powerful Western Union Company went into competition with a subsidiary, The American Speaking Telephone Company, which held the patent rights of Gray, Edison, who had developed a much superior carbon granule microphone, and others. The Bell company brought suit in 1878 and won. The deciding factor was the fact that Bell's patent included the principal of the variable resistance microphone for which he was able to prove first conception. In personal terms, the court case established Bell as the inventor of the telephone and relegated Gray to the status of a historical footnote. More important, the settlement put Western Union out of the telephone business for good, and gave the Bell interests the rights to all Western Union's telephone patents—including Edison's microphone—in return for 20 percent of Bell's receipts over the next seventeen years. The ultimate success and power of the American Telephone and Telegraph Company was due in no small measure to its start free of competition, a direct result of Patent No. 174465.

Chapter

6

Universal Service

Following the invention of the telephone, Bell worked incessantly in the dual role as perfecter of the technology and promoter of the concept. The centennial exhibition in Philadelphia in 1876 gave him an early opportunity to promote his invention. President Rutherford Hayes was among the most enthusiastic of the observers, and he later became the first president to bring a telephone into the White House. Bell and his partners set about to raise money, install wires, manufacture instruments, and begin to offer service. There was no question of government involvement—the telegraph experience had left electrical communications firmly in the private sector.

While Bell enjoyed the lecture demonstrations at the centennial exhibition and elsewhere, he soon tired of all the other aspects of the process of entrepreneurship. Like Morse some thirty years earlier, he soon dropped out of active participation in the exploitation of the new device, leaving the issues of business management and development to others. In mid-1877, Bell married Mabel Hubbard, his student and the daughter of his partner, and the two set sail for England, where their first child was born and where they were to remain for more than a year, during the formative years of the Bell Company. When he finally returned, his partners put him in harness to play the primary role in the suit against Western Union. Once that was over, he was free to disappear as an active player in the company's affairs.

Within a few years, all the original partners withdrew from active management, leaving the principal role to Theodore Vail, a distant cousin of Morse's colleague, Alfred Vail. Although Hubbard's tenure in the leadership of the company was short, his contributions to the ultimate success of what would become the American Telephone and Telegraph Company were profound. In addition to providing the guiding hand to his future son-in-law during the invention process, he led the first entrepreneurial efforts. It was Hubbard's decision, for example, to lease service rather than sell equipment, a decision that had far reaching effects over the years. But perhaps his most important management action was in bringing into the company a manager of the caliber of Vail. Ask an old telephone hand to name the most influential pioneers in the industry, and the answer is almost invariably Bell and Vail. Once Hubbard withdrew, it was Vail more than any other who shaped the course that the company was to follow. It was not always easy. He had two tenures leading the company, leaving in 1887 after a disagreement with the board and returning in 1907 as new forces took over the company's direction.

But before he left active participation, Bell made another contribution that was arguably as significant as his invention. It was only natural for people to think of using the telephone in the same way as a telegraph. But Bell's appreciation for the human voice led him, from the very beginning, to conceive of the telephone as a user-to-user device. In 1878, during his year in England and only two years after his invention of the first telephone instrument, Bell wrote this extraordinarily prophetic piece in a letter to a group of British investors:

> The simple and inexpensive nature of the Telephone . . . . renders it possible to connect every man's house, office or manufactuary with a Central Station so as to give him the benefit of direct telephonic communication with his neighbors at a cost not greater than that incurred for gas or water.

> At the present time we have a perfect net-work of gas-pipes and water-pipes throughout our large cities. We have the main pipes laid under the streets communicating by side pipes with the various dwellings enabling the inmates to draw their supplies of gas and water from a common source.

> In a similar manner it is conceivable that cables of telephonic wires could be laid underground or suspended overhead communicating by branch wires with private dwellings, Counting Houses, shops, Manufactuaries, etc., etc., uniting them through the main cable with a Central Office where the wires could be connected together as desired establishing direct communication between any two places in the city. Such a plan as this though impracticable at the present moment will, I firmly believe, be the outcome of the introduction of the telephone to the public. Not only so, but I believe that in the future wires will unite the head offices of Telephone Companies in different cities and a man in one part of the country may communicate by word of mouth with another at a distant place.

> I am aware that such ideas may appear to you Utopian . . . . Believing, however, as I do that such a scheme will be the ultimate result of the

introduction of the telephone to the public, I would impress upon you all the advisability of keeping this end in view that all present arrangements of the telephone may eventually be utilized in this grand system.[25]

While Morse had predicted the web of wires that would cover the nation converting it into one neighborhood, neither he nor anyone else associated with the telegraph had foreseen a truly user-to-user service. Telegraph service was from telegraph office to telegraph office. A person would write out his or her message and deliver it to the local office. The recipient would receive the message when it was delivered from the receiving office. While there were a few examples of direct telegraphic business connections, the idea of all subscribers being in communication with one another without the intervention of someone else was not within the realm of possibility for a service requiring skill in Morse code.

But this user-to-user service is precisely what Bell foresaw for the telephone. Essential to making such a scheme workable was the idea of *switching* that Bell introduced in his remarkable letter. It is clear that if every telephone is to be able to talk to every other telephone, there have to be wire connections between every such pair of telephones. It does not take too long to come to the realization that actually stringing a wire between every pair of telephones is completely impractical. Most people talk to a small selected subset of other people most of the time. Look at all the wire that would be wasted!

The answer to the problem of universal connectivity was Bell's central office. All the telephones in a neighborhood would be wired to the office. Then some mechanism within the office would connect a caller to his or her destination. Initially, that mechanism was a person, the telephone operator, who would manually connect the appropriate wires together. Later, a mechanized version of a telephone operator, called a switch, that could recognize a dialed telephone number and make the proper connection, replaced the operator for all but special cases. Telephone systems still work this way. Of course with worldwide telephone service, many switches are required to connect a caller in New York with a party in, say, Bombay, but the principle is still the same as that foreseen by Bell in 1878.

In those first years, though, the technology was so primitive that two-way conversations could only be supported over very short distances. So, in his early lectures at the U.S. Centennial Exposition and elsewhere, Bell dazzled his audiences by including with each lecture a demonstration of the transmission of music over a wire to the lecture audience, the application that anticipated the radio broadcast. There is no indication that Bell had any intention whatsoever of capitalizing on the potential of the telephone for broadcasting. Bell's letter to potential British investors indicated that as early as 1878 Bell understood that the destiny of the telephone was as a vehicle for two-way communication. Such *broadcasting* demonstrations were strictly in the realm of public relations. The telephone was to be guided in the direction of universal two-way connectivity not broadcasting.

It is an interesting historical curiosity to note that there was a serious attempt to apply the telephone to such a broadcasting application a few years later, not in the United States but in Hungary. When telephone service was initiated in Budapest in 1893, it was in the form of a broadcast service called the *Budapest Register* or *Gazette*, nicknamed "The Pleasure Telephone," that was to presage what was to happen more than twenty-five years later with the over-the-air radio and seventy-five years later with cable television.[26] The *Register* broadcasted a regular schedule of features over its wires including news, music, stock market prices, poetry readings, and lectures. Within five years it could boast of having 6,000 subscribers using its 220 miles of wire. There were sporadic versions of broadcast services similar to this in Britain and elsewhere, but none with the formality and success of the Budapest system. However, none lasted more than a few years, so powerful was the eventual pull toward universal two-way connectivity.

The first commercial uses of the telephone followed the lead of its predecessor. The telegraph of the day was widely used in private line connections between business offices. And in its first installations, the telephone was simply a one-for-one replacement for the telegraph motivated by the fact that the telephone eliminated the Morse operator. Just as stockbrokers were among the first to make use of the telegraph, so their successors two generations later found similar utility in the telephone. There were applications in which one telegraph operator relayed a message to another. When the telephone was substituted for the telegraph, this manual relay would often remain. It just never occurred to them that the telephone, unlike the telegraph, could be patched straight through completely eliminating the middleman. There was some analogy between these initial perceptions of the uses of the telephone and Edison's initial thoughts on uses for the phonograph, which he had invented at about the same time. Edison thought of the phonograph as a means of recording messages that would be transmitted by phone from one place to another for playback. It took him fifteen years to recognize its entertainment potential.[27]

Vail was quick to recognize the importance of universal service and began to establish service based on the notion of user-to-user connectivity almost from the beginning of his service with the company. The pattern in those early years was to install telephone service wherever the population was large enough to support it. It is understandable that the greatest perceived need was for this local service—even today most calling is local. Nevertheless, Vail recognized the importance of long-distance service very early, building the first such line from Boston to Lowell, Massachusetts, in 1880. Other such lines followed quickly as the Bell system established long-distance service as a way of interconnecting the various local systems. Organizationally, Vail established each local organization as a separate company, with the parent company owning a controlling interest in each, while long-distance service remained as a function provided directly by the parent company. Vail also had the foresight to recognize early the importance of engineering and manufacturing, buying Western Electric, the company started by Bell's old rival Elisha Gray. Though scarcely ten years old, it was already a vertically integrated monopoly that would ultimately become the largest corporation in the world under the name of The American Telephone and Telegraph Company.

Chapter

7

Establishing Telephone Service

There were many practical problems to be overcome before the telephone could become accepted by the general population. There was, for example, the problem of how to run the wires. Wires could be strung above ground on poles or buried under the ground. Burying the cables was more expensive initially, but buried cables were not put out of service by the weather, as happened during the great *Blizzard of '88* to many of the above-ground installations. And the more universal the medium became, the more important it was to maintain continuous reliable service above all else.

The most fundamental of these problems illustrated an important difference between telephone and telegraph signals. By the time that Bell first demonstrated his rudimentary telephone instrument in 1876, the nation was wired up for telegraphy. The technique of running telegraph wires reliably was well understood. But the technology needed for wiring the nation for the more complex voice signals was different enough from what it had been for the telegraph signals to force the telephone pioneers to break new ground. The process had to begin all over again for the new medium, and it turned out to be so much more difficult that spanning both coast-to-coast and overseas distances took much longer to realize than was the case with the telegraph.

It soon became apparent, for example, that it was not sufficient to run a single wire between cities with the circuit completed through a ground return as with the telegraph. To be sure, the ground is a conductor, but not a very good one when compared to a copper wire. The resistance of the ground connection not only impedes the current flow, but is also the source of interference between one telephone signal and another, since the same ground carries the return path for many circuits. Both these effects tended to limit the distance over which satisfactory telephone service could be established. But the introduction of wire pairs instead of single wires only solved part of the problem. Even though copper is an excellent conductor, it still has some resistance. Since the larger the diameter of the wire, the lower its overall resistance, the telephone pioneers began to use larger wire to obtain greater distances. But the larger the wire, the heavier and more expensive it is, and the greater the cost of the installation.

Using this brute force technique helped to some limited extent, but it was clear that more sophistication was needed to make the telephone truly useful over long distances. The savior in those early years was the *loading coil* invented in 1899 by Michael Pupin, a Columbia University professor.[28] The concept was developed concurrently by a Bell engineer, George Campbell, but so important was the invention that the telephone company did not hesitate to pay Pupin a total of $255 thousand for the rights to his invention and avoid the time-consuming litigation over who did it first that would impede its application to the practical business of expanding the telephone system. On the face of it, the loading coil was simple enough—just a coil of wire, inserted in the telephone line at periodic intervals to alter its transmission characteristics in such a way as to compensate for the natural degrading effects of long wires. But the process of determining first that it was a coil and not something else that was needed, and then of calculating its size took a deep theoretical understanding of the new electromagnetic theory of James Clerk Maxwell that was leading to the invention of radio. It is interesting to note that this understanding came to the American and not the British telephone engineers, in the same time frame in which Guglielmo Marconi was doing his pioneering wireless work in England.

The reason why this is so is a commentary on the state of electrical science and engineering at the close of the nineteenth century. Electrical engineering did not exist as a discipline until that time. All the advances in understanding electrical phenomena were made by physicists, and the practical applications either by some of the same physicists (recall that Joseph Henry tried his hand at a practical telegraph) or by intuitive self-trained inventors such as Morse, Edison, and Bell. It was the knowledge of the advanced mathematics required to understand and apply Maxwell's work that distinguished between the two groups, in the main. And it was this mathematical approach that made it possible to define electrical engineering as an academic discipline. For example, in 1882 the Massachusetts Institute of Technology became the first American institution to give electrical engineering official recognition by establishing it as an option within its physics department. Twenty years later, this option grew into a full-fledged department.[29]

Similarly, it was not until around the turn of the century that the makeup of professional societies in the field began to reflect the presence of university-trained people—The Institution of Electrical Engineers (IEE) in the United Kingdom started out in 1871 as the Society of Telegraph Engineers, and the American Institute of Electrical Engineers (AIEE) founded in 1894 was similar.

People such as Pupin in the United States and Oliver Heaviside in Britain were men of the new school. Sir William Preece, the chief engineer of the British Post Office and the dominant force in British communications, was of the old school. It is to Bell's credit that he recognized that he could go just so far without a proper grounding in mathematics. Edison would never admit it and continued to disparage the new-style engineer. Once the new century came along, the days of the old-style inventor were numbered. Advancement in electrical technology was becoming just too complex and mathematical for the old-style inventor.

What was it about telephone transmission that required this deeper, more mathematical approach not needed for telegraph trasnmission? The essential reason lies in the fact that voice signals contain a wider range of frequencies (or, what is the same thing, a wider *bandwidth*) than do telegraph signals—the range of speech frequencies runs up to about 8,000 cycles per second or hertz, as compared to a few hundred, at the most, for Morse code. Eliminate some of these frequency components in the process of transmitting the speech, and the received speech sounds distorted. Eliminate enough of them and the speech is rendered unintelligible. When a wire carries a Morse signal, it need have only a bandwidth a few hundred hertz in extent. A wire suitable for carrying speech must have a bandwidth about ten times as large.

The bandwidth of a wire is analogous in many respects to the capacity of a roadway to carry automobile traffic. Using this analogy, a telegraph wire is comparable to a narrow dirt road that can carry a small amount of lowspeed traffic. This dirt road must be widened a bit and paved before it can handle the vehicular equivalent of the human voice. Even then, the longer it is, the less traffic it can handle. Similarly, the frequency-carrying capacity of a telephone wire degrades the longer it is. The loading coil deliberately cuts off some of the less important high-frequency components in return for boosting the mid-range frequencies most important for voice intelligibility enough to carry them over longer distances. It is hardly a high-fidelity system, but it passes enough frequency components to achieve the modest fidelity that is generally acceptable for voice conversations.

To achieve better quality, we need still more bandwidth such as is provided by radio broadcast channels. An AM radio channel, more like a city street, achieves better voice quality and modest music quality, and an FM channel, analogous to a secondary highway, achieves still greater fidelity. A standard television channel, more analogous to a high-speed freeway, has a bandwidth thirty times as great as an FM channel to enable it to carry all the information in the color video signals. Now near the end of the twentieth century, bandwidths have become large enough to merit the electronic superhighway metaphor, a fact that is well known from its use by the Bill Clinton/Al Gore presidential campaign in 1992 as one of the vehicles for restoring economic growth and prosperity to the nation. More about that later in Chapter 31.

All these various wireline techniques introduced to facilitate telephone transmission had one thing in common: they reduced the amount of signal degradation with distance. But while very helpful, these were not sufficient in themselves, because, in the end, reducing signal degradation was not sufficient. What was needed to carry the voice signals over cross-country distances was a way of actually strengthening the signals— a process called *amplification*. But the telephone industry had to wait several decades for the emerging wireless industry to give birth to the technology of the vacuum tube that made the amplification process possible.

By 1915 the new invention finally made its impact on the telephone system when AT&T turned the initiation of coast-to-coast service into a great media event. The company sent Thomas Watson, Bell's original assistant, to San Francisco and had Bell in New York repeat his famous first telephonic sentence: "Mr. Watson, come here; I want you." Mr. Watson's inspired reply, ". . . if you want to see me, it will take me almost a week to get there," expressed the very essence of the difference between communication by electricity and by transportation. Even with the invention of the amplifier, it still took another forty years before the first Atlantic telephone cable was laid, some eighty years after the invention of the telephone.

It was business policy every bit as much as technical considerations that determined the character of the early telephone service and, in particular, its rate of growth. For example, telephone service was almost exclusively for business purposes in the early years for economic reasons. The pricing was flat rate, that is, for a fixed rate, a subscriber could make an unlimited number of calls. These rates were generally too high for the average family to maintain a telephone at home. Such household members would obtain access to the system through public telephones that were installed almost from the inception of service either within or in the vicinity of popular neighborhood stores. The single action that began the personal use of the telephone in earnest was a change in pricing policy. In 1896, New York Telephone Company abolished the flat rate, replacing it with a message-sensitive rate that brought the cost to a level that low-volume users could afford. As a result, the number of subscribers doubled in the next three years. This rapid growth continued to such an extent that by 1914 there were as many as 10 million telephones in the country.

As the number of subscribers increased, it became clear that the process of making and breaking telephone connections had to be automated in some way if the cost of the personnel required for manual switching was to be restrained. It is curious that once an automatic switch was invented, it was the new so-called independent telephone companies that arose after the original Bell patents expired, rather than AT&T, which grasped the significance of the technology. Vail, whose judgment turned out to be so good in most areas, was inexplicably slow in appreciating the necessity of introducing automatic switching into the Bell system, probably because of its large investment in manual switchboards. Finally, in 1911, Vail succumbed to pressure from his chief engineer, John J. Carty, and began to introduce the automatic switches.

In a more logical world, one would expect that the economic impossibility of retaining manual switching in a rapidly growing network would have motivated the development of the first automatic switch. But this was not the case. The motivation for the first switch was economic, to be sure, but of a very different kind. It seemed that a Kansas City undertaker named Almon Strowger suspected that he was losing business because the town's telephone operator was directing all requests for funeral services to a competitor to whom she was related. We do not know how talented Strowger was as a mortician, but he has gone down in history for his electromechanical talents in developing an automatic switch in 1889 that was first installed in LaPorte, Indiana, in 1892. History does not record how this affected his undertaking business.

Technical challenge was only one of the inhibitors to telephone expansion. Politics was an equally important challenge, especially in Europe. Since the telegraph's expansion in Europe and elsewhere in the world had been almost as rapid as in the United States, one would have thought that the same human impulse to talk at a distance that made telephone growth so rapid in the United States would have been the same everywhere in the world. The fact that this was not the case in Britain and France can be attributed to self-serving governmental attitudes. In 1870, the British Post Office took over the telegraph as a government monopoly, and by the mid-1880s, it was generally agreed that Britain had the finest communication system in the world, with telegraph traffic at the 50-million level in 1886. The telegraph establishment viewed the telephone as an interloper into its domain. The official government position was that the mail and telegraph services were necessities deserving of public subsidies, while the telephone was a luxury that had to pay its own way. This is how Preece, the chief engineer of the British telegraph, justified this position in the House of Commons in 1879:

> I fancy the descriptions we get of its use in America are a little exaggerated, though there are conditions in America which necessitate the use of such instruments more than here. Here we have a superabundance of messengers, errand boys and things of that kind . . . . The absence of servants has compelled Americans to adopt communication systems for domestic purposes. Few have worked at the telephone much more than I have. I have one in my office, but more for show. If I want to send a message—I use a sounder or employ a boy to take it.[30]

This attitude of the communications establishment aroused the ire of many in the business community. Five years after Preece's testimony, the *Spectator* wrote:

> The New Yorker of means is understood to be no more able to do without his telephone than the Englishman without his Penny Post. We are the most letter-writing country in the world . . . it is most probable that had it not been for the hateful effects of state monopoly we should have been the most wire-speaking country in the world.[31]

Even as late as 1902, *The Times* of London was still not convinced that the telephone was to play a major role in British society:

> When all is said and done the telephone is not an affair of the million. It is a convenience for the well-to-do and a trade appliance for persons who can very well afford to pay for it. For people who use it constantly it is an immense economy, even at the highest rates ever charged by the telephone company. For those who use it merely to save themselves trouble or add to the diversions of life it is a luxury. An overwhelming majority of the population do not use it and are not likely to use it at all, except to the extent of an occasional message from a public station.[32]

As an example of the slow spread of the telephone in the business community, the exclusive London department store, Harrods of Knightbridge, did not obtain telephone service until 1908, at a time when the telephone was well on the way to becoming universal in the United States. Finally in 1912 after considerable pressure, the telephone was nationalized and thereby admitted into the establishment. It was only then that telephone growth comparable to that in the United States could proceed unhampered by prejudices and enlightened self interest.

Growth of the telephone in France was also slow compared to that in the United States, but for different reasons than in Britain. Until recently, the French telephone service was among the worst in the world, a direct consequence of the attitude of the government since the nineteenth century. That attitude is wonderfully expressed in the wording of a bill to establish a government-owned visual semaphore system in the regime of Louis Philippe between 1830 and 1848:

> governments have always kept to themselves the exclusive use of things which, if fallen into bad hands, could threaten public and private safety: poisons, explosives are given out only under State authority, and certainly the telegraph, in bad hands, could become a most dangerous weapon. Just imagine what could have happened if the passing success of the Lyons silk workers' insurrection had been known in all corners of the nation at once.[33]

The French were not prepared for democratic communications that encouraged reciprocity. When telephone systems were established, the control was localized under politicians who were not interested in its growth as a democratic medium. Fortunately, these attitudes have changed in more recent years, and French telecommunications have been in the pioneering forefront in many areas.

While there was no entrenched government interest to inhibit telephone growth in the U.S., there was the enlightened self interest of the increasingly powerful AT&T, which did not appreciate the competition of the independent telephone companies beginning to emerge in the 1890s as soon as the Bell patents expired, any more than any monopoly appreciates an intrusion on its operating style. That this competition constituted more than a minor nuisance is demonstrated by the fact that by 1907 the independents had half the market. AT&T flexed its monopolistic muscles in every way it could to maintain its dominance, aided by the fact that Theodore Vail was back at the helm, the result of the success of the financier, J. P. Morgan, in wresting control of the company from the Boston financiers who had controlled the company since its inception and who had forced Vail out twenty years earlier. One obvious tactic was to buy up any of the competitors that it could and to exert economic pressure on others to drive them out of business. In some cases rivals set up operation in cities that already had a Bell company. AT&T's response was to refuse to interconnect its circuits to those of a competing company, forcing those individuals and businesses who had the need to talk to subscribers of both systems to maintain two telephones. Bell's leverage was especially strong in the long-distance area where there were no competitors. By denying connectivity to the independents, it effectively barred their subscribers from long-distance services.

By 1913 these monopolistic practices were placing AT&T in the same position as Western Union had been forty years earlier. Indeed, by this time Morgan had even gained control of Western Union by buying its stock secretly at above market prices. This combination of events finally forced the Justice Department to take antitrust action. A court action was not necessary. AT&T agreed to interconnect with the independents and to stop acquiring them, and Morgan gave up control of Western Union. This action was just the first in a sequence of actions by the government to regulate and restrain the enormous powers of the great telephone monopoly held by the old AT&T and its successor companies of today. Vail saw the handwriting on the wall. He was setting the pattern for most of the century by agreeing to regulation as the price for recognition of his monopoly status.

During World War I, the government flirted with taking over the company, following the model of the British in 1912. Woodrow Wilson's Postmaster General Albert Burleson was the principal exponent of this action within the government. Vail's politically astute leadership succeeded in fending off the government for a while. By changing the company's emphasis from stockholders' profits to improved service, he was able to modify the image of the company to the general public. However, once the United States entered the war in 1917, the government finally took over the telephone system as part of the war effort, and AT&T carried the brunt of army communications during the war with its *Bell Battalions* stringing telephones throughout France. But more about this in Chapter 11.

These skirmishes between the government and the Bell telephone monopoly were to continue steadily in the face of a changing competitive situation and of explosive technological change, culminating finally in the momentous agreement between the company and the Justice Department in 1982 mandating that AT&T divest itself of its local service. Some eighty years earlier, the tension between the government and the powerful Western Union monopoly simply went away by itself, as that once powerful corporation went into a long period of decline. This decline did not happen overnight, but rather over a period of time beginning with the appearance of the telephone. It is not that the need for telegraphy disappeared when telephony appeared; quite the contrary, telegraphy has continued to remain important for many applications. But the telegraph industry has not expanded in importance, nor has its existence spawned new applications. In contrast, the telephone networks have expanded their scope. In addition to handling ever increasing volumes of voice traffic, beginning in the 1920s, they became indispensable to the emerging broadcast industry as vehicles for distributing network radio and later television network programming. And in the latter half of this century, its networks have carried an increasing amount of the computer-to-computer traffic that is the most modern version of telegraph traffic and that developed quite outside the telegraph mainstream.

Technology changes, and applications of the technology change at a rapid rate. While Western Union's network was basically special purpose in its dedication to the specific applications of the telegraph, AT&T with its universal network was better prepared to grow with the technology. Its magnificent research and development capabilities through its Bell Laboratories was, in fact, the leading developer of this technology placing it in a virtually unchallenged position in the U.S. communications industry.

Of course, the industrial lineup has changed in our day. And communication has expanded to include many things other than voice transmission. But the telephone has not lost its primacy as had the telegraph in the previous century. On the contrary, despite the modern diversity, the telephone has become and remains the essential piece of communications equipment, because the human voice remains the *natural* way in which we communicate.

Chapter

8

Extending the Personal Presence

> The great advantage [the telephone] possesses over every other form of
> electrical apparatus consists in the fact that it requires no skill to operate
> the instrument. All other telegraphic machines produce signals which
> require to be translated by experts, and such instruments are therefore
> extremely limited in their application, but the telephone actually speaks,
> and for this reason it can be utilized for nearly every purpose for which
> speech is employed.[34]

With these words, part of that now-famous letter to British investors,
Alexander Graham Bell emphasized the fundamental difference between
the telephone and its telegraph predecessor. Aside from some degree of
amazement at the whole notion of a *talking* wire—the press was filled
with awestruck comments such as "almost supernatural" and "weird"—
most people were inclined to think of the telephone in telegraphic terms.
Of course, in a technical sense, the two are similar; in each system,
information is converted to electrical form, transmitted over a wire, and
then converted back to its original form. But human communication is
more than the transfer of information from one place to another. The
form of the information and the way in which it is converted from human
form to electrical form play a large role in determining the characteristics
of the communication. The direct use of the human voice in the process
is something very special because it is an important, perhaps the most
important, part of the personal presence. It was this aspect of the human
voice that convinced Bell that telephone connectivity had to be universal.
Had a person without Bell's grounding in human speech been the
inventor of the telephone, the notion of universal connectivity probably
would not have come so naturally or quickly.

Even without comprehending the full implications of Bell's vision, everyone could certainly agree that direct user-to-user connectivity made the telephone an inherently faster medium of information exchange than the telegraph. Of course, both Morse code signals and voice signals travel with the same speed of light. But the true measure of speed is how long it takes the information to go between one subscriber and another, and this depends upon more than the propagation speed. The telegraph system required intermediaries who knew Morse code. The sender had to write out a message, give it to a Morse operator who encoded the message and sent it to another operator. The message reached its destination only after decoding by the second operator and delivery to the recipient. As fast as the transmission might be, the writer-to-reader time had to include the time required to compose the message and get it to the sending operator, the time it took to key in the message, and, finally, the time required by the receiving operator to deliver the message to its final destination.

These characteristics of the telegraph meant that for all practical purposes a message and its reply together consumed an amount of time measured in hours. A competing system that reduced this time to minutes would, of course, be very useful and perhaps even crucial in some circumstances. But the telephone did more than that. Once the connection was established, it effectively reduced the time to zero; the listener hears the talker as he or she talks and the other party can then reply just as if the two were face to face. This instantaneous feedback gives telephone communication a completely different character, making it into something that the telegraph never could be: a social as well as a business instrument. The time would come, Bell said, when Mrs. Smith would spend an hour with Mrs. Brown "very enjoyably cutting up Mrs. Robinson" over the telephone.[35] (As sexist as this may sound to modern ears, it cannot be denied that women, more attuned to intimacy than men, are more likely to use the telephone in social ways.) The telephone is therefore a multipurpose instrument meeting many societal needs. In John Brooks's words: "it impartially disseminates the useful knowledge of scientists and the babble of bores, the affection of the affectionate and the malice of the malicious."[36] The telephone was truly an extension of the self, and, as such, struck a responsive chord in a broad cross section of society.

Crucial to the difference between the telephone and telegraph is the fact that the human voice conveys more than the content of the words alone. It also communicates information about the talker, not only his or her identity, but also his or her state of mind while speaking. No two voices are exactly the same; some are high-pitched and some low; some are accented and some not. And there are many other characteristics that cannot be quantified with any accuracy that give each voice its own unique sound. Thus two people can say exactly the same words but the information transferred is different. Even for a particular speaker, the character of the voice depends on how he or she feels at that particular time. Is the talker calm or agitated? Is he or she talking slowly or rapidly? All these things add information to the basic content of the spoken words.

This aspect of voice communication meant that the telephone was to play a far different role than the telegraph. The telegraph simply transmits facts. The human voice can also communicate specific pieces of information, and many of the telephone's applications depend on this. But its most unique applications rest no more on the fact that information is being transferred than the fact that it is the human voice that is doing the transferring. In contrast to the telegraph that replaced the transportation of things, the unique personal quality of the telephone enables it to replace the transportation of people or personal travel. "Reach out and touch someone" is the way the modern AT&T advertising describes this ability of the telephone to transfer an important aspect of the personal presence along with factual data.

No two methods of communication are exactly the same in all dimensions. When a new communication system comes into existence, it creates new applications and takes applications from the older systems. But it does not replace the old systems. Rather, the new system adds to the choice available to the public. Thus, the telegraph did not replace the mail. It added a quicker option to the transmission of the written word. Those who did not need the additional speed or for whom the extra cost was burdensome continued writing letters. Similarly, the telephone has not replaced either written communication or personal contact; it has added the option of remote voice conversation to be used where speed and convenience are important. The telephone, therefore, augments our ability to talk face-to-face by relaxing the condition that we have to be in the same location. It permits similar but not identical interactions to occur between people at a distance, whenever, in the judgment of the participants, it is the preferable mode of interaction.

We all recognize that there are times and circumstances in which the telephone is not an adequate replacement for a face-to-face interaction. Because while audio information may well be the most important component of sensory communication, it is by no means all there is to it. When two people talk face to face, more than speech is communicated. Information is also transferred by what is seen, touched, smelled, and tasted, and also by behavioral patterns reflective of multiple sensory indications. Does the person look you in the eye? Does he smell of alcohol? Is his handshake firm or wishy-washy? All these things impart information along with the spoken word. For reasons such as this, we often find it congenial to discuss business affairs over lunch or over a golf game. Family members interact while eating or watching television or driving in the automobile. All the same subjects may be discussed over the phone but with an element of artificiality in being constrained to devote our attention to talking without the mediating effect of the other activities.

Transportation can never compete with the telephone in cost and speed. A coast-to-coast telephone interaction today takes a few minutes, the time it takes to put on one's coat and step out of the office. It costs at most a few dollars for a long conversation, far less than even local travel. Yet, if we think that the interaction is important enough, we are likely to take the trip to transfer the information in person, spending the hundreds of dollars and the days necessary for a personal face-to-face interaction. We all draw the line in different ways. Most people agree that the speed and economy of telephone contact is the best way to handle routine transactions and that personal contact is desirable for important deals. For those transactions in between we all make our choices. Typically, business people will conduct many of the preliminaries to an important deal by telephone. But more than likely the deal will be consummated by a series of personal contacts. After all, you cannot have a drink together when you are not together. You cannot work out the details of the deal over lunch when you are thousands of miles apart.

The same considerations hold on the personal level. The telephone is the tool of intimacy for people whether in the same town or across the country. Teenagers for whom peer relationships are crucial augment their frequent face-to-face encounters with long telephone conversations. Family members separated by many miles will maintain contact by phone on a regular basis, but will take the time and spend the money for the occasional visit where the interaction means more than exchanging words. A man and woman can flirt with each other by telephone. One of them can even propose marriage over the telephone. But ultimately the distance must be bridged in person.

Similarly, there are times when we recognize the superiority of writing over speaking either personally or over the telephone. Oral communication is highly perishable. It is just not practical to use the voice to convey more than a few sentences worth of hard facts. How often do we find ourselves writing down information received in person or over the telephone? It cannot convey quantitative information with high precision, especially when there is a lot of it. Similarly, we like the human presence in radio and television, but recognize that newspapers provide coverage of news events at a depth that the electronic media rarely approach. Thus, even while we may prefer sensual communication, we recognize that written communication has had the more profound long-term impact. Great ideas are communicated in writing, not orally. To be sure, there is the spellbinding orator who can move his listeners to action, but do you remember those words thirty minutes later? Lincoln's Gettysburg address had little impact when delivered. But just consider the effect those words have had on later generations in written form. To be sure, in the ancient world, when written communication was difficult, history was preserved by oral traditions. Story tellers would commit long sagas to memory in order to transmit the information as accurately as possible. Even when important history and literature was written down, its dissemination was severely limited by the fact that writing was so labor-intensive and expensive. The printing press, the great invention of the middle ages, changed society profoundly by making written communication and its dissemination relatively easy.

The meteoric rise of facsimile communication in the past decade demonstrates how popular written communication can be when it is fast, convenient, easy-to-use, and universal. Before its general availability, you might have read selected portions of a multipage letter over the telephone to get the most important points of your message across. But transmission of the entire letter would have to wait for the mail, either regular or, if time was of particular importance, overnight. Electronic mail is another option that is becoming more feasible now that the computer is almost as ubiquitous as the telephone in the business environment. Both of these modes are preferable to the voice under many circumstances. For example, when you call your local movie theater to find out the time of the next showing of a particular film, or your supermarket to find out the price of lamb chops, you do not really care that a human being at the other end provides the information. Most people currently have no other way short of travel to find out the information. Because the human interaction is sometimes unimportant, this is the kind of information most likely to be recorded. And it is also the kind of information that could be accessed by an electronic mail system when available as universally as the telephone.

But conveniences such as fax and electronic mail are modern devices that only came into their own a century after the telephone. In those intervening years, the telephone system with its great speed, convenience, and ubiquity became the universal mode for remote communication, used for all kinds of applications transcending those that demand some aspect of the personal presence. How much easier it is to phone rather than write a letter. Indeed, social commentators have lamented the fact that the telephone has all but destroyed the ancient art of personal, as opposed to business, letter writing. From the very beginning, people would use the telephone rather than the telegraph to send relatively limited amounts of information, even when it suffered the disadvantage of limited intelligibility often requiring the repetition of words and even spelling them out. Such effort is a tribute to the convenience of oral communication.

But what is so obvious to us today was hardly so to most of Bell's contemporaries who continued to think of the telephone in terms of its telegraphic heritage. Because of this attitude, it took decades before the telephone was able to gain full acceptance as a social instrument. In its first decades, it followed in the footsteps of the telegraph as a tool of business, but, interestingly enough, not primarily as a one-for-one replacement of the telegraph. For example, some were reluctant to switch to the telephone, despite its obvious speed advantage, because it lacks the written record provided by the telegraph. (It is interesting to note that there were also some who turned this lack of a written record into an advantage, since it left them free to deny what was said at a later time.) Rather, the telephone began to be used in new ways primarily as a convenient way of sending information around town. Instead of going some place in person or sending a messenger, a quick phone call would do the trick. Doctors and drugstores, for example, found the telephone to be an indispensable tool from its very beginning.

The sociologist, Claude Fischer, explains the initial reluctance of people to use the telephone for reasons other than business with the observation that basic social patterns are not easily altered by new technologies.[37] The forces of habit are very strong. Since the telegraph was primarily a business tool, why should the telephone be any different? To use the telephone as a social tool was considered by many to be the height of frivolity, following in the footsteps of Thoreau who had expressed himself so vigorously on the evils of the telegraph. Thoreau died in 1862 at the young age of forty-five, well before the advent of the telephone. One can only imagine how this lover of solitude would have greeted this medium which, more than any other, interrupts ones privacy equally well for the insignificant as for the significant. Even today, answering the ringing of the telephone usually takes precedence over anything else we are doing.

The notion of excluding the telephone from frivolous use was initially reinforced by the telephone industry itself, many of whose personnel came out of the telegraph industry. They expressed their emphasis on business use in their pricing policies. In the few years between the successful suit against Western Union and the expiration of the Bell patents, the telephone company did what any monopoly would do: It charged as much as it thought businesses would pay, effectively limiting home use for economic reasons. The prices began to drop once competition began in the 1892, and usage increased. But the method of pricing also tilted toward business. As I noted earlier, the prevalent flat-rate pricing, while ideal for business users, effectively priced residential users of modest means out of the market. Rather than maintaining a telephone at home, individuals would obtain access to the system for important uses through public telephones that were installed almost from the inception of service either within or in the vicinity of popular neighborhood stores. And as I also noted earlier, the single action that began the personal use of the telephone in earnest was the New York Telephone Company's institution of a message-sensitive rate that brought the cost to a level that low-volume users could afford and doubled the number of subscribers in the three years after its inception.

Even as the telephone became more affordable, the Bell system's advertising continued to be aimed at the telephone as a practical instrument of business rather than an instrument of sociability. People were encouraged to install telephones in their homes, but discouraged, at the same time, from using them frivolously. For one thing, usage-based pricing discouraged long conversations. For another thing, many residential users were connected on party lines and long social conversations prevented other subscribers on the same line from using the phone for *useful* purposes. It was only after World War I that the attitudes changed enough for the company to begin actively encouraging the use of the telephone for social purposes.

Even though the Bell system was slow to exploit the potential of the telephone as a social instrument, there were subscribers in all sectors of society who did. Particularly noteworthy was its popularity in rural America. Between 1908 and 1920 the percentage of farm homes with telephones actually exceeded the urban percentage.[38] Early in the century, there was some concern that with more and more of the population leaving the farms for the cities, America was losing its essentially rural character, and some were predicting that the telephone would stem this movement. President Theodore Roosevelt's Country Life Commission designated the telephone as one of foremost influences for the "solution of the rural problem." This did not turn out to be the case as the migration from farm to city continued unabated. But the telephone did alleviate the extreme isolation felt by farm families, especially the wives, permitting them to maintain social contact with one another. To quote Fischer again, "The telephone resulted in a reinforcement, a deepening, a widening of existing lifestyles more than in any new departure."[39] The fact that rural connections were made to party lines added another source of amusement for the entire farm family. Party-line subscribers would use the operator for personal services—"Ring me up in 15 minutes so I won't forget to take the bread out of the oven." Since party lines were not restricted to rural areas—even as recently as 1950, 75 percent of all residences were not equipped with private lines—many others could experience the pleasures of eavesdropping on their neighbors. Fortunately or unfortunately, depending on your point of view, the number of party-line residences was reduced to 27 percent by 1965, and today, it has virtually disappeared.[40] Perhaps we have lost some sociability at the price of gaining privacy.

This sociability factor is probably what accounted for the telephone's relative popularity in rural areas, but this popularity did not last long. The rural percentage began to decline in the mid-1920s, and its comeback was slow—it wasn't until 1950 that it reached its 1920 level. There are rarely simple answers to social trends of this sort. One factor cited by Fischer is that the growth of the telephone paralleled the growth of the automobile and the radio in the 1920s (see Figure 1).[41] Both of the latter grew in use much more rapidly than the telephone and, perhaps, competed with the telephone as a source of social fulfillment. In fact, among working class, urban and rural alike, autos were more

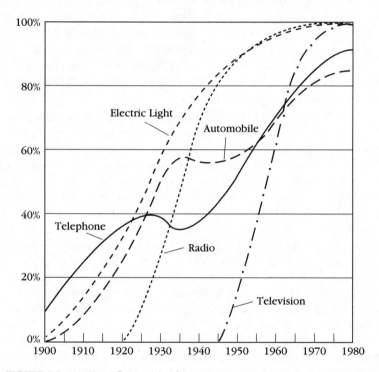

FIGURE 1 Penetration of new technologies in American homes beween 1900 and 1980 taken from U.S. Census Bureau data. Note the very rapid growth of radio and television, the former even during the depression when telephone and automobile penetration were slowed or even reversed. (From *America Calling: A Social History of the Telephone to 1940*, by Claude S. Fischer, University of California Press, Berkeley, 1992. Courtesy of Claude Fischer.)

popular than telephones in the 1920s. At the same time, the telephone companies did little marketing among the rural communities. Of course, the continued decline in the 1930s can be attributed to the economic depression. It is noteworthy that even in the height of the depression, when both rural telephone and automobile usage were in decline, the numbers of people buying radios and electrifying their homes continued to rise. Perhaps it was an indication that the telephone had lost its glamor and had become humdrum.

The urban usage pattern was somewhat different. The telephone was slower to take hold in the cities, but once it did, people were more inclined to keep the service. During the 1920s, when the rural percentage was declining, the urban percentage continued to rise, only flattening out during the depression years. By 1930, more than 40 percent of urban homes had telephone service, and with numbers such as that it was possible to state that telephone service was reaching the universality of Bell's vision, at least in the upper socioeconomic groups. It was not until the post–World War II years that this universality could be said to encompass almost the entire American population. Now, near the end of the century, the telephone is in more than 90 percent of American homes, exceeded in ubiquity only by electric lights, television, and radio, all of which are close to the 100-percent mark. The telephone has truly become part of the American infrastructure.

It is precisely because of this universality that social scientists have had a difficult time in assessing the impact of the telephone. There have been commentators galore, both professional and amateur, on the societal effects of newspapers and the radio and television broadcast media where a small number of people determine what is read, heard, and watched. It is also easy to point to the specific industries such as the press, railroads, and financial services that benefited particularly from the early telegraph. But the fact that the telephone system is used by so many under such a wide variety of business and personal circumstances makes it difficult to quantify its societal impact. One of the few examples of a whole industry being influenced by the telephone is indicated by the fact that people began to call prostitutes *call girls* near the turn of the century, reflecting the fact that prostitutes no longer had to advertise their wares in person. Probably the best way to describe the telephone's position in society is to cite the fact that, from the very beginning, it began to insinuate itself into the societal infrastructure along with the railroads, the electric wires, the gas mains, and water and sewer pipes. It became just as natural to use the telephone for business or personal reasons as to take a glass of water from the tap or turn on the lights.

In no area is Fischer's comment about the slowness of social patterns to change more applicable than in the matter of social etiquette. As a case in point, by as late as 1890, the etiquette books were not sure of the propriety of using the mail as the vehicle for extending social invitations. By 1900, the mail had become quite acceptable, but not the telephone. According to Fischer, one etiquette book dictated that an invitation by telephone "is never excusable, save among very intimate friends" or in an emergency, but even then it required an apology for such a departure from established norms.[42] There was also the quaint old custom among the social elite of establishing *at-home hours* during which others would pay a social call long enough to drop off their calling cards. While it would appear that this custom was falling into disuse even before the telephone became popular, its demise was certainly accelerated by the new technology. Today's equivalent to the calling card would be the telephone call with a message left on an answering machine if the receiving party turned out not to be at home. The very existence of the telephone makes the older practice seem not only quaint but overly intrusive. But is an interruption in the flesh any more intrusive than an interruption by telephone? I would say that the marginal decrease of intrusiveness is compensated for by a decrease of sociability. Has calling become a substitute for visiting? Some would claim so. But others claim that the contrary is true, that the convenience of the telephone for making contact actually facilitates personal interactions. Broad sociological questions such as this are not answered easily.

Broad societal effects are almost never due to a single advance in technology. For example, the dispersion of urban populations and businesses from the city to the suburbs is usually attributed to the automobile and massive efforts at highway construction. Of course, these transportation technologies made the suburbs physically possible. But would this dispersion ever have happened had not the telephone been there to provide the instant human contact between the separated people? Modern Americans have become the most mobile people on Earth as a result of the automobile and the jet aircraft, but this mobility would have been far less appealing without the comforting telephone to hold together the dispersed families. It is doubtful if the more impersonal and nonuniversal telegraph could have substituted for the telephone in these broad sociological trends.

The telephone was also a contributor to vertical dispersion within the city itself. Through most of the nineteenth century, businessmen stayed physically close to their colleagues within the city: there were wool districts, millinery districts, and so on. Late in the century, urban designers began to build skyscrapers to make more economical use of expensive urban real estate, thereby permitting these various commercial districts to expand vertically. It was improvements in materials and construction techniques that made the skyscraper a physical possibility. When this new building technology was combined with the telephone, the huge structures became social possibilities. Here is how John J. Carty, the chief engineer of AT&T, put it in 1908, "Suppose there were no telephone and every message had to be carried by a personal messenger. How much room do you think the necessary elevators would leave for offices? Such structures would be an economic impossibility."[43] This was, of course, amateur sociology. While it is known that skyscrapers were built before the telephone became widespread, Carty's comment has something of a ring of truth about it.

Now that modern methods for transmitting written information are available in very convenient and economic ways with universality approaching that of the telephone, there is less excuse for using voice communication in their place. We may even see the video equivalent of the telephone make inroads into the market place. But communication by the human voice will always remain with us. Bell's invention and his foresight set the pattern that will remain with us as long as human beings communicate with one another.

Part

II

Communication
Without Wires

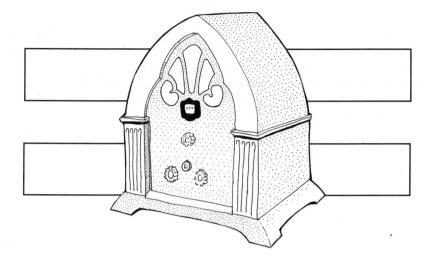

By the turn of the century, communication by wire had passed from the realm of the mysterious to that of the commonplace. The telegraph was more than a half-century old. The telephone was a quarter-century old. Both devices had been integrated into the personal and business lives of millions of people throughout the world through networks of wires. Then, shortly before the nineteenth century was to conclude, another mystery was beginning to unfold. A young Italian Irishman had demonstrated conclusively that wires were not necessary.

It was a mystery then, and even today, almost a century later, when radio has become as integral to society as wire communications was earlier, the reason that it works still remains a mystery to the vast majority of people. But mystery or not, this new ability to communicate without wires has truly transformed the world. Some of the ways in which this has happened are obvious: communication to ships and airplanes, radio broadcasting, television broadcasting, walkie-talkies, radar, the communications satellite.

But could anyone have expected that the emergence of wireless was to be the principal technological event that distinguished the new century from the old in so many ways? Both the telegraph and telephone were discrete devices that had a profound influence on the way we communicate. But the wireless was more than a discrete device, and it influenced more than communication. From it came the vacuum tube and, as a result, the technology of electronics that was to influence almost everything else that was to be developed in the new century. Communication was no longer a discipline apart from all others. It was now bound irrevocably to technological progress in all areas, some of which were far removed from what we ordinarily think of as communication.

The wireless also represented the beginning of the end of the intuitive inventor/entrepreneur. Technology was becoming too complex for the inspired tinkerer in the image of Morse, Bell, and Edison, all of whom achieved hero status in the eyes of the public. Marconi, a man in this image, achieved great success. But those who were to follow began to fit the twentieth-century mold of the well-trained, largely anonymous scientist working in a substantial laboratory.

Chapter

9

Through the Ether

In September, 1899, crowds began to gather in New York harbor to welcome home Admiral George Dewey, the hero of the battle of Manila Bay. But shortly thereafter another event was to occur just outside New York harbor that was to have far more impact on the world than the American victory over Spain. The America's Cup competition, the prestige event of yacht racing, was underway. At the finish line some distance from shore was the steamship *Ponce,* rigged up with a peculiar wire hanging from its mast. As soon as it became clear that the American entry, *Columbia*, was going to beat Sir Thomas Lipton's *Shamrock* across the finish line, a telegraph message was sent from the steamship to midtown Manhattan a few miles away with the report on the race results. Scarcely a half-century after the first flash of Morse's lightning line, another news scoop made history, one that was to alter the face of the world as had no invention before it.

On the ship transmitting the news was Guglielmo Marconi, a man who had reached the age of twenty-five years but still looked like a boy, despite the mustache that he had grown for the occasion.[44] His New York demonstration was to establish him as an instant hero in the eyes of the American people. But he was already famous in England where his achievements in transmitting wireless messages over ever greater distances had caught the fancy of the whole country, including its ruler. So famous had he become that the seventy-nine-year-old Queen Victoria requested a wireless connection from her royal cottage to her yacht. Marconi's daughter tells the story of how her father, in the process of installing the equipment at the cottage, intruded upon her majesty's private garden sitting area. She immediately barked out "Get another electrician," only to receive the reply that "England has no Marconi." At this point the queen forgave Marconi's indiscretion. In a subsequent publicity stunt, he covered the Kingstown regatta for the *Dublin Daily Express*. It was the success of this demonstration that induced the *New York Herald* and the *Chicago Times* to sponsor the similar America's Cup event in New York the following year. The press was maintaining its tradition of using whatever communication technique was available to scoop the competition.

Today the word *radio* is virtually synonymous with broadcasting. Nothing could have been further from the mind of Marconi as the nineteenth century was coming to a close. To him the new invention meant the ability to extend telegraph services to places such as the steamship *Ponce*, that could not be reached by wires, in other words, wireless telegraphy—perhaps wireless telephony would follow later when the technology was up to it. And *wireless* was the name by which it was called everywhere in those early years. The French term *radio* began to be used in the United States about ten years later, but did not come into regular use for another ten years when broadcasting was first introduced. Wireless remained the common term in Britain until the 1960s.

Marconi was very much in the tradition of Morse, Bell, and Edison, an ingenious young man driven to succeed in his electrical pursuits, but without much in the way of the formal training in science that was to become so essential in the new century. His father was an Italian country gentleman from Pontecchio, near Bologna. His mother, Annie Jameson, was from a prominent Irish family from county Wexford, well known as brewers and distillers. Annie had a beautiful singing voice and wanted to sing in the opera at Covent Garden. When her parents refused to allow it, she was given a trip to Italy as a consolation prize, and it was there that she met and fell in love with the Italian many years her senior, much to the consternation of her parents. Young Marconi received his formal education in Bologna and Florence, and, at age thirteen, began to study science in Leghorn. When his all-consuming interest in wireless developed, his mother induced Professor Augusto Righi to allow the young man to audit his lectures on electricity and magnetism at the University of Bologna.

We do not know exactly what it was about the new science of radio that fascinated the young Marconi. We know that he became so interested in electricity that he felt impelled to repeat some of the classic experiments of Franklin and Faraday. We also know that he was unique among his contemporaries in being an engineer seeking practical applications rather than a scientist like the others, including Righi, who were seeking further understanding of the new phenomenon through laboratory and field experiments. Even with his orientation toward the practical, he managed to develop enough scientific knowledge in the process that he was to earn international acclaim as a scientist to the point of winning the Nobel Prize in physics in 1909.

Marconi's contribution was fundamentally different from that of either Morse or Bell. Both of the latter had used a known medium for transferring energy from one place to another—the flow of electric current through a wire. The telegraph and the telephone were devices for impressing information on and extracting information from the electric current. In contrast, Marconi laid the groundwork for the exploitation of a wholly new transmission medium in which energy was transferred from one place to another without wires.

Marconi did not *invent* the new medium; he was the most successful of a group of people trying to exploit a recent scientific discovery. The fundamental scientific contribution that made the work of Marconi and all the others possible came from the Scottish physicist, James Clerk Maxwell. Maxwell was one of those rare creative giants of the caliber of Sir Isaac Newton in the seventeenth century and Albert Einstein in the twentieth. All during the latter part of the eighteenth century and continuing into the nineteenth, physicists were gradually obtaining an understanding of the phenomena of electricity and magnetism and the relationship between them. (I had occasion to make reference to some of these earlier in telling of the background to Morse's development of the telegraph.) Maxwell's greatness lay in his ability to put together the bits and pieces of knowledge obtained by his predecessors and synthesize from them a comprehensive theory. Not only did this theory, published in 1873 in his *Treatise on Electricity and Magnetism*, provide a common basis for understanding all the phenomena previously observed, but it led to something startling in its implications.

This theory predicted that if an electric current were to surge back and forth through a wire very rapidly, then some of the energy in this current would radiate from the wire into space as a so-called electromagnetic wave. Such a wave is made up of related electrical and magnetic fields vibrating at the same rate or frequency as the current vibrations in the *aerial* or *antenna*, the names given to the radiating wire. Maxwell's theory also predicted that these waves would travel at the speed of light, leading to the remarkable conclusion that light itself was electromagnetic in nature, differing only in that its frequency was many times higher than that of waves derived from electrical vibrations. But it left open the tantalizing notion that, some day, light could be generated analogous to the way in which radio waves are generated from electrical vibrations, impossible in Maxwell's day but commonplace today with the laser.

Electromagnetic waves are like sound waves in some respects. They travel through the air similar to the way in which sound does, only about a million times faster. Each is characterized by a frequency, with that of the electromagnetic wave derived from an electrical source and that of the sound wave from a mechanical source such as a tuning fork or a violin string. But there are also profound differences. Sound propagates by causing the particles of air to vibrate; it could not propagate at all, if there were no physical medium such as air. The nineteenth-century scientists, Maxwell included, believed that such a medium was needed for light propagation as well. Since most of space through which the light from stars reaches us is empty of normal matter, the scientists were forced to invent a propagation medium which they called *ether*, a name that we still use poetically to describe empty space. But the fact of the matter is that neither light nor any other kind of electromagnetic wave requires any physical medium at all. Once they are generated, the electrical and magnetic oscillations set up in space by a radio antenna simply move by themselves at the speed of light.

If this was hard for the professional scientists of the nineteenth century to come to grips with, it is no wonder that the phenomenon remains difficult to this day for nonscientists who are content to accept such things as radio and television simply because they work. Thus, Morse and his fellow laymen could discuss electricity and magnetism in the 1830s as part of their social discourse, while their successors today find it much harder to do so, so nonintuitive has much of modern physics become.

The process of reducing Maxwell's theory to things that the eyes could see began shortly after the publication of his treatise. The process is the same one that we often see today in the physics of elementary particles, where mathematical theories are developed followed by attempts at experimental verification. One major difference lies in the fact that some experimental verification today can be so expensive that it makes a serious impact on the national budget. Fortunately this was not so in the aftermath of Maxwell's theory. In the period between 1885 and 1889, Heinrich Hertz, a German physicist, succeeded in actually generating electromagnetic waves in the laboratory. His apparatus was so crude that these waves traveled only a few feet, but Maxwell's theory had been verified.

Hertz was content to stop at this significant achievement. He was not interested in exploiting the new medium for information transfer, but the seed was there. Sir William Crookes, a well known British scientist, wrote an article in 1892 in which he predicted that the new phenomenon would one day be harnessed to permit telegraphy. Two years later Sir Oliver Lodge succeeded in sending a signal the length of a football field. It was an article by Professor Righi on Hertz's experiments that first lit the spark in young Marconi, and the flame was fanned by Crookes's article, which spurred him to learn more about the new phenomenon from Righi.

The more he learned, the more the twenty-one-year-old Marconi became obsessed with the idea of building a practical wireless system. He began his experimental work on the grounds of his father's estate in 1895, achieving modestly successful results using a transmitter and receiver similar to those that Righi had demonstrated in his lectures. His parents differed in their response to their son's ambitions. His father initially felt that these scientific endeavors would never amount to anything, and he soon became impatient with his son's activities, influenced, no doubt, by the fact that Guglielmo's academic achievements were so weak that he was unable to gain admittance to formal educational institutions. However, once his son gained some success, achieving the unheard of range of a kilometer, his attitude became more supportive, and he assisted his son in applying to the Italian navy for support.

Annie Jameson Marconi had been her son's strongest booster from the start. When the Italian navy declined the opportunity offered by Marconi, Annie and Guglielmo left for England, there to seek the aid of her influential family. It was there that he filed for his first patent in 1896, assisted financially by his cousin, Henry Jameson-Davis. He also succeeded in meeting and impressing Sir William Preece, the chief engineer of the British Post Office. Apparently Preece did not consider the wireless the threat that he did the telephone a few years earlier. On the contrary, he viewed the new invention as something practical that might help him in fulfilling his own responsibilities, such as the need to communicate with lightships to inform them of the approach of severe storms thereby reducing the loss of life that often occurred in heavy weather.

Marconi proceeded to carry out demonstration after demonstration, improving his crude technology and extending the range of his wireless, acquiring his fame in the process. In 1897 he built a station at The Needles on the Isle of Wight and used it to communicate to a tugboat eighteen miles away, the first recorded transmission to a ship at sea, thereby presaging the principal use to which the new technology would be applied in those early years. As he refined his techniques, he was able to communicate over ever greater distances, until in 1901 he managed to span the Atlantic ocean from Poldhu in Cornwall to St. John's in Newfoundland. The intended receiving site was in Wellfleet on Cape Cod, Massachusetts, but Marconi had sufficient difficulty in erecting his large antenna in the face of severe weather that he settled for the somewhat shorter distance to Newfoundland using a large antenna supported by balloons. That transmission consisted of a succession of three dots, the Morse code for the letter *s*. Here is the way in which Marconi described his great triumph:

> It was shortly after midday on December 12, 1901, that I placed a single earphone to my ear and started listening . . . . I was at last at the point of putting the correctness of all my beliefs to the test. . . . The chief question was whether wireless waves could be stopped by the curvature of the earth. All along I had been convinced that this was not so, but some eminent men held that the roundness of the earth would prevent communication over such a great distance as across the Atlantic. The first and final answer to that question came at 12:30. . . . Unmistakably, the three sharp clicks corresponding to three dots sounded in my ear, but I would not be satisfied without corroboration. "Can you hear anything, Mr. Kemp?" I asked handing the phone to him. Kemp heard the same thing as I . . . I knew then that I had been absolutely right in my calculations.[45]

Despite Marconi's corroboration, this was hardly a convincing demonstration. After all, it was very difficult to distinguish three dots in a high noise background. Those with faith in Marconi accepted it, while many others without such faith treated it as premature or even a hoax. But in the following year the doubters were converted to believers when Marconi managed to send a whole message from Cornwall to the finally completed Cape Cod station.

One of the reasons why so many demanded more proof than offered by that first transatlantic demonstration was the fact that, according to the conventional scientific theory of the day to which Marconi referred in the above quotation, it was not possible to transmit wireless signals over distances beyond the horizon. Everything in Maxwell's theory indicated that wireless waves should propagate just like light waves. The only difference between the two kinds of waves is their frequency, and this should not affect the way they propagate. Anyone who has ever used a flashlight recognizes that light travels in straight lines unless it strikes an opaque object that blocks it or one that reflects it like a mirror, or that bends it like a prism or a lens. Thus, in the absence of such a perturbing object, it was preposterous that one could shine a light, no matter how powerful, in England that could be seen on Cape Cod.

But there were perturbing objects. One of them was the ground itself. Marconi was certain that there was something about the Earth that permitted radio waves to bend so as to follow its contour and achieve these phenomenal distances. During those first experiments in Italy, his mentor, Professor Righi, visited his laboratory one day and, noting that his apparatus was not connected in anyway to the Earth, told him that he would not succeed in transmitting over very long distances "senza presa di terra," that is, without the "grasp of the earth."[46] Guglielmo followed his advice, grounded his antenna, and immediately extended the distances over which his transmissions flowed. He also noted that the lower the frequency of the wireless signal, the more reliable was this transmission over the horizon. However, he also noted that he could also achieve long distances with higher frequencies but not as reliably.

As it turns out, there is no single phenomenon that explains all these effects. The behavior at low frequencies results from the fact that waves can, in fact, travel through the Earth near its surface but at a different speed than through the air. Combinations of these transmissions in air and through the Earth produce the apparent bending of the rays along the Earth's surface. But high-frequency waves cannot penetrate the Earth's surface, and so this so-called ground wave does not propagate at high frequencies. To explain Marconi's over-the-horizon transmissions at these higher frequencies, physicists came to the conclusion that something must exist in the atmosphere that is transparent to ordinary light but that causes the wireless waves to bend. As early as 1902, two of them, A. E. Kennelly, an American, and the English Sir Oliver Heaviside postulated the explanation that the bending of the wireless signals was caused by the existence of belts of ions (electrically charged atoms) surrounding the Earth, produced by the interaction of the sun's rays with the upper atmosphere. These belts, originally called the Kennelly-Heaviside layers but now usually referred to as the *ionosphere*, are known to extend from 50 miles to 250 miles above the Earth. They are transparent to light, just as ordinary clouds that absorb light are transparent to radio waves, and just as the layer of ozone at the top of the atmosphere absorbs the sun's ultraviolet rays (rays with frequencies just above the visible) while it allows the visible light to pass unimpeded.

Though Marconi understood very little of these physical phenomena, he had an instinctive sense of what was possible. In this respect he fit the image of his nineteenth-century-style predecessors Morse and Bell. But he differed from them in his natural flair for entrepreneurship. Neither of the early inventors played much of a personal role in exploiting their devices after the original patents and demonstrations, leaving the entrepreneurship to others. In contrast, Marconi's personal instincts were entrepreneurial from the very start. Not only was he more interested in applications than in science, but he was interested in making money from these applications. Thus, he rejected Preece's offer to buy his inventions for the British Post Office, and shortly after patenting his system, he set up his first company, Wireless Telegraph and Signal, Ltd., again with the help of his cousin. Then, after his New York Harbor triumph made his name world famous, he felt that it was good business to change the name to Marconi's Wireless Telegraph Co. Ltd. He subsequently established another company, the Marconi International Marine Communication Co. Ltd., dedicated to pursuing business opportunities in the area that he felt would be the main stream for the wireless.

He also went international in 1899, with the founding of the Marconi Wireless Telegraph Company of America, as a subsidiary of his British company.

All this business activity was accomplished on the basis of exceedingly crude transmitter and receiver technology. For example, the early receiver was a device called a *coherer* that was nothing more than a container filled with iron filings with a wire connected to each side. One of the early experimenters made the brilliant discovery that the iron filings would fuse together slightly or *cohere* in the presence of an electromagnetic wave, and the electrical resistance of the device would decrease. Therefore, when a coherer was connected between the terminals of a battery, the current would increase in the presence of an electromagnetic wave. The problem was that the filings had to be *decohered* by shaking to make them ready to detect the next Morse code symbol.

The transmitter was, if anything, even cruder. In those days the only way of producing the signals that oscillated back and forth rapidly was to impress suddenly a high voltage between a pair of metal balls until lightninglike sparks passed back and forth from the one to the other— short duration sparks for dots and longer ones for dashes. This is how Hertz generated the radiation that verified Maxwell's theory. Nikola Tesla, a brilliant Croatian emigré to the United States, paved the way for Crookes and then Marconi by improving the technique with a device that came to be known as a "Tesla coil". Tesla went on to invent prolifically during his long lifetime, but is best known for his coil, which continued to be used for many years to generate very high voltage, high frequency discharges. This artificial lightning that was barely adequate for generating Morse code was out of the question for voice signals. It was quite impossible to generate wireless signals that were in any sense proportional to audio signals until fundamentally different transmitter and receiver technology was developed. Radio-telephony would have to wait.

Marconi's patents did not protect him the way Morse's and especially Bell's had protected their inventions. His inventions consisted of particular approaches to the transmitter, receiver, and antenna technology. But since there were many potential ways of improving on this crude technology, it was quite possible for many competitors to enter the field without infringing upon the patents of the others. As one might expect, certain technical approaches eventually demonstrated their superiority. But the fact that no single competitor was able to monopolize this advanced technology led to an impasse during World War I and its aftermath, the resolution of which changed the course of the history of the radio in a fascinating way.

While the Americans were not the first with the wireless as they were in many other technological areas, once Marconi had shown the way, several Americans followed. It is fascinating to observe how different Marconi's American competitors were from him. He was a brilliant tinkerer in the mold of Morse and Bell and a successful entrepreneur. They were all scientifically trained in the spirit of the new century, and this training was to make its mark in the superior quality of their technical exploits. But, to a man, their technical proficiency was matched by personality quirks and entrepreneurial ineptitude.

The best known of these competitors was Lee De Forest.[47] Armed with a Ph.D. from Yale's Sheffield Scientific School in 1899, he achieved a measure of fame following in Marconi's footsteps, by competing with Marconi in reporting the yacht races in 1901, a competition that provided a graphic demonstration of another deficiency of the early systems, the fact that the wireless signals generated by their untuned transmitters interfered with one another. Today's radio and television broadcasting stations generate their electromagnetic signals on frequencies controlled precisely to keep this interference from happening. The early spark-gap transmitters could not do this. Their zig-zag sparks generated waves on a spread of frequencies. This wide bandwidth became a severe problem as the new wireless spread, and spurred the development of tuning techniques for minimizing the problem.

One would have thought that De Forest, with his strong background, would have taken a primarily scientific approach to improving Marconi's technology. But it was fame and fortune that drove him, not technical excellence, and, time and time again, it was this instinct that got him into trouble. He established a company in partnership with a mysterious and unscrupulous character named Abraham White. White was an old fashioned scam artist who took the opportunity to use De Forest's name to promote public investment in the company. Whether the company earned anything to justify the investment was apparently a secondary consideration. The result was a rash of problems with the law.

De Forest is, of course, best known for his invention of the Audion, the forerunner of the vacuum tube. His motivation to undertake this project stemmed from perhaps his most serious ethical lapse. It seems that the receiver which he had been using bore such a strong resemblance to one invented and patented by Reginald Fessenden, another of the early wireless competitors, that Fessenden finally sued for patent infringement. The plausibility of Fessenden's charge was borne out by the fact that De Forest's new receiver had made its appearance shortly after he had hired one of Fessenden's former assistants. Fessenden, who had developed the receiver to replace the essentially unsatisfactory coherer, won his suit and De Forest and White were required by the court to stop using the technology and to pay damages. They were so slow in complying with the court order that they were cited for contempt. In fact, De Forest had to flee over the border to Canada to avoid being jailed while White was raising the money for the damages. Finally White paid up, saving his partner from a prison term by the skin of his teeth. Ironically, it was at this point that White kicked De Forest out of the company. Now in the depths of despair, the chastened inventor had to look elsewhere for receiver technology, and the Audion was the inspired result.

A self-educated academic, Fessenden was born in Canada in 1866 and became interested in Hertzian waves at an early age from his reading. After teaching at the secondary level for a while, he moved to the United States and acquired his inventive spurs working for Edison. He subsequently left Edison to teach engineering at Purdue. From there he moved to the University of Pittsburgh because of its proximity to Westinghouse, where he had research interests.

Fessenden had a burning ambition to transmit audio as well as dots and dashes. From the very beginning of his wireless career, he sought out technology that would bring his goal into the realm of the possible. This goal was what motivated his early work in finding a replacement for the coherer receiver. But what could be done about the unsuitable spark gap transmitters? There were some who were attempting to obtain improved performance by refining the spark-gap technique. For example, in 1902 a Danish engineer, Valdemar Poulsen, developed a variation called a continuous-arc transmitter that generated waves from a series of short arcs. While this transmitter was hardly ideal, Fessenden seized upon it to make history by conducting the first radio broadcast. It was Christmas Eve in 1906, and many ships at sea were startled to hear, just barely, songs coming out of their wireless sets. The songs were accompanied by all kinds of noise but were nevertheless recognizable as Christmas carols and the singer was none other than Reginald Fessenden himself who completed the program with recitations and some recorded music.

Despite this history-making achievement, Fessenden was well aware that the spark gap was fundamentally unsuitable for speech and music, and he set about to develop an alternative. What was needed, in fact, was some way of generating alternating electrical currents in a controlled way that did not require the taming of erratic bolts of artificial lightning. Doing this today with our advanced electronics is a routine affair. But in the first decade of this century when electronics had not yet been invented, the only possible way to generate alternating current was mechanically, and to do so Fessenden came up with a novel kind of alternator. Many people today are familiar with a component under the hood of an automobile that goes by the same name. Both the automotive alternator and Fessenden's wireless transmitter have in common the fact that they convert direct current (DC) that flows in one direction from one terminal of a battery to the other into alternating current (AC) that flows back and forth in a smooth and predictable way.

By this time AC had won out over DC as the preferred way of supplying electrical power. High-power alternators were being manufactured by companies such as Westinghouse and General Electric. But there was one large difference between these alternators and one that could meet Fessenden's needs. The AC power in your wall outlet alternates fifty or sixty times per second, depending on where in the world you live. To be useful for radio transmission, the oscillations have to occur tens of thousands of times per second, no mean feat for rotating machinery. Fessenden devised a way of achieving oscillations as rapid as 100,000 times per second, and he contracted with General Electric to build such an alternator. The project was a success due to the ingenuity of Ernst Alexanderson, who had emigrated from his native Sweden to work with the legendary Charles Steinmetz at General Electric.[48] However, the ingenuity of Fessenden's invention was more than counteracted by his utter lack of business sense, and, even more, by his overwhelming and all-consuming paranoia. There is a pathetic story that illustrates the latter more than any other occasioned by his having been awarded the Institute of Radio Engineers' medal of honor in 1921.[49] He suspected that his medal was of gold plate rather than solid gold which he believed Marconi to have received the previous year. When an analysis of his medal proved him right, he angrily returned it. The IRE finally prevailed upon him to take it back with its apology that gold plate was all it could afford for all its medals, including Marconi's.

With all his brilliance, Fessenden never became much of a factor in the emerging industry. De Forest may have lost the suit that Fessenden brought, but he won out in the end. The vacuum tube, it turns out, can not only amplify signals, but can also generate oscillatory signals. Once the ability to do this was established, transmitters as well as receivers were brought into the electronic domain, and Fessenden's alternator became a historical curiosity. It is also interesting to note that recognition of the vacuum tube's ability to generate oscillatory signals was also to become the source of almost endless litigation, this time between De Forest and a brilliant and highly inventive younger contributor named Edwin Howard Armstrong. But that is a story best left until later (in Chapter 14).

Significantly Fessenden, De Forest, and another American engineer, John Stone Stone—apparently his mother wished to preserve her own maiden name to the point of redundancy—all developed technology superior to that of Marconi. They all started companies that, at various times, sold service and equipment. Yet, in contrast to Marconi, their companies had no lasting impact on the wireless scene. It was the American Marconi Co., almost an afterthought of the British parent company, that dominated the competitive scene in the United States during those early years, just as the parent company did in Britain. And the arena in which most of this competition took place was the sea.

Chapter

10

The Wireless Goes to Sea

In the more than half century that had passed since the first telegraph, communication by wire had settled into the world's infrastructure. The telegraph was old hat; its wires spanned most of the civilized world. Even the telephone was becoming relatively commonplace, certainly in the United States. The one major gap in worldwide connectivity was getting to places that wires could not reach. It is, therefore, only natural that the first area to be exploited by the new technology was in bridging this gap between land and sea. This was the environment in which Marconi had earned his worldwide fame. And this was the application that was to dominate the first twenty years of the wireless.

While the wireless represented new technology, its promotion still had to be based on sound business practices, something that Marconi understood. One of his earliest decisions was to follow the lead of the telephone and telegraph companies and sell services rather than systems. If a shipping company were to buy a system, it meant a significant investment in shipboard equipment, in shore stations, and in the supervision of Morse operators. With a leased service, the initial investment was very small, and the service could be discontinued if it turned out not to be satisfactory. In addition, selling the service meant supplying the Morse operators rather than leaving that important part of the system to the customer where standards of proficiency were likely to be lower. Then there was the additional advantage that all Marconi customers would be able to intercommunicate if necessary over a common network. Having made this decision, Marconi established his maritime company, built a series of shore stations, and began selling service.

By the time the wireless came along, a tradition of monopoly had already been established in the area of wire communications. It happened in various ways in the United States and Europe, but the tradition was entrenched. One can, perhaps, make the case that this condition was inherent to a business that depended on covering the world with a network of wires. Under this assumption, duplicating wire connectivity was just so inefficient that eventually one of the contenders had to dominate. But whether or not this argument was valid, it certainly could not apply to the wireless. Marconi did not deal with wires. Rather, he dealt with the "ether". Yet, this fact did not stop him from seeking to dominate his industry just as his wire-based predecessors had done before him. To this end, he adopted some of the same practices toward his competition that AT&T had found useful in thwarting its rivals who began springing up in the 1890s after the original Bell patents had expired. For example, he would not interconnect with competitors. His rule was that Marconi operators communicated only with other Marconi operators. Thus, a ship with someone else's equipment on board had to have Marconi service in addition if it was to talk to Marconi's relatively large complement of ships and shore stations. In just a few years, he had succeeded in signing up many steamship companies, Lloyd's of London—the leading maritime insurer—and the Italian and British navies.

He also had a secondary objective to compete with the transatlantic cable company, which had earned the enmity of the people on both sides of the ocean for its predatory pricing policies. However, the inherent shakiness of the transatlantic radio service precluded it from being a serious competitor in those early years. In fact, more than a decade later when the technology had advanced to the point where voice service could be supported by radio, it became the only way to carry the telephone across the ocean. Yet transatlantic calling was never terribly satisfactory both because of its poor quality and its high price until the first cable was installed in 1956 .[50]

The adoption of the wireless by the United States navy was an example of the right invention coming at just the right time. Just as the telegraph had made its appearance at the right time to assist the emerging Penny Press, so the wireless appeared at the opportune time to assist the United States in its new flirtation with imperialism. Following the Spanish-American War, the United States found itself a world power through its control of the former Spanish colonies of the Philippines, Guam, Hawaii, Puerto Rico, and Cuba. In the previous century, the British had demonstrated how communication in the form of undersea telegraph cables helped them maintain control of a worldwide empire. For the United States to do the same in the new century required a powerful navy responsive to the president, with the new wireless as the vehicle for assuring this responsiveness. Theodore Roosevelt, first as assistant secretary of the navy, then vice president, and finally, president, was a firm supporter of the new navy as the vehicle for his *big stick* policy, following the precepts laid down by the naval theoretician, Alfred Thayer Mahan. Thus, for the first time since Morse's demonstration from Baltimore to Washington, the government of the United States was to become involved in communications in a first-order way.

But the road was far from smooth for several reasons. The Congress and public were far from unanimous in favoring this new policy. There was opposition in Congress and the press to the whole idea of America as an imperialistic power. Nor was the navy unanimous about the desirability of installing wireless sets on ships at sea. Its ambivalent attitude toward this new capability is an interesting commentary on the clash between navy traditions and the changing needs of the nation.

The navy chose not to buy Marconi's monopolistic services or those of any of his inept American competitors. Rather, it operated its own services with shipboard equipment purchased from German companies and four shore stations—at Key West, Cuba, Puerto Rico, and the Canal Zone—purchased from De Forest in 1904. Technical difficulties resulting from the primitive state of the technology and the inexperience of the navy in operating its own services were the least of the problems. More detrimental was the reluctance of the navy to come to terms with a technology that diminished the authority of the commanders on the scene by letting the Washington brass interfere with the time-honored prerogatives of the captain of a ship. With communication back to Washington, even poor sporadic communication, the captain was no longer on his own once he left port.

Old traditions die hard, and the autonomy of a ship's captain is one of the oldest. The problem of making the operating navy (as opposed to the Washington navy) enthusiastic, or at least comfortable, with the wireless was analogous to that of making the field army accepting of the telegraph when it was first introduced. If anything, the problem was greater with the navy, and vestiges of it still remain almost 100 years later. This is what retired Admiral Lucien Capone referred to as the *Nelsonian syndrome* when he wrote in 1979: "We demand instant, rapid, reliable, and secure communication with our subordinates—but we prefer to hear from higher authority once a year by slow mail."[51] The independence of the ship captain from outside *meddling* is the very personification of naval tradition. To these traditionalists, radio was an intruder that would force time-honored doctrine to be changed, and, above all, threatened to allow the politicians to meddle in the preserve of military professionals.

It is not surprising, then, that the operating navy was as uncooperative as it was unenthusiastic. It did not train its operators adequately and failed to integrate the new capability into the modus operandi of ship-board life. As a result, the wireless created hardly a ripple in the day-to-day life on board ship. Even though it was slow to have an operational effect on the navy, it did have a political effect. The Depart-ment of the Navy may have been an inept user of the wireless, but its attempts served to establish it as the major governmental player in the new wireless business.

Thus, when international conferences on wireless took place, it was the Navy Department that represented the interests of the United States. International cooperation is essential for communication of all kinds to assure that standards are maintained that permit the systems of one nation to interoperate with those of others. They were especially impor-tant for wireless not only because ships operated in international waters but also because of the interference problems. The essential reason for this interference potential highlights the difference between communi-cation by wire and by wireless. A telegraph or telephone wire connects two specific points. A telegraph signal on a wire run between telegraph offices in New York and Philadelphia does not interfere with the signals on a wire running from New York to Pittsburgh or, for that matter, on another wire between New York and Philadelphia. A wireless signal, on the other hand, does not go from one point to another specific point, but rather to an area the size of which depends on the characteristics of the antennas used. This means that any receiver in that area has the potential ability to pick up the signal, a property that is precisely what is desired for broadcasting. But it is not desirable at all for ship-to-shore or ship-to-ship communication. For one thing, it means that discipline of some sort has to be imposed to allow more than one simultaneous communication in the same geographical area, the problem that came up earlier when both Marconi and De Forest tried to report the results of a race at the same time. The other problem is one of privacy. An eavesdropper has to go to the trouble of overtly tapping a telephone line to listen in on a private conversation. In contrast, *ether-tapping* comes naturally.

Once schemes were developed for tuning transmitters, frequencies could be assigned to various users permitting them to share the ether. Users constrained to use the same frequencies had to be disciplined to listen before sending and wait for the completion of one message before trying to send another one. The problem of privacy was dealt with by scrambling or encrypting the message to make eavesdropping difficult or impossible. Interestingly enough, these problems remain with us today in using modern radio media such as communications satellites and cellular radio systems. And the spectrum of solutions that exists for us today is not terribly different from that available to the wireless pioneers almost 100 years ago, even though the implementation technology is far different.

These fundamental facts of wireless life made some kind of international regulation necessary to assure satisfactory service to the maritime users. Some of the European participants also had the hidden agenda item of breaking the Marconi monopoly. The world radio conference in 1906 hit directly at Marconi's refusal to interconnect with outside systems by recommending a treaty requiring all shore stations to exchange wireless communications with any ship. The British, in support of the Marconi interests, held out for a while but ultimately had to ratify the agreement, compensating Marconi in return. On the other hand, the U. S. Senate declined to take any action at all. High on the agenda of the Congress at the time was debate on antitrust, child labor, and pure food and drug legislation. Regulation of radio communication was simply low-priority compared to these other regulatory matters.

Of more practical importance at home was legislation proposed by the navy to regulate the growing cult of amateur radio operators. The cost and complexity of running wires effectively eliminated any but serious commercial or governmental organizations from standard telegraphy and telephony. But liberated from the constraints of wires, anyone who could afford the radio equipment could communicate with his or her fellows just as well as the professionals. Thus amateur radio became a great national hobby, and, in those early years, many of the amateurs were more proficient than the navy, had better equipment, and often made a sport of interfering with maritime communication in a way that is reminiscent of how some of today's computer hackers take pleasure in disturbing establishment computer facilities. This first proposed regulation never made it through the Congress. As is so often the case, it took a well-publicized disaster to make the American people and their elected representatives in the Congress sit up and take notice.

That disaster was the sinking of the *Titanic* in 1912. The heroic actions of the ship's telegraph operator earned him, and the radio telegraph, wide publicity. And the fact that some amateur transmissions interfered, in part, with the *Titanic's* emergency transmissions led to the first regulation in the United States. The Senate Commerce Committee investigated the disaster soon after the event, and, in four months, there was legislation stipulating that transmission was a privilege assigned by the state and not a right, that property rights could be established in the airwaves, and that institutional users were the main claimants to those rights. Amateurs were required to be licensed and were assigned certain frequency bands separated from those used for maritime communication.

Finally the navy itself began to take the wireless more seriously and took steps to use it in a more professional way. Woodrow Wilson's navy secretary, Josephus Daniels, was the prime mover, in concert with a young naval officer named Stanford C. Hooper. The first step was to reorganize the navy to make it more responsive to the secretary's direction. At the time, the navy was divided into bureaus each of which was responsible for a particular area. The admiral heading each one could expect only the most general guidance from the civilian Secretary to whom he reported. At Daniels's urging, Congress established the position of Chief of Naval Operations as the senior officer in the navy. In the new scheme, the CNO sat at the secretary's level, enabling the secretary to maintain a tighter level of control over the bureaus. Significantly, the naval radio service was attached to the CNO thereby gaining the prestige necessary to integrate it into the way the navy was to do business in the future. All these steps meant that when World War I broke out in 1914, and especially when the United States entered the war three years later, the navy was finally ready to make effective use of the wireless telegraph.

11

World War I and Its Aftermath

As a wartime emergency measure, the U. S. government took over the railroads, the telephone system, and, along with these, most of the commercial wireless shore stations. In each case the rationale for this action was somewhat different. In the case of the wireless, the circumstances were quite extraordinary.

The navy, in fact, had to take actions more drastic than simply taking over the shore stations, actions which were to play a large role in determining the characteristics of the radio broadcasting boom after the war. The wireless had now been in existence for close to two decades. The technology of transmitters and receivers had advanced well beyond that of the early years, and yet the industry was still so highly fragmented that no one company could build an advanced system without running the risk of infringing on some other company's patents. In order to buy the best equipment it could for its ships, the Navy Department, in effect, absolved its contractors of this risk and assumed it for the government. With this action, the navy was now free to buy the most modern equipment from the several American manufacturers. Gone was the amateurism of the earlier years. The navy was now in the wireless business in a serious way and made effective use of it during the war.

The prime example of this technological chaos that motivated the navy's action was the vacuum tube, the device that, for the first time, permitted weak electrical signals to be strengthened or amplified. It was the singular great contribution made by De Forest at the time of his deepest despair in the wake of his legal struggles with Fessenden. Behind it all was a phenomenon that had been first noted by Edison who, while studying the properties of electric light bulbs, had observed that a heated wire filament gives off electrons. But he never did any more with his discovery. Subsequently, Sir William Preece of the British Post Office studied the phenomenon, and it was he who coined the name "Edison Effect" to describe it. But he could not exploit it either. This was left to another Englishman, James Fleming, who in 1896 inserted a second electrode in the form of a metallic plate into the bulb. When he impressed an oscillating signal between the two electrodes, the plate collected the electrons boiled off by the filament when it was positive relative to the filament but not when it was negative. This two-electrode bulb, or *diode* (a contraction of di-electrode), therefore had the ability to convert oscillating signals into unidirectional currents and, hence, to serve as a wireless receiver. It is crucial to the events that were to follow that Fleming subsequently went to work for Marconi. But Marconi was not impressed with the practicality of the device. He was more interested in another detector that used a piece of crystalline material to do the same thing.

De Forest's novel idea was to insert a third electrode in the form of a mesh structure or grid into the bulb between the other two, thereby creating a *triode*. Electrons still flowed in one direction, as in the diode, from the hot filament to the plate, passing through the holes in the grid. But the intensity of the flow depended on how the grid was electrically charged, the more positive the charge the greater the electron flow, the more negative, the less the flow. It followed that an oscillating signal impressed on the grid produced an oscillating electron flow. This property, in itself, was unremarkable. However, what was remarkable was the fact that these current oscillations represented an enhanced version of the signal on the grid. The amplifier was born!

De Forest's Audion was not a vacuum tube as we know it, because the bulb or tube housing the electrodes was not evacuated of gas. In fact, De Forest mistakenly thought that the performance of the new device was somehow related to the presence of the air in the chamber. Even the name Audion connecting audio and ion indicates his conception of the key role played by the gas. It was only later that Harold Arnold of AT&T and Irving Langmuir of General Electric more or less simultaneously recognized that the gas was not only not helpful but harmful. They pumped out the gas thereby giving birth to the true vacuum tube triode.

It is difficult to overstate the significance of the vacuum tube. It converted the radio receiver from a finicky device that required an expert to operate into something that the average citizen could use—*user-friendly* in today's language. As noted earlier, the vacuum tube had a similarly important effect on radio transmitters, both from its ability to generate oscillatory signals and to amplify them to the high power levels necessary to achieve long communications ranges. But it soon became apparent that radio was not its only area of applicability. The vacuum tube was exactly what AT&T needed to send telephone signals over long distances. It was also the device that liberated the phonograph from the recording and playback horns in the 1920s, and it made the digital computer possible in the 1930s and 1940s. In short, the vacuum tube was the component that created an entirely new field that came to be called electronics.

AT&T had bought the rights to the Audion from De Forest in 1913 for the bargain basement price of $50,000, taking advantage of De Forest's financial straits. Over the next few years, AT&T entered into additional agreements with De Forest that gave it rights to wireless telephony with the Audion and, later, exclusive rights to all De Forest's vacuum tube inventions, those in the past and for seven years into the future. This agreement with AT&T marked De Forest's departure from commercial wireless telephony, retaining the right only to manufacture equipment for amateurs and "for the distribution of music and news," functions that AT&T held in low esteem. As a result of these arrangements, AT&T was able to follow its first cross-country telephone connection by wire with a wireless connection, and by 1915 both the navy and AT&T had demonstrated transatlantic voice transmission.

With the invention of the vacuum tube, the wireless industry now seemed to be in a position to spurt ahead with vastly improved equipment. But this position was more apparent than real because of a legal problem that stemmed from the checkered history of the device. Marconi held the patent on the diode as the result of Fleming's work, and AT&T, as the successor to De Forest, held a patent on the triode. But Marconi claimed that the triode patent was invalid because it conflicted with the prior patenting of the diode, on which it depended. As long as the courts could not decide the issue unambiguously, the whole ownership situation was up in the air. And as long as the issue was in doubt, the only unequivocal technology for high-power continuous transmitters was the General Electric alternator that stemmed from Fessenden's original work. The Marconi Company belatedly recognized this coming trend, and, not having the technology of its own, endeavored to buy the alternators from the American source. The first of these was installed in an American Marconi shore station just in time to be taken over by the navy as the United States got into World War I.

But the situation with respect to the rights to the vacuum tube was only the most dramatic of the patent issues. Just as important was the fact that the scattered ownership of the many patents on various aspects of radio technology prevented any one company from fielding an optimum system. It was only by taking the drastic step of protecting its vendors against possible lawsuits that the navy was able to take care of its wartime needs.

The navy may have been the leader in the exploitation of the wireless, but the army, too, was beginning to apply the new medium. Of all army applications the one closest to the naval application was in communicating with its new Air Corps. The airplane made its military debut in World War I. While the problem of communicating with aircraft bears some technical similarity to that of communicating with ships, the emotional hurdle that confronted ship captains was entirely absent in the airplane because, while armies and navies have existed throughout history, the invention of the airplane followed the invention of radio. The air forces of the world had no histories and traditions to be perturbed by the invention.

When the U. S. Army first acquired aircraft not long after the first demonstrations of flight early in the century, it placed them under the command of the Signal Corps. This ostensibly strange assignment followed from the perceived potential of the airplane as a high observation platform, following the precedent established earlier with the use of balloons for this purpose. Thus, by the onset of World War I, military aircraft had already appeared. And even that early, the role of the aircraft expanded to the more modern roles as bombers and fighters, even giving rise to a new category of military hero with flyers such as Captain Eddie Rickenbacker, and the German Baron Manfred von Richthofen, the Red Baron (alter ego of Snoopy in the *Peanuts* comic strip). The use of wireless telegraphy between air and ground made its appearance even before the war and was of particular importance to the wartime observation role.

The new airplane played only a minor role in World War I, a situation that was to change radically in the approximately twenty years, from the end of this "War to end all wars" to the onset of the next world war. It played a crucial role in that war both as a fighting machine and as a transport vehicle. In the years since then its fighting and transport roles have continued as new roles have been added. And these roles have been increasingly dependent on the ability to communicate.

The wireless played only a small role in the ground fighting of World War I, not because there was no need for it, but rather because of the limitations of the available technology. One of the reasons for this situation was sheer capacity. Ground forces with massive troop deployments require massive communications. While a single radio channel between a shore station and a naval task force can mark the difference between victory and defeat, this is not usually the case in modern ground warfare where so much can be happening to so many people. Even with the availability of the vacuum tube, only a limited number of channels could be supported without interfering with one another. The place where radio found its major application was in the relatively low-capacity role of connecting General John Pershing, the commander of the American Expeditionary Force (AEF), to Washington across the Atlantic by telegraph where normal service was being hampered by the Germans cutting the transatlantic cables with regularity.

In contrast with this limited use of wireless, the army used wire communication massively in a way that was patterned after the use of the telegraph during the Civil War more than fifty years earlier, that is, as a way of connecting the battlefield forces back to the higher echelons of command. When the AEF landed in France, there was a major dispute over how it would be deployed. The British and French military leadership wanted American troops to supplement or replace their own exhausted forces. But Pershing was adamant about establishing an undiluted American presence on the battlefield. He demanded and finally received a piece of the front lines as his own. To control his forces, he demanded an extensive communication system behind the front, in effect a commercial-style system to connect his forces throughout France and from there to Washington. By its wartime takeover of the telephone system, the government was able to enlist the services of the Bell system in the formation of the Bell Battalions, under the command of John Carty, AT&T's chief engineer, who was given the rank of colonel in the Signal Corps. Carty's troops installed wire communications for both telephony and telegraphy to augment the existing French plant. The extent of this activity was quite remarkable: 2,000 miles of pole lines using 28,000 miles of wire. In conjunction with this, they installed 134 telegraph offices and 273 telephone exchanges. All this equipment, of course, connected the higher echelons of command with one another and to the rear where the higher-level headquarters were established. This massive effort, commensurate with the massive use of ground forces, established the precedent that was to continue during the remainder of the century.[52]

This was the case in World War II, Korea, Vietnam, in Europe during the long cold-war era, and in Saudi Arabia during the Gulf Crisis. Military units, usually Army and Air Force, were moved to semipermanent locations where they established communications that bear strong similarities to the fixed plant systems that are found in the commercial world. Sometimes the semipermanent locations take on all the characteristics of permanent locations as in Europe and Korea.

The years between the two world wars marked the maturation of the use of radio as a point-to-point medium in both the civil and military domains. Since the transoceanic telephone cable did not appear until after World War II, the wireless remained as the only way of supporting transoceanic telephony in either domain. While the importance of its commercial use in this way was eclipsed by the newly emerging radio broadcasting, this was not so in the military domain where its improved performance and reliability was instrumental in its acceptance as an important part of the military infrastructure. Even though the army made increasing use of the radio, it remained most closely identified with the navy, a consequence of its history and the fact that the navy, alone among the military branches, has the problem of keeping in touch with its mobile forces spread throughout the world in times of peace as well as war.

Advancing technology made what is known as *short-wave* radio feasible, and, from the mid 1920s on, this became the dominant mode for most applications, displacing the *long-wave* communication that had been prevalent in the earlier years. Almost from the very beginning of his career, Marconi had a fondness for the short-wave or high-frequency end of the spectrum, leaving it only for practical reasons. Later in the 1920s, he had the luxury of returning to study the propagation of these high-frequency waves.

The reason for the distinction between the long and short waves has to do with the way in which they are affected by the ionosphere. I noted earlier that low-frequency waves propagate following the surface of the Earth as so-called ground waves. One of the mechanisms for this bending of the waves is propagation through the Earth's surface, but there is also another mechanism. Very-low-frequency waves also propagate as if they are trapped between the Earth and the ionosphere; that is, they follow the contour of the Earth by hugging the surface of the Earth on one side and the lower layers of the ionosphere on the other. If the Earth and the ionosphere were perfect reflectors, then these waves could travel indefinitely far by a series of reflections. But since they are not perfect reflectors, at every reflection the waves lose some energy, and ultimately the waves dissipate with distance. The higher the frequency, the greater the dissipation and the harder it is to achieve long distances in this way.

When the frequency gets high enough, another mode of propagation sets in. These high-frequency signals pass through the lower layers of the ionosphere and are bent back to Earth by the upper layers much as a light beam is bent by a prism or a lens. Beginning in the 1920s, when the technology for generating and receiving at these higher frequencies became more common, this so-called sky wave became the technique favored by most for long-distance radio telegraphy and telephony.

It is not that there is a sharp dividing line between long- and short-wave propagation. It is more that the higher the frequency, the more the ground wave is dissipated, and the lower the frequency, the less likely it is that sky waves are possible. Because of this characteristic, there is a frequency region in which both modes can occur. The AM broadcast band is in this ambivalent region. Most of the time, especially during the day, AM broadcast signals propagate as ground waves achieving modest ranges of forty to fifty miles. But at night, they sometimes propagate erratically as sky waves disturbing the reception of stations hundreds of miles away on the same frequency.

When the frequency becomes high enough, the waves pass right through the ionosphere just as light does, and the distance they travel on Earth is usually limited by the horizon. The frequency bands used for FM radio and television broadcasting are in this very-high-frequency part of the spectrum, which explains why the ranges for these signals are quite limited. Of course, such frequencies were out of the question for Marconi and the others in the early days of radio. They did what they could at the low-frequency end and struggled mightily to gain an entrepreneurial foothold while improving their technology as best they could.

One of the advantages of short-wave propagation, and one of the primary reasons for its popularity, is the fact that it can span long distances with modest amounts of transmitted power. But along with this advantage, it has the significant disadvantage that its coverage area has gaps in it, and locations of these gaps vary with time and are difficult to predict. Thus, if the navy headquarters wishes to contact a particular ship at a particular time, it can never be sure that its message will arrive. This unpredictability was one of the major reasons why short-wave radio almost disappeared from the scene in all contexts in the latter part of this century, replaced by the new technology of satellite communications. Today it is staging a mild comeback for certain military applications, due largely to a greater understanding of the vagaries of its propagation and the development of techniques to overcome some of these.

The source of these difficulties is, of course, the ionosphere itself. Recall that the ionosphere is caused by the effect of the sun's rays on the Earth's atmosphere. Its properties depend on the extent to which the air molecules are ionized by the sun's radiation. It is obvious that the extent of this ionization should be different at night than during the daylight hours. It is by no means obvious but nevertheless true that the sun's radiation varies not only from day to night, but also from month to month and year to year as sunspot activity varies. Modern cameras and binoculars have built-in mirrors that reflect the light in appropriate ways. Just imagine the kind of photographs you would obtain from a camera whose mirrors were subject to fluctuations over which you had no control. Present day short-wave technology can compensate for some of these problems, but this is a rather recent phenomenon.

It is for reasons such as these that in the years between the two world wars, the navy found that a more reliable, if more procedurally awkward, way to communicate to its ships was by the use of low-frequency or long-wave signals. This propagation required very large and expensive shore stations to develop the high powers necessary to cover the oceans, but cover the oceans they did in their brute-force way. At low enough frequencies the long-wave signals are capable of propagating over thousands of miles—hence, the reliance of the navy on these frequencies to reach ships all over the world.

The other penalty paid in the use of these very-low-frequency signals is low bandwidth, meaning low communications capacity. Just to give an example, the entire low-frequency range contains the equivalent capacity of about 25 voice channels, the AM broadcast band contains 10 times as many, and the short-wave band contains 200 times as many, or 5,000 equivalent voice channels. It is clear from these numbers that the use of voice is an expensive luxury at low frequencies; the only practical thing is to reserve this band for telegraphy. Therefore, the modus operandi established by the navy that continued through World War II and even beyond, was based on a *Fleet Broadcast* communication system by which large shore stations sent a continuous sequence of Morse code or teletype messages to all ships at sea in a kind of one-way party line. Radio operators on board each ship would watch for messages addressed to their ship and direct them to the captain. If a reply was warranted, the ship would send it by short-wave radio to whatever shore station could pick it up for relay to its ultimate destination. Shortwave was used for the replies from the ship to shore both because it was difficult to generate the very high power low-frequency signals on a ship and because the lack of reliability for the sporadic replies or for the messages originated by the ship was of less consequence than for the heavy continuous broadcast traffic.

Since telegraphy was the only practical way to communicate to and from ships and the most practical scheme for general overseas communication, written message communication remained the standard for official communication, both military and nonmilitary. The secretary of state communicated with overseas ambassadors by message either carried in the diplomatic pouch or transmitted electrically. In fact, the message as a vehicle for military and other official communication is as old as mail service. If the king entrusted waging of war to his generals, he and they exchanged information via the military messenger. The message served another function that transcended its utility as a bandwidth saver. An authenticated message has the force of law. When sent from a higher level to a lower level, it is a command as valid as if delivered in person. Even with modern communication bandwidths in which voice is usually technically permissible, the written message is the technique for issuing a directive. The military has developed structured procedures to preserve the authority of the message by demanding that a message be approved by a higher authority before it is sent out, and a structured way of preserving the record of what transpired by maintaining an archive of message traffic that permits events to be reconstructed at a later time. As convenient as the telephone may be, no ephemeral telephone message conveys the authority of the written message.

Organizations often have trouble adapting their tried-and-true procedures to new technology. The written message is an excellent case in point. The early military message systems were modeled after Morse's telegraph systems. They were not user-to-user. Rather, the originator would write out a message, get the commanding officer to sign off, and deliver the approved copy to the military equivalent of the Western Union office. Today when a person can sit at a computer terminal, compose a message, and then send it off as a piece of electronic mail, these older, labor-intensive procedures seem as antiquated as the Model T Ford. But how does an official user insure that an electronic-mail message is properly approved by higher authority? Authentication has been a problem that has impeded the introduction of modern messaging techniques for the traditional message role. Since the decade of the 1980s, when this technology was becoming widespread, the Defense Department has struggled with two systems: modern electronic mail for *informal* message traffic, the written equivalent of a telephone conversation—and the old telegraphlike system for *formal* message traffic. As time goes on, the older system will wither away, to be replaced by a user-to-user electronic-mail system that incorporates the electronic equivalent of the old sign-off process. I have more to say about this in Chapter 24.

There is still another important, peculiarly maritime, advantage in using the low-frequency end of the spectrum. Since sea water is a reasonably good conductor of electricity, it effectively shorts out any electromagnetic waves that strike its surface. However, if the frequency of the waves is low enough, the waves will penetrate the water to some small extent, the lower the frequency, the greater the depth of penetration. The principal advantage of nuclear-powered submarines over the older diesel-powered boats is their ability to remain submerged for very long periods of time, thereby decreasing the chance that they will be detected by hostile ships and aircraft. When the higher frequencies are used in communicating with submarines, the boats are required to surface. And every time they do this, they place themselves in jeopardy of being detected. However, when very low frequencies are used, they are able to remain below the surface even if their antennas have to float close to the surface. At still lower frequencies, even the antenna can be submerged well below the surface. Of course, the lower the frequency, the lower the bandwidth and the lower the rate at which information can be transmitted. The result is that minimal amounts of information can be exchanged with submerged submarines, enough to maintain some level of coupling between the submarine skipper and his superiors ashore.

In the commercial maritime domain, where assured reliability at all times was less of a concern, the short-wave radio became the dominant mode of communication. The same, of course, was true for all point-to-point applications, such as intercontinental telephony. But in the post-World War I years, the use of electromagnetic waves as wireless connections to locations without wires was fast losing its preeminence. Rapidly taking its place was the new concept of radio broadcasting.

Chapter

12

The Origins of Broadcasting

At 8:00 P.M. on November 2, 1920, radio station KDKA in Pittsburgh went on the air with the first returns from the presidential election in which Warren G. Harding defeated James M. Cox, thereby turning out of office Woodrow Wilson's Democratic party that had led the nation to its wartime victory. It was the world's first radio broadcast that could be called commercial. A year and one-half later, Herbert Hoover, then the secretary of commerce, described the radio boom that followed as "one of the most astounding things that has come under my observation of American life."[53]

To the casual observer, broadcasting came out of the blue. Even to the noncasual observer, with some awareness of the immediate background to the historic event, the speed with which it came was unexpected. But whatever one's reaction to the events surrounding this first broadcast, what happened thereafter was nothing short of startling. The telegraph and the telephone, the phonograph and the motion picture were all great successes that met with immense popular approval in the years following their first introduction, but the reception accorded the radio outdid them all.

How did this happen? More than twenty-five years earlier, there had been experiments with wireline broadcasting in various places in the United States and Europe, the most successful and long-lasting of which was the Pleasure Telephone of Budapest. But there is no evidence that any of these played any role in what followed with radio broadcasting. It would appear that the idea of broadcasting entertainment, news, and sports was an idea that sprang up independently and spontaneously wherever the technical and economic conditions were right. If anything appears to be an inherent natural desire of people, it is to be entertained. The phonograph, invented by Edison at the time of the telephone, had made it possible for ordinary people to hear music previously out of reach of all but the upper rungs of society. The motion picture that made its appearance in the 1890s truly democratized entertainment. Millions of people who had never had the opportunity or the money to attend the theater were able to watch dramas in thousands of nickelodeons that sprang up all over the country. The radio, like its wireline-based predecessors, combined some of the features of both. Like the phonograph it brought music into the home. In fact, much of the programming in the first years of radio consisted of recorded music. The radio also brought drama, a new kind, to be sure, that reached its audience by sound without sight. It also brought news bulletins and special events. There seemed to be no limit to the variety. There was something for everyone.

Phenomena like the radio boom may seem to spring up as if from nowhere, but they cannot happen just at any time and in any place. The conditions have to be right, and the United States in the aftermath of World War I provided the right conditions. One of the necessary conditions for such a boom was reliable, easy-to-use technology. There would be no boom if the broadcast transmitters did not work well enough to sustain a consistent schedule and if the receivers were not operable by the average citizen without a technical bent. The improved technology that had resulted from the war and from the actions of the Navy Department that made this technology available for military use was one of the preconditions that prepared the stage for the events that were to follow.

Another precondition lay in the political events that made this same technology available commercially after the war. Recall that Josephus Daniels, Wilson's secretary of the navy, had established a virtual government monopoly over the wireless in America during the war, with the navy as its agent. His wartime action in taking over most of the commercial wireless assets and, especially, of getting around the fundamental issue of scattered patent ownership enabled the navy to take care of its wartime needs. Now that the war was over, Daniels saw many advantages to the country in retaining this same arrangement.

The navy's wartime management of the wireless industry had been highly successful. With the impetus of winning the war, the government was able to have the use of all the American patents under one roof, a monopoly of technology that had never existed previously. Daniels appeared to feel that monopoly was inherent to the industry, and, if that were the case, the monopoly should be American. The prewar Atlantic wireless traffic had been dominated by the British, who also dominated the undersea telegraph cables through their control of the gutta percha material used to render the wires waterproof. Thus, he viewed with some alarm an impending deal between General Electric and Marconi in which the latter would have essentially exclusive rights to the alternator, still the only really satisfactory transmitting device. We also know that he viewed wireless as too important for the national interest to be dependent on foreign technology or to allow strategic American technology to fall into foreign hands. (This latter aspect sounds familiar to us today in a very different set of circumstances.) In fact, one of his first postwar steps was to attempt to buy those remaining Marconi shore stations that the government had not taken over during the war. But the Congress was not to allow Daniels to have his way. For one thing, it was just not within the American tradition. In addition, the government operation of the railroads and telephone systems during the war had not been nearly as salutary as the navy's operation of the wireless. Government ownership of basic industries was something that might be tolerated in time of war, but not in peacetime.

Recognizing that Daniels's desire for continued government control of wireless was beyond their grasp, the navy sought another method.[54] First they requested that General Electric hold off on the impending alternator deal with American Marconi until the company could hear the navy's views. Subsequently, Captain Stanford C. Hooper, considered the Father of navy radio, and Admiral W. H. G. Bullard made the proposition to Owen D. Young, GE's vice president, that the electrical giant get into the wireless business by taking over the patents that the navy had acquired and adding them to the patents that GE already owned. The appeal was based on the patriotic idea that it was in the national interest not to allow anything as important as wireless to remain controlled by foreign interests.

Young was evidently impressed by the navy's arguments, but he extended the government's plan in an ingenious way. General Electric was an equipment manufacturer, not a provider of communications services. Rather than going into an entirely new line of business in competition with Marconi, why not buy out American Marconi and run it as a GE subsidiary? Then Marconi's patents would be added to the others. It would be a marriage made in heaven, between the largest American manufacturer of electrical equipment including the alternator, and the leading wireless service company. E. J. Nally, American Marconi's president, was enthusiastic about the idea. Daniels went along with the arrangement after a last try with Congress failed; if he could not have a government-controlled monopoly, the next best thing was a government-sponsored industrial arrangement that would achieve some of the same results. American Marconi had little choice but to accede to the novel proposal, largely because the government was still holding the shore stations that it had taken over during the war. The screws were tightened still further when the stockholders of the British subsidiary were led to believe that their chance of receiving government business would be much greater as an American company.

Thus was born the industrial giant known as the Radio Corporation of America. Young became the board chairman of GE's new subsidiary. The remainder of the leadership consisted of the old American Marconi officers: Nally became president, and David Sarnoff, later to be the name most identified with broadcasting and a long-time employee of American Marconi, became the commercial manager. Interestingly enough, this unprecedented action involving government and industry that played fast and loose with the nation's antitrust laws was taken with a minimum of publicity. Radio, now almost twenty years old, had ceased to be good copy. As it turned out, the agreement ultimately succumbed to these antitrust laws, but by the time that this happened, the government's objectives had been fulfilled.

The new company was to play the role in the commercial world that the navy had played during the war. It was to provide central control for all radio telegraphy in the country, ". . . to link the countries of the world in exchanging commercial messages," according to the press release announcing the formation of RCA. One of these objectives, that of removing wireless services from foreign control, was clearly achieved by the plan. The plan also laid the groundwork for patent sharing. But additional arrangements were needed to achieve the same level of patent sharing in peacetime that government control had accomplished during the war. The key patent holders outside the RCA fold were AT&T and Westinghouse. Westinghouse, like GE, its major competitor, was a manufacturers with no prior interest in communications except as an outlet for its products. AT&T was the monopolistic telephone company with no obvious interest in radio. Indeed, its interest in the vacuum tube to begin with was motivated by the revolutionary effects that the new device would have on telephony. It participated minimally in the wireless business but held in reserve the option to do so under the right circumstances. In public it maintained a contemptuous attitude toward the wireless while privately maintaining its technological proficiency.

It was particularly important to bring AT&T into the patent-sharing deal, primarily to clarify, once and for all, the legal status of the vacuum tube by placing under a single umbrella the De Forest triode patents now owned by AT&T and the Fleming diode patents now owned by RCA, the inheritor of the American rights to the Marconi patents. After the two companies reached an agreement, the vacuum tube was finally freed of its shackles. It was not very long after that it was applied to the important high-power transmitter application and the hitherto importance of the alternator began its decline. The alternator's moment of glory occurred during the war with the construction of 200 kilowatt transmitters for the navy. After a few years most of these had disappeared in favor of tubes, although, curiously enough, one historical relic was still operating in Sweden as recently as 1986, perhaps as a tribute to its native son, Alexanderson, and a descendent continued to be used by the Italian navy into the 1990s.

In return for the patent sharing, each of the players was assigned a unique piece of the radio communications turf. RCA was to have exclusive rights for transoceanic wireless telegraphy and ship-to-shore communication. AT&T's domain was radio telephony with exclusive rights to its use for toll (long-distance) service, and with exclusive rights to manufacture wireless telephone transmitters. GE was to have exclusive rights to manufacture radio receivers. It is especially interesting that the concept of broadcasting was nowhere to be found in these agreements. And all this maneuvering happened in 1919, the year after the armistice and the year before KDKA. Broadcasting was farthest from the minds of the participants.

It seems that the only person connected with forging the agreements who had any interest in the potential of broadcasting was David Sarnoff.[55] Sarnoff had immigrated to the United States as a child from the Pale of Settlement, a swath of land in the old Russian empire running from the Baltic countries in the north to the Ukraine in the south, covering portions of what is now Poland, Hungary, and Romania as well as portions of the former Soviet Union. It was here that most Jews in the Czarist empire were compelled to live. Young Sarnoff started with American Marconi in 1906 as a floor sweeper and began to learn the business. He achieved some measure of fame during the *Titanic* disaster as one of the Morse operators who received the ship's SOS messages. As early as 1916, he wrote a memo to Nally in which he predicted that broadcasting would become a significant factor in the industry. But no one in the conservative Marconi organization could see beyond wireless telegraphy or perhaps telephony. Three years later at the fledgling RCA, Sarnoff again promoted his ideas on broadcasting and convinced Young to take some first steps in developing a radio receiver. It was these first tentative steps that enabled RCA to hit the ground running once Westinghouse showed the way.

Westinghouse was the odd man out as far as the RCA patent-sharing agreements were concerned. It was a major patent holder, having acquired the rights to both Fessenden's and Armstrong's patents. This omission of Westinghouse from the RCA pact was to play a role in the introduction of broadcast radio; but the road was far from direct. First, Westinghouse attempted to compete in RCA's domain, but was effectively shut out by RCA's aggressiveness in locking up exclusive arrangements with foreign countries for intercontinental radio telegraphy. It was only after the KDKA broadcast that Westinghouse joined the radio club. To obtain the rights to the key Westinghouse patents, RCA entered into a cross-licensing arrangement with Westinghouse that had as one of its provisions an agreement by RCA to share its receiver orders between GE and Westinghouse on a sixty-forty basis.

But commercial broadcasting did not spring into existence from nowhere; it simply followed in the footsteps of the amateurs. Lee De Forest could lay claim to being the patron saint of these amateurs. Recall that in his agreements with AT&T, the one right he continued to reserve to himself was that of manufacturing equipment to be sold to amateurs. In fact, De Forest, with his usual modesty, claimed to be the inventor of broadcasting in 1906, the same year in which his old nemesis, Fessenden, broadcast a program of carols on Christmas Eve. Those were the days of his deepest troubles with Fessenden's patents and the law. One of the great passions of his life was opera, and during those troubled days he would often attend the opera in the cheapest available seats to lose himself in the music and drama. "I look forward to the day when opera may be brought into every home. Some day the news and even advertising will be sent out over the wireless telephone," he said to reporters.[56] But in those early years, the technology was so crude that very few took his prophesy very seriously. He went so far as to attempt a broadcast of a Metropolitan Opera production of two short operas commonly presented together, *Cavaleria Rusticana* and *I Pagliacci*, starring Enrico Caruso and Emma Dustin. While we do not have a record of how good the performances were that day, we do know that De Forest's radio audience did not hear anything well enough to exercise any judgment.

The legislation of 1912 that introduced regulation into radio for the first time initially discouraged the cult of the radio amateur. But after this initial setback, the hobby began to flourish with renewed vigor. One indication of this growth is the fact that the number of licensed amateur operators increased from 322 in 1913 to 13,581 in 1917, with estimates of as many as 150,000 unlicensed. While most of the traffic was still Morse code, the improved technology based on the vacuum tube for the first time allowed voice and music transmission. The market share for this use as opposed to telegraphy was continually increasing. De Forest, himself, inaugurated nightly programs of phonograph music, and he would also air special events such as the Harvard-Yale football game and the presidential election results in 1916. He also claimed to be the first to carry advertising over the air. Other amateurs began to emulate his practices. After being shut down during the war, they returned with renewed vigor in 1919, taking advantage of the refined equipment available as a result of the war effort that improved their ability to send speech and music.

The radio hams of the first part of the century seem to have been motivated by many of the same factors that motivate today's computer hackers. They were participating on the frontier of a new technology and contributing to the advance of that technology. They delighted in demonstrating their superiority over the professionals in their field, a characteristic that got them into trouble around the time of the *Titanic*, just as a few hackers have run afoul of the law for illegal penetration of computer systems. They were interested in the radio for the excitement of communicating over long distances as well as in the technology of the radio transmitters and receivers. Once they succeeded in making contact with one of their fellow hams, they would chat for a while to get acquainted. It cost money to do this on the telephone but was free on the wireless. They might bring their companion up to date with the news from their town. Running out of things to say, they might play a new phonograph record. These things are natural consequences of the desire to communicate. While some amateurs may have intended their transmissions to be private, all were, in fact, broadcast to anyone in the signal path who cared to listen in.

The most famous of the amateur broadcasters was Frank Conrad, a Westinghouse employee. He followed a more or less regular schedule in his broadcasts of both live and recorded music and developed a wide following largely in the Pittsburgh area but also wherever his fellow hams could pick up his transmissions. The Joseph Horne Department Store cashed in on the radio craze and, in turn, fueled it by selling receivers for $10. This was the sequence of events that prompted Harry Davis, a Westinghouse vice president and Conrad's boss, to conceive the idea of doing the same commercially. After obtaining a commercial license with the now-famous call letters KDKA, he hired Conrad to begin broadcasting just in time to carry the results of the presidential election of 1920.

Chapter

13

Radio Broadcasting Captures the Nation

Frank Conrad's idea spread like wildfire. Commercial stations were licensed in all the major cities. From January to May 1922, the number of stations grew from twenty-six to ninety-nine. Finally, the unprecedented popularity of the new medium began to convince the wireless giants that there might be something to radio broadcasting after all. The realization shook RCA to its very roots. Its management finally understood where the business was going. It finally struck them that Sarnoff's view was the correct one: broadcasting, rather than point-to-point service was to be radio's destiny. Once it overcame its initial psychological block, RCA jumped with vigor into both broadcasting and the sale of radios together with its manufacturing partners GE and Westinghouse in accordance with its agreements. So did AT&T, a company not usually associated with radio broadcasting. Yet the telephone company was also to be one of the major players in the formative days of broadcast radio.

Many other radio manufacturers entered the field in competition with RCA, General Electric, and Westinghouse. With the unprecedented boom, there was room for many in this amazing business. The receiver manufacturers, struggled to supply enough sets to meet the enormous demand. Receiver sales grew from $60 million in 1922 to $358 million in 1924.[57] By 1928, only eight years after commercial broadcasting began, 7.5 million homes had radios.[58] Herbert Hoover, the secretary of commerce, was forced against his will to introduce some minimal regulation simply to keep the burgeoning station population from interfering with one another. The sheer numbers of broadcasters who started up made this minimal regulation ineffective. After the courts ruled that the Commerce Department did not have the authority to regulate, Congress passed the Radio Act of 1927 providing a Federal Radio Commission (later replaced by the Federal Communications Commission) with this authority.

Improved user-friendly receiver technology fueled this growth. Many of the radio amateurs were tinkerers who relished playing with their antennas, transmitters, and receivers to increase their range. The typical amateur receiver was a crystal set in which the crucial component was a piece of crystalline material, carborundum or silicon, to which two wires were attached. It was the solid-state equivalent of the vacuum tube diode in that it conducted current in one direction, and its discovery in 1906 was what made Marconi lose interest in Fleming's diode as a radio receiver. The crystal was, in fact, a crude predecessor of the silicon technology that was to replace the vacuum tube later in the century. With its virtues of simplicity and low cost, it was a vast improvement over its predecessor receivers, and, until the vacuum tube was perfected and freed of its legal shackles, the crystal was the principal receiver technology. Nevertheless, it was quirky and finicky. No one really understood how it worked, and there was some element of art in placing the wires—called catwhiskers—on the crystal to obtain the maximum asymmetry of current flow. By the time broadcast radio came along, it remained as the mainstay of the receivers used by amateurs because of its low cost. But in the wake of the war, the improved triodes were becoming available at lower prices, resulting in more reliable and higher performance receivers for commercial broadcasting.

The amateurs powered their receivers by batteries, not the dry cells so prevalent today, but wet cells similar to automobile batteries. Wet cells may have been fine for hobbyists, but not for the general public, interested in radio for its content. The first commercial radios also used wet cells, but housewives would not allow these sets in their living rooms out of fear that battery acid would spill on their carpets. Once the *plug-in* variety became available, the receivers were installed in handsome cabinets that began to grace the living rooms of America. The receiver circuits were themselves upgraded to use several tubes to improve the quality of the audio and its resistance to atmospheric noise. Loudspeakers were soon introduced replacing the older earphones, thus allowing the whole family to listen at once.

All the characteristics of radio broadcasting that were later assumed by television as well were developed during those first few formative years. The programming was varied, including news, time checks, and religious broadcasting. But the dominant program fare was music, mostly recorded because it was so convenient, but also live performances. In the beginning, the music was almost exclusively classical, performed by the most noted musicians of the day in concerts and operas. This trend reached its climax with the founding of the NBC symphony under Arturo Toscanini, the most famous conductor of them all.

Radio was the vehicle by which jazz became the popular music idiom of the twenties and thirties. It is difficult for us living in these days of blatantly sexual music freely performed on radio and television to understand the mentality of the 1920s that barred jazz from the air as undignified. Only when Paul Whiteman began to popularize Gershwin's *Rhapsody in Blue* in 1924 did it achieved sufficient respectability to be allowed on the air. By 1930, all the familiar patterns of today's television broadcasting were there: the sports broadcasts, the continuing situation comedies epitomized by *Amos and Andy*, the soap operas, and the comedians, who were to forsake vaudeville for the new medium where they could perform for millions instead of hundreds or, at most, a few thousand.

Radio became the main vehicle for news and entertainment, in short, the main communications vehicle for just about anything. It was another example where the whole is more than the some of its parts. The essayist E. B. White ascribed divine properties to its impact when he wrote in 1933:

> I live in a strictly rural community, and people here speak of *The Radio* in the large sense, with an overmeaning. When they say *The Radio* they don't mean a cabinet, an electrical phenomenon, or a man in a studio, they refer to a pervading and somewhat godlike presence which has come into their lives and homes.[59]

With the rapid growth of radio broadcasting in its early days came perhaps the biggest question of all: how could broadcasting be made commercially viable? Westinghouse's original notion was to use the medium as a vehicle for selling receivers, and there were some who proposed building on that idea by levying a tax on receiver sales. But this approach was not in the cards for a country as the United States that always sought to avoid government involvement in what was considered a private-sector affair. It was, however, in Britain where the tradition was quite different. From the beginning, the United Kingdom made it a matter of national policy that the new radio was to be used for the public good. It began broadcasting in 1922 with a public company and, five years later, chartered the British Broadcasting Corporation to be funded by a license fee on every radio (and later, television) set.[60] It was much later that the United States government became involved in broadcasting when it established the Corporation for Public Broadcasting supported by the taxpayer.

Interestingly enough, the notion of supporting programming with advertising began with AT&T in a manner that stemmed from its experience with telephone service. Why not sell time on its powerful New York station WEAF just as it did for toll calls on its long-distance network and create, thereby, *toll broadcasting* in which a company could broadcast anything it chose during the time that it bought and pay AT&T for the privilege. AT&T had no more desire to dictate the programming in the advertiser's time slot than to tell its telephone subscribers what to say during a toll call. But when individual advertisers did not respond with their own programming, the stations had to step in reluctantly and begin the kind of system that we have today in which the stations or networks select the feature programs and then sell them to advertisers. Broadcasting was becoming truly autocratic, with the majority of its programming coming from a few broadcasters who had to satisfy their perception of the tastes of the listening public and the advertisers who footed the bill. It is interesting to note that simply calling the principle by the name *toll* was enough to convince the Commerce Department to give WEAF a unique frequency because of the association of its radio service with its universal toll service.

It was not too long after the inception of broadcasting, that the concept of the broadcasting *network* arose as the vehicle for bringing common programming into many cities at the same time. It began informally when AT&T set up multiple-station hookups for special broadcasts using its telephone circuits to provide the interstation connectivity. When RCA tried to do the same, AT&T astonished it by refusing to provide the telephone circuits. It claimed the right to do this by citing the patent-sharing agreement in which it was given exclusive rights to wireless telephony. After all, it claimed, what was broadcasting if not a form of wireless telephony. This action forced RCA to buy poorer-quality telegraph circuits from Western Union, with correspondingly poor results.

This set of occurrences was to mark the beginning of the end to AT&T's brief career in broadcasting and, shortly thereafter, of the navy's and Young's carefully crafted plan. A bitter legal dispute developed between the two broadcasters based on their conflicting interpretations of their agreements in 1919 and 1920. They finally agreed to binding arbitration in 1925, and most of the issues in contention were decided in RCA's favor. But this was a case in which the result of binding arbitration did not settle the issue. Rather, it led to further legal wrangling. For AT&T's rejoinder was that if the arbitrator were correct, then the original agreements between the two companies must have been illegal. The situation was finally settled when AT&T decided abruptly to get out of the broadcasting business and sell its broadcasting assets to RCA, with the statement that broadcasting was too far removed from the mainstream of the telephone business. Another unstated reason was probably the fact that both RCA and AT&T were the subjects of a great deal of unfavorable publicity during the prolonged dispute, and AT&T, as the telephone giant continuously under the eye of the Justice Department, felt it necessary to retain the goodwill of the public that it served.

In 1926, the two companies agreed to carve up the communications pie in accordance with what each saw as its basic interests. AT&T retained those aspects of radio that were central to the telephone business, that is, both wire and wireless telephony, and RCA agreed not to compete in these areas nor in wire telegraphy. AT&T was also to supply network relays by wire or wireless to RCA on an exclusive basis. Following this agreement, RCA formed a broadcasting subsidiary called the National Broadcasting Company with two networks: the former AT&T network with station WEAF as its flagship became the NBC Red Network, the ancestor of today's NBC, and the former RCA network, with station WJZ as its flagship station, became known as the NBC Blue Network, later in 1943 to become the American Broadcasting Company, when the Federal Communications Commission forced NBC to divest itself of one of its networks.

NBC enjoyed its broadcasting monopoly for two years until competition arose in the form of the Columbia Broadcasting System. Initially AT&T refused to lease telephone lines to CBS as part of its agreement with NBC. But it did not take long for the Federal Trade Commission put a stop to that when it forced AT&T as a common carrier to lease lines to anyone who wanted them.

It was, therefore, the emergence of this enormously popular phenomenon of broadcast radio that began the conversion of AT&T's public network from total dedication to telephone service to the more general function of providing connectivity for information in any form that was appropriate. The expansion of the system beginning immediately after World War II was to create the capacity not only for increased telephone service but also to support the then mature radio broadcasting industry, the emerging television broadcasting industry, and the digital revolution that were to follow in the second half of the century.

The bitter litigation between RCA and AT&T that culminated in the withdrawal of AT&T from broadcasting was just the beginning of the end of the great RCA experiment. AT&T had cast doubt upon the validity of the arrangements that had been so carefully crafted in 1919. The Justice Department brought an antitrust suit against RCA in 1930, contending restraint of trade in the provision that divided the receiver manufacturing pie between General Electric and Westinghouse to the exclusion of the other manufacturers—almost 750 had been established between 1923 and 1926, but only 72 lasted until 1927. The action ended in 1932 with the parties accepting a consent decree that separated the two manufacturing giants from RCA. RCA would continue to administer the patent pool in a nonexclusive way, and General Electric and Westinghouse were to be allowed back in the receiver manufacturing business after two years.

But this turn of events cannot by any stretch of the imagination be considered a defeat for the objectives of the government. RCA had become a powerful *American* corporation and the dominant force in transatlantic communication. But, of course, this was all beside the point, because transoceanic communication had been dwarfed by the new role of radio as an entertainment medium, an event unforeseen by any of the parties to those postwar agreements. And it was this broadcast role that led to television and its enormous impact on so much of our society.

It is ironic that decades after these changes the situation was to revert back to the earlier days in many respects. Who would have imagined that this powerful American electronics manufacturing dominance would again slip into foreign hands, and that this would be one of the contributing factors to the sale of RCA and its NBC subsidiary back to General Electric in the late 1980s?

Plus ça change, plus c'est la même chose.

Chapter

14

Video Enters the Picture

No previous invention had ever captured the heart and soul of America as had the radio. In less than twenty years it had become the principal way in which the average American received his or her news and entertainment. And yet, on the threshold of World War II, at the pinnacle of its success, it was on the verge of being displaced by something else in the hearts of its subscribers.

At first glance, the transition from radio to television appears to be similar to that between the telegraph and the telephone sixty years earlier. Here was a newer technology beginning to supplant an established technology because it added a new dimension that improved the friendliness of the communication. But this similarity is superficial at best. The telephone indeed replaced the transmission of words with the transmission of the human voice saying those words, but there was a lot more to it than that. For the very nature of voice transmission led naturally to the concept of universal service with instant feedback, something quite foreign to the telegraph. In addition, telephone service was brought into being by entrepreneurs outside of and, hence, in competition with the telegraph mainstream. All this made telephone service something qualitatively different from telegraph service—a bolt from the blue with a revolutionary effect.

It was not this way with television. Rather than being something qualitatively different, television was more an enhanced version of the same thing, an extension or evolution of broadcast radio. It was brought into the home in just the same way. The industry that developed it was the same as the one currently bringing radio into millions of homes. And the programming and advertising formats for the new medium were natural extensions of the ones that were proving so successful with the audio medium.

While the advent of television broadcasting is a post-World War II phenomenon, the first few broadcast stations went on the air before the war. The previous two decades had seen engineers, fascinated by the notion of being able to transmit video as well as audio, develop the basic technology, with the intuitive feeling that once they were successful, the value and importance of their efforts would be recognized by a population eager to see as well as hear. Once they were successful, the broadcast industry, led by David Sarnoff of RCA, picked up the ball, only to be delayed until the war was over and American industry could shift from military to civil production.

What comes as a surprise in the story is that the first efforts to invent the technology needed for television occurred in 1884, well before the radio, the vacuum tube, or even the motion picture existed. The pioneer was the German inventor, Paul Nipkow. Nipkow had all the right ideas but was unable to implement them adequately because of a lack of technology. His vision was to be able to send pictures, even moving pictures, over telegraph wires. His big contribution was the invention of a rudimentary mechanical scheme for scanning a scene and converting the image to electrical form. But the technology of the day was so primitive that despite his ingenious idea he was never able to demonstrate even a crude system.

Many authors refer to Nipkow as the Father of television. I prefer to bestow that honor on the two individuals of more modern vintage whose inventiveness led directly to the television that we know today. And what a disparate pair: an aristocratic Russian emigré and an Idaho farm boy! But it was not only their countries of origin that distinguished the two. Vladimir Zworykin was the very epitome of the modern technologist. He received his education at a celebrated institution of higher learning, the Saint Petersburg Technological Institute, and worked on his ideas on television at the Russian Wireless Telegraph and Telephone Co. He left Russia for the United States in those days of ferment following World War I at the age of thirty and continued with his research in large corporate institutions, first at Westinghouse and later at RCA.[61]

Whereas Zworykin conformed to the new pattern of the inventor as the employee of the industrial research laboratory, Philo T. Farnsworth, true to the image of the nineteenth-century inventor/entrepreneur, was too independent a soul to work for someone else, particularly a corporate giant. He became fascinated with science at an early age, with the important assistance and encouragement of his teachers who recognized the ability and zeal of their student. His contributions to television began in the early 1920s while he was still in his teens. In the spirit of his inventor predecessors, he formed his own company in California. But even a rugged individualist entrepreneur needs money. After exhausting all his private sources, he finally had to accept financing from Philco, a leading battery manufacturer soon to make its mark in the radio business, but he managed to retain control of his company.

Both Zworykin and Farnsworth made their seminal contributions to the television art at approximately the same time. Both patented their inventions and, in keeping with the traditions of the field, contested each other's patents in the courts. As happened so often before, there were suits and countersuits. The first decision was in favor of Zworykin, but a later decision upheld Farnsworth's claims. It was clear to RCA that a successful commercial television system would require control of both sets of patents, and so it attempted to buy out Farnsworth. But the last thing that the individualist Farnsworth was about to do was to sell out to an establishment corporation. In the end, the company that was founded in the endeavor to consolidate all patents under one roof was obliged to obtain a license from Farnsworth and, for the first time in its history, to pay royalties to someone else.

It is hard to know precisely what motivated either or both of these inventors to work on picture transmission. The older Zworykin started his work before World War I when wireless was in its early years and radio broadcasting existed only as dreams in the minds of the likes of Lee De Forest. Farnsworth, born in the same year as De Forest's Audion, began his work a few years later in the early days of broadcasting when at least the idea of television might be viewed as a continuation of radio. It is that much more remarkable that the notions of television were first worked on so much earlier by Nipkow.

The thing that made Nipkow's concepts feasible were previous discoveries that certain materials had electrical properties that changed when they were illuminated. In some cases, their electrical resistance changed as light impinged upon them. Other materials were found to give off electrons in the presence of light. The explanation of this latter photoelectric effect is what earned Albert Einstein his Nobel Prize, and not the theory of relativity for which he is best known to the public. Nipkow and his contemporaries recognized that the most straightforward way to convert a picture into electrical signals was to focus it on a mosaic of such materials and then convert the brightness of each element of the mosaic into a proportional electrical signal. But the thing that made this approach impractical in Nipkow's days was the sheer number of elementary picture elements—tens of thousands—required to represent a picture with acceptable definition. It became apparent, therefore, that some kind of scanning system was required, one that would cover the picture one small element at a time rapidly enough to fool the eye into thinking that each picture element was being observed in a continuous fashion, capitalizing on the physiological process called *persistence of vision* in which a visualization of an image remains in the brain for a fraction of a second after the image itself disappears. It was the same phenomenon that made it possible to create motion pictures out of a rapid succession of still pictures of a scene.

The problem was how scanning could be reasonably accomplished, and this was what Nipkow set about to investigate. The heart of his scheme was to move a narrow beam of light across the whole scene until the entire picture was covered and then repeat the process as the scene was changing. If this were done often enough, then the eye would be fooled into seeing continuous motion. His clever scheme for doing this was to shine the light through a rotating disc covered with a spiral pattern of small, closely-spaced slots. As the disc rotated, the light beam would pass through each slot in the spiral in succession causing the beam to cover the entire field of view in small increments. The light-sensitive surface would then respond with a series of electrical signals in proportion to the brightness of each element of the picture. This succession of electrical signals would be transmitted to another location by wire and then reconstituted into a picture by a reverse process in synchronism with the scanner. Implementing this scheme was a tall order in those early days, and Nipkow was never able to do anything practical once he patented his invention. Despite his personal failure, his ideas on mechanical scanning were highly influential on others who followed him. Particularly noteworthy were the efforts of J. L. Baird in England who was probably the first to actually succeed in transmitting video, albeit crude, in the 1920s using refined versions of Nipkow's technology.

As ingenious as these first attempts might have been, their pictures were entirely too crude for commercial application, due to fundamental limitations in the mechanical scanning process. The answer was electronic rather than mechanical scanning and the vacuum tube was the invention that made it possible. But it was a different kind of tube from that of De Forest. Instead of the grid that De Forest inserted to modulate the intensity of the beam of electrons on its way from the cathode source to the collecting plate, there was a mechanism, either electric or magnetic, for deflecting the beam. The heart of electronic scanning is to use this deflection mechanism to scan the electron beam across the collecting surface in a regular pattern. You can think of the beam starting at the upper left-hand corner moving from left to right until it reaches the right edge, then flying back to the left edge very rapidly and moving down by a small amount for the next left-to-right scan, continuing in this way until the entire picture is covered. By analogy with the mechanical process, the picture to be scanned is focused on the collector, which is made of a material that emits electrons when struck by the beam, the number of electrons being proportional to the brightness of the picture at that point. A receiving scanner would work in synchronism with this electronic camera. Only now the electron beam would be varied in intensity in accordance with the transmitted electrical signals and these would excite a surface that would give off light when struck by the electron beam of intensity in proportion to the beam intensity. The beauty of the electronic scheme is its flexibility in being able to trace out a scanning pattern with high definition rapidly enough to fool the eye. Of course, the problem was to reduce this beautiful concept to practice in the early days of vacuum tube technology.

The pioneering work on electronic scanning for both the camera and projector was done in both Russia and England. As it turned out, both groups were investigating essentially the same techniques, but it was the approach of Professor Boris Rosing in Leningrad that ultimately gained the most recognition through the work of Zworykin, one of his students. The combination of war and the Bolshevik revolution made the Russia of those years an inhospitable place, and the young Zworykin left it for the United States in 1919. It was there that he made his great contribution with the invention of the *iconoscope*, the first successful electronic scanning camera and the ancestor of today's cameras.

The basic principles behind the iconoscope were in Zworykin's mind before he emigrated. He joined Westinghouse shortly after arriving in the United States, and by 1923 he had developed his ideas enough to apply for a patent. His management at Westinghouse was not particularly interested in his innovations, and he was only allowed to continue when Sarnoff of RCA expressed enough interest to contribute some support. The meagerness of this support is evident from the fact that it took another five years after the patent application before he was able to perfect his invention sufficiently to warrant a demonstration. It was fortunate for Zworykin that shortly thereafter RCA took over all radio research from General Electric and Westinghouse including the television development.

But in 1922 the sixteen-year-old Farnsworth already had the idea for what he called an image dissector tube, an alternate approach to a television camera. By 1927 he had put together a demonstration, a year before Zworykin's first demonstration. It was this concurrency of their work that led to the ambiguity of who did what first and their bitter patent litigation.

There was no event comparable to Marconi's reporting of the America's Cup races that heralded the arrival of television. Nor did the first public television broadcast make the splash of the first commercial radio broadcast. Television was something that crept upon the scene in the mid 1930s. The BBC started it in 1936 using two competing technologies, an electromechanical system by Baird and an electronic system developed by a former colleague of Zworykin, Isaac Schoenberg, who went to England to work for the phonograph company, EMI. Even though Baird's system was much improved over his pioneering systems of the previous decade, the cause was lost and, within a few months, the descendent of the old Nipkow technology breathed its last breath. Thus when the BBC broadcast the coronation of King George VI in 1937, the system was electronic. Experimental video broadcasting began in New York also in 1936, with the first officially authorized public broadcasting in 1941, a few months before the United States entered the war. No new technical development devoted to civilian living could be afforded in a time when all the resources of the allied nations had to be devoted to winning a war. But once the war was over, commercial television had its second start and began the process of taking over in a way comparable to the early days of radio following KDKA.

All this ferment in the gestation period of television was taking place while broadcast radio was in the period of its maximum growth, becoming established as a fixture in American and world society. And concurrent with the development of the basic television technology, major technical advances continued to be made in radio technology. The most important of these was the development in 1934 of *frequency modulation* (or FM, for short) by Armstrong.[62] The term *modulation* designates the way in which the audio is impressed on the radio waves. The scheme used in the early days and still considered standard is called *amplitude modulation* (AM), a technique in which the amplitude or strength of the radio signal is made to vary in proportion to the amplitude or instantaneous strength of the audio signal. In frequency modulation, the amplitude of the radio signal remains constant. Instead, the frequency of the radio signal is made to change in proportion to the amplitude of the audio signal, that is, large swings in audio signal strength are converted to large deviations of the frequency. As it turns out, interfering signals from electrical storms and other noise sources are quicker to affect the amplitude than the frequency of a broadcast signal, giving FM the greater resistance to such interference. The price FM pays for this desirable feature is bandwidth. Today's FM channels are twenty times as wide as are the AM channels. They would not have to be quite that wide if noise suppression were the only consideration. But with this additional bandwidth, they also carry the high frequency audio sounds that the narrow AM channels cannot support, giving it a more natural sound.

There was something tragic about the lives of the American radio pioneers, De Forest, Fessenden, and Stone, all of whom were far less successful in their endeavors than they might have been given their natural gifts. Edwin Howard Armstrong, who followed these three by a few years, was an even more tragic case. His life seemed almost predestined for tragedy. He was uncommonly bright and inventive. As a student at Columbia in 1912, seventeen years De Forest's junior, he recognized the fact that one could take an amplified signal from the plate of a vacuum tube and feed it back to the grid to greatly enhance the sensitivity of the triode as a wireless receiver. Armstrong called this circuit that he developed a *regenerative receiver*. It was just a simple conceptual step beyond this to increase the amount of feedback to cause the triode to become an oscillator. De Forest contested Armstrong's patents of these ingenious applications citing notebook entries as proof of his prior conception of these ideas. After years of bitter litigation and appeals, De Forest was finally upheld in the Supreme Court in 1934. However, most of their engineering peers were on Armstrong's side, feeling that Justice Benjamin Cardozo, brilliant in most instances, had been in error in this case. Since that time, most historians have also come down on Armstrong's side.

The superheterodyne receiver was another of Armstrong's inventions. Its great virtue was that it used a circuit configuration that permitted the receiver to tune in weak signals very accurately with a single tuning knob. Its combination of high performance and operational simplicity was one of the major factors contributing to the radio boom. Even though today's technology is now vastly different, the principles behind Armstrong's inventions remain as fundamentals of the radio art. These inventions brought him great fame and fortune, but these were more than counteracted by the pain and anguish that led to his untimely death.

The development of FM was Armstrong's most important invention and, at the same time, the source of his greatest tragedy. His work had originally been inspired by his friend Sarnoff, now the head of RCA, who was looking for something that would improve the noise resistance of radio signals. Armstrong's success in achieving this improvement with the concept of frequency modulation exceeded everyone's expectations. It was such a great step forward in broadcast radio, that it was reasonable for Armstrong to expect it to lead all radio broadcasting to migrate from AM to FM.

But Sarnoff, the dominant executive in broadcast radio, who had the power to lead the industry in this direction, had a change of heart. He now felt that while the quality improvements that FM could achieve were undeniable, the price to be paid in shaking up this fantastically successful new industry was just not worth it. The broadcasting stations would have to move to a new frequency band wide enough to accommodate the wider-band FM channels. Even more important, millions of radio listeners would be forced to invest in new radios capable of receiving FM broadcasts. But there was a still more important reason that dampened Sarnoff's enthusiasm. Even if he made the move to FM successfully, the only result would be a better quality radio broadcasting system. As desirable as this might be, it was not likely to revolutionize radio and the profits of his company. On the other hand, there was a truly new technology that had the potential to do just that. And so, Sarnoff deemphasized FM and hitched his and RCA's wagon to television. It's not that there was no activity in FM broadcasting. It is rather the case that FM grew only in modest proportions along with, instead of in place of, AM.

This defeat at the hands of his erstwhile friend was a crushing blow to Armstrong. But he did achieve success on one front, and, ironically, it turned out to be the source of his great tragedy. The FCC approved the use of FM for the audio portion of the TV broadcasting standard, forcing the TV manufacturers to pay royalties to Armstrong for the use of his invention. But RCA, determined not to repeat the unfortunate experience with Farnsworth, developed its own FM system in which it tried to get around the Armstrong patents. Armstrong brought suit and eventually RCA was forced to pay royalties. However, the payee was not Armstrong but his estate. The unhappy inventor had committed suicide by jumping out of a window before a final settlement could be reached.

The rivalry between the proponents of FM and TV was also evident in the standards arena in which both had to compete for broadcast spectrum allocations. Television, of course, had much greater demands, ultimately receiving channel allocations six megahertz wide, 30 times that of the FM channels and 600 times that of the AM channels. The TV channel bandwidth accommodated the standard that was adopted in the U. S. in the early 1940s after years of ferment, using a frame of 525 horizontal lines to scan the picture transmitted 60 times per second. Previous experience with motion pictures had indicated that a minimum of 50 frames per second were needed to prevent the eye from observing flicker in the picture. It is interesting to note that the European standard uses about the same bandwidth but with a somewhat different format, transmitting 50 frames per second with 625 lines per frame giving higher definition than the American standard. An earlier, lower quality UK standard stemming from 1936 is no longer in use. The difference between the two standards is both practical and logical, stemming from the fact that the most convenient way to synchronize the frames is to use the frequency of the electric power source, sixty hertz (alternations per second) in the U.S. and fifty hertz in Europe. Today's developmental *high-definition television* uses about twice as many lines per frame to obtain the higher resolution.

Then, too, it had to be decided where in the band the FM and TV channels should be located, a subject much in dispute during those years. To obtain the requisite amount of bandwidth, they had to be placed much higher than the AM broadcast band (between .550 megahertz and 1.5 megahertz) and, in fact, considerably higher than the shortwave band used for sky-wave radio telephony and telegraphy (2 to 30 megahertz). The TV channels were established first. Then after pressure from the FM interests, the TV channel designated as channel 1 was assigned to FM. Later, after FM broadcasting had begun in this designated channel, a change was made instigated by RCA, to the anger and dismay of Armstrong, when it was agreed to place FM broadcasting in the higher-frequency band between 88 megahertz and 105 megahertz, with TV channels both below and above this band. These FM and TV channels are high enough above the short-wave band for the ionosphere to be transparent. Their broadcasting range is, therefore, limited by the horizon to approximately fifty miles, a little less than the range of AM broadcasting.

All these wrangles over frequency allocations were finally concluded just as the United States was entering World War II, and commercial TV broadcasting was making its first tentative start. A total of only six commercial television stations had been installed in the United States by the time of Pearl Harbor. At the same time, there were some four dozen FM stations broadcasting mostly classical music that could benefit from the improved fidelity of FM. Further construction had to stop so that the nation could devote all its resources to the war effort. Then, once the war was over, came the spectacular growth in all forms of broadcasting, but especially television, justifying Sarnoff's business intuition. Almost from the beginning, the public demonstrated a willingness to purchase television sets costing hundreds of dollars when radios were available at small fractions of those sums. It was more than simply the novelty of it all. It was the fact that now more than disembodied voices could enter the home. The public were voting with their pocketbooks that pictures were important.

Chapter

15

The Power of the Picture

Television's influence over society has been so pervasive that it has done much more than simply replace radio as the dominant entertainment medium. It has also affected the competing media in very significant ways. Even more than that, it has changed our whole outlook on life, the way we view ourselves and our own culture, other cultures, and world events.

When television is used to its greatest advantage, its effect is nothing short of astonishing, especially when dealing with the news, the same area in which radio made its early triumphs. We first became impressed with the power of the picture during the presidential election campaign of 1952, the first such campaign to receive widespread television coverage. It shed a new light on the national presidential nominating conventions with all their strengths and weaknesses. And what spectacles they were. We had previously heard only the speeches. Now we could watch the delegates fidget in their chairs, sleep through impassioned rhetoric, wear party hats, dance jigs, and do many of the other silly things that conventioneers do. The conventions have never been the same since, nor have the other aspects of political campaigns.

Since then television has given us an unprecedented view of world events. Who can forget the live coverage of Lee Harvey Oswald's shooting in 1963, the first moon landing at the end of the decade, and the live coverage of the Watergate hearings a few years later? And, more recently, I will never forget an astonishing scene during the Gulf War in 1990 when a CBS crew entered Kuwait City ahead of the advancing coalition troops, who had stopped to mop up the Iraqis at the airport, and began interviewing everyone in sight in front of the American embassy, not knowing whether any residual Iraqi forces were still there.

But good television reporting of world events does more than inform us or entertain us. It influences us individually and collectively, and, when this happens, it influences world leaders and events. For example, we only have to ask ourselves whether the interventions of the United Nations in such places as Bosnia and Somalia might ever have taken place had it not been for the pictures of human suffering that television brought into the homes of hundreds of millions of people throughout the world.

Of course, most television news is not so impressive. When television simply provides *talking heads*, such as when a news reporter does little more than read the news from a teleprompter, the picture adds almost nothing to the voice. The same thing is true for much TV news coverage where the video is so banal that it adds little to the story. But even in those normal situations when the news of the day is not out of the ordinary, the picture adds enough to have made television the news medium of choice for most people, so that by as early as 1960, it was estimated that half the country depended on TV as the primary source of its news.

Today's television coverage is considerably more responsive to issues of public importance than it was in the early years. In those days, the major commercial networks dominated all aspects of television including news and derived the bulk of the advertising revenues. They formed an oligarchy in league with the advertisers, which manifested itself in a programming philosophy that catered to the lowest common denominator in tastes and, especially, with a much greater timidity than the print media in confronting important social issues from the demagoguery of Senator Joseph McCarthy in the 1950s to the Vietnam war in the 1960s and Watergate in the 1970s[63]. Ironically, it was television that ultimately broke the back of McCarthy, but it did not come easily. Edward R. Murrow, probably the most eminent radio broadcast journalist during the war, made a highly successful conversion to television after the war. His program, *See It Now* was an attempt to cover the important public issues. When he turned his attention to McCarthy, CBS reluctantly let him proceed, but balked at advertising the show in the papers thereby forcing Murrow and his producer, Fred Friendly, to pay for the ads out of their own pockets.

Although this show marked the beginning of the end of the McCarthy phenomenon, it did not change the attitudes of the networks and advertisers in any significant way. Here is how Friendly, one of the most successful of the news producers in the early decades of television, stated it in the late 1960s, some fifteen years after that famous broadcast:

Three soap companies . . . account for about 15% of the nation's total television sales. This is one reason why Americans know more about detergents and bleaches than they do about Vietnam or Watts. The three great printing presses in their seven-day-a- week continuous runs are so oriented to advertising and merchandise that after a single day of viewing television, a visitor from another planet could only infer that we are bent on producing a generation of semiliterate consumers.[64]

In the end, it was the fulminations of media critics such as Friendly that made television news more responsive to world events, through the vehicle of competition. The direct result of this kind of criticism led to the inception of public television in 1967 when Congress established the Corporation for Public Broadcasting. But the really significant competition occurred later with the rise of cable as a significant force in the industry. With the multiple sources of television coverage now including the Cable News Network and C-SPAN as well as the Public Broadcasting System (PBS) in addition to the commercial networks, it is a rare event of even modest public interest that escapes being televised.

Thus while government intervention started the process of making television news properly responsive to the needs of the public, it was ultimately the American tradition of free enterprise that completed it. It was not this way in Britain where the broadcast media were established with public support from the outset as vehicles for public service. Thus, the BBC, supported by radio and TV set license fees rather than advertising, gained a reputation for first-rate news reporting from its early radio days on. It also gained a reputation for stodgy entertainment programming prompting the establishment in 1954 of the competing, advertising-based Independent Television (ITV) network, to broaden the entertainment choices to include more popular programming. The ITV turned out to be so popular that the BBC had to establish a second channel to compete with it and gain back some of its lost viewers. Along with its American-style entertainment programming, the ITV also offered highly regarded news services in the tradition of the BBC. In the many decades that have elapsed since then, only a modicum of additional competition has developed in the United Kingdom, far less than in the United States. In particular, cable TV with its multiplicity of channels has burgeoned in the United States but has never been successful in Britain.[65]

Radio and television together have brought about great changes in their old competitor, the newspaper, both as a disseminator of news and as an advertising vehicle. The radio initiated the process of replacing the paper as the source of fast-breaking news. Then the television with its ability to deliver the news not only rapidly, but also in an articulate, colorful, and entertaining way changed the character of the newspaper. Gone are the extra editions hawked by the newsboys to bring news flashes. Gone also are most of the afternoon or evening papers, replaced by television as the primary source of information and entertainment at the end of the day. The newspapers have attempted in various ways to adapt to their changed environment. Instead of aiming for the fast-breaking news, they compete in other ways, giving more in-depth information about any topic in the news that the broadcasters can hope to provide, especially in those aspects of the news that depend more on the skill of the reporter than on the medium.

Thus, it is not surprising that the economics of the newspaper industry has changed substantially over the latter half of this century. According to the *New York Times*,[66] even the morning paper has become more of a weekly or, perhaps, a three-day-a-week journal. The Sunday edition, carrying the bulk of the week's advertising, dominates with a total circulation equal to that of the other six days of the week combined. Somewhere behind it in popularity are the Wednesday editions with food advertising and the Friday papers with entertainment advertising. Monday, Tuesday, Thursday, and Saturday bring up the rear. The net result is that the number of newspapers in the United States has dropped sharply in the latter half of the century—from a robustly competitive environment, most communities, even sizable ones, have only a single paper and the largest have perhaps two or three. Their total circulation, which had risen steadily until the mid 1960s to around 62 million copies per day, has remained at about that figure ever since despite the increasing population.

The fact that the decline of newspapers began in the 1960s, coinciding with the coming of age of television, is certainly circumstantial evidence that television is the main culprit. Simply observing that broadcast advertising revenues reached the billion dollar mark in the decade of the 1950s lends economic credance to this argument. But the role of television in this decline is less important than its broader role as an entertainment, not simply a news, medium, and the impact of its growth has to be viewed in this light. For example, reading, in general, has declined markedly, blamed by some on the ubiquity of television, just as early generations had blamed the telephone for the decline in letter writing. And reading is only one of many ways in which people find entertainment. Most of the other sources of entertainment have also been affected first by radio and then television in rather complex ways.

Take music, for example. How important is viewing a group of musicians in performance as opposed to listening to the music alone? At one level it is the music that counts, not the visual images of the performers. This fact is certainly borne out by the continued popularity of audio recordings—the long-playing record, which revolutionized the recording industry in its day, coincided with the onset of TV broadcasting, and the more recent compact disc boom demonstrates the persistent strength of the recording industry. Yet, the interest in television shows and video recordings of popular music demonstrates how important the visual element can be to music lovers.

At the same time, as popular as broadcast and recorded music presentations may be with or without video, people still flock to live concerts—from rock to classical—where they may pay premium prices for seats presenting views vastly inferior to those provided by television. There is something exciting in the live performance that goes beyond sound and sight. It is, perhaps, analogous to our preference for face-to-face meetings over telephone conversations.

That the same preference is not true when it comes to sporting events is evident from the way in which television has changed sports over the past fifty years. In contrast to concerts, in sports the sight is everything and the sound is almost inconsequential. The camera often gives TV watchers close-up views beyond the sight of anyone in the stadium. Contrast this experience with, say, baseball broadcasts that were popular in the early days of radio, especially the telegraphic recreations that were aired when there was no on-the-spot radio coverage. A radio broadcast of any sporting event turns us into second-hand observers, at the mercy of someone else's eyes. And no matter how much sports fans enjoyed the radio broadcasts when there was nothing else available, they were quick to change their allegiance to television sports. In fact, I often regard the sometimes inane comments of the television sportscasters who feel obliged to fill up the audio space as unwarranted intrusions on the visual scene. It is no wonder, then, that not only does TV win out handily over radio, but also that many of us prefer to watch the events from the comfort of our living rooms and avoid the hassle of the trip to the stadium or arena, despite the undeniable thrill of participating in the event by being there in person. This transfer of the audience from the stadium to the home has altered the economics of sports in ways that no one would have predicted when TV was in its infancy. Television revenues dominate today. Schedules are adjusted to the convenience of the TV viewers. Star players have been converted from local to nationwide and even international heroes, and they command salaries that are commensurate with their fame.

Drama—and this includes everything from serious drama to situation comedies—lies somewhere between music and sports in the relative importance of the visual and audible. It was very popular in the days of radio. But once television came along, virtually all dramatic programs migrated to the new medium, with the partial exception of Britain where some radio drama continues to be popular. Without denying the obvious advantages of the pictures in these contexts, we have lost some of the magic of the imagination. Some of the popularity of the early radio dramas was contributed by the listeners trying to imagine what was happening when their only information was the dialog and sound effects.

Opera is another interesting case—a form of drama in which the audio is the most important component. In fact, since the acting standards in opera have not always been as high as its musical standards, the visual effects can often detract from the overall emotional impact of the production. So important is opera to its devotees, that the Metropolitan Opera Saturday matinee performances continue to be broadcast over the radio since the late 1930s with the same commercial sponsorship. Opera standards have changed over the years, so that today's audiences demand more realistic acting than in previous generations. It is much less acceptable now for an aging overweight soprano, no matter how great her vocal gifts, to play the role of a beautiful young woman dying of consumption. The increased availability of opera on television has undoubtedly played a part in modifying our standards of taste.

But clearly, the main impact of television drama has not been on radio drama or on opera but rather on the motion picture. In some ways, it is similar to the effect early radio had on vaudeville. But whereas vaudeville eventually disappeared as a result of the competition, the motion picture has been resilient enough to adapt after an initial drop in movie attendance of from 20 percent to 40 percent in 1951. The bitter rivalry that developed in the early days between the two industries was replaced by the inevitable marriage of convenience in which the motion picture industry provides much of the program material for broadcast and cable television and also in videotape form for delayed home viewing. From the early days to the present, there has been an almost constant evolution in the ways in which drama of all sorts is brought into the home and in the industrial lineup that provides it, most of which was difficult to foresee. And there is no indication that this evolution will change as we move into the future.

Television has, therefore, taken the place of radio as the principal broadcast medium, but it has not *replaced* radio. It is more accurate to say that television has changed radio's role. Radio remains as the medium of choice in circumstances in which television is not possible or acceptable for an audience, such as when walking down the street, driving in the automobile, or sitting in the office. It now performs a primarily local rather than national function. It remains invaluable as the disseminator of news and especially of music, and it has become increasingly popular as the vehicle for the public to express its opinion through call-in shows. As cruel as Sarnoff might have been to Armstrong, it is clear that when he chose investing in television over FM radio, his business sense was absolutely correct. The picture adds so much information to the sound in so many contexts that television's rise to become the prime broadcasting medium was inevitable once the technology to do it was available. Now, more than a half-century after television first made its appearance, it has become firmly established in the world's communications infrastructure, and broadcast radio has assumed a secondary role.

While the public has indeed voted that the picture makes a difference when it comes to broadcasting, video has had very little impact on the other great audio medium, the telephone. Should it surprise us that one immensely popular audio medium has become dominated by video whereas the other has been virtually unaffected? The fact of the matter is that the similarity between radio broadcasting and telephony based on their common audio roots masks the essential differences between the two media. The radio is a medium of entertainment. The telephone is a vehicle for personal and business communication. It is the means by which anyone can send any kind of information to anyone else, provided the information can be represented by the spoken word.

Yet the notion of adding the picture to the voice is an obvious extension of the telephone. AT&T had experimented with television in the 1920s, and this was the application that fascinated them. While it may have been an article of faith to some in the telephone company, nevertheless even after television broadcasting hit the scene and captured much of the market that radio had previously had to itself, there was no observable groundswell of demand for a video telephone. Even if there had been, the issue would have been academic until such time as the video camera could become sufficiently economical to take its place beside the ubiquitous telephone instrument in its subscribers homes. And so, aside from issues of desirability, the application to video telephony had to wait many decades for the technology to be suitable for that application.

In the 1970s, AT&T finally introduced an experimental video telephone service called *Picturephone*. It did not meet with success. Its quality was quite acceptable, especially considering the fact that it was transmitted over ordinary telephone lines. But it was expensive, due in part to the high the cost of all the ancillary equipment needed to achieve this quality. Of course, such is often the case when a new product is introduced. Then, if and when the product meets with some market success, the cost comes down. But this was not the case with Picturephone, and AT&T discontinued the service.

Since then, another kind of interactive video, the video teleconference, became available for business customers in many forms. The quality achieved was much higher than that of the Picturephone, but the equipment was still more expensive. Part of the reason for the improved quality was the use of a greater bandwidth than the universal telephone system could provide, and for which special transmission facilities were needed. AT&T provided this service only from particular conference center locations, in effect, video studios that could be rented by conferees by the hour. These were relatively economical, but the inconvenience of having to leave one's office at the appointed hour detracted from the desirability of the service. Some companies found it economical to establish their own private video conferencing services connecting their own locations to enable them to conduct conferences in a convenient environment. A typical application is the demonstration of new products to large numbers of people at the same time, avoiding the expense of sending salespeople to many locations. These private systems have the convenience of locating the video on company premises, but the amount of use must be sufficiently large to justify the expense of a private system. Their use, therefore, is still confined to the larger, especially international, companies.

AT&T carried out studies in the wake of the Picturephone disaster that showed some subscribers are not just indifferent but actually hostile to the idea of the video telephone, leading some (even in the telephone industry) to feel pessimistic about its viability.[67] That these industry doubters were in the minority is borne out by the fact that in the early 1990s the telephone industry was testing the market once again with contemporary, but still expensive, successors to the old Picturephone with guarded optimism regarding its prospects. All the old arguments for the value of the picture were resurrected. One of these is the presumption that adding video allows business calls to take on more of the characteristics of face-to-face interactions. One industry spokesman noted that a video conversation forces the participants to devote all their attention to the interaction rather than listening with one ear and paying attention to other issues simultaneously. Thus the video conversation could have a special advantage over the ordinary telephone in carrying out business affairs, even to the point of replacing travel in some cases. One can also think of circumstances in which the advertising slogan "reach out and touch someone" would have more meaning if the picture added to the voice permitted family members and close friends to maintain more intimate contact when geographically separated. This would be especially true for grandparents who do not have the opportunity to see their grandchildren as often as they would like.

But I think there is even more to this dispute than the current arguments, both pro and con, would indicate. History has shown that new communications capabilities spawn new applications in unpredictable ways. The true test of the viability and usefulness of a video telephone service will not come until we have available a modern video telephone making available good quality video at prices reasonable enough to make an initial market penetration. Then a market-place evaluation can determine whether enough subscribers believe that the video adds enough to the conversation to warrant an additional expenditure, or, in the extreme, whether the video exchange can conceivably cut into the travel-based face-to-face interaction. The picture quality of the new video telephones is not as good as it would be if the telephone connections were improved. I discuss in Chapter 30 why these improvements will inevitably come about for other reasons, and when they do, we will have the opportunity to see whether the person-to-person audio medium ultimately succumbs to the same forces as the century comes to an end as did its broadcasting cousin at mid-century.

Chapter

16

The Wireless Makes a Comeback

In the years that followed World War II, a new bowl-shaped architectural form began to appear on the landscape. In populated areas they were mounted on the roofs of buildings. In open spaces they were mounted on towers, often in clusters, giving the appearance of peculiar telephone poles. In the early installations, the bowl was oriented on its side pointed toward the horizon, but by the 1970s, some of them would be tilted to point well above the horizon.

These bowls, or dishes as they were usually called, were a new kind of radio antenna. Although their appearance was far different from the odd shapes that Marconi and his successors had used in their wireless experiments, or from the vertical wires used by the radio and television broadcasters, or the peculiar pieces of bent wire that began to appear on rooftops to pick up distant television signals, their function was nevertheless the same. The difference in shape was the result of the fact that they were using electromagnetic waves at frequencies far higher than those used heretofore, frequencies high enough for their antennas to look superficially like the lenses and mirrors that had been used for centuries to focus the extremely high frequencies of visible light.

What these antennas were doing on mountain tops, towers, and roofs was augmenting and eventually replacing wires to carry information from place to place in order to meet the demand not only of the new television networks, but also the telephone requirements of the surging postwar economy.

Telephone service is part of the infrastructure that we have all come to take for granted. When any of the utilities—water, gas, electricity, telephone—functions properly, we hardly give them a thought. But lose them, even for a short period of time, and we feel helpless and deprived. Less dramatic than an actual utility outage, is the degraded performance that goes with the inability to satisfy demand. The individual homeowner only notices the large demand for electric power to feed air conditioners on a sultry summer day when the power company is forced to institute brownout procedures by lowering the line voltage. Similarly, no individual telephone subscriber notices when the number of calls per day increases tenfold until he or she keeps getting a busy signal, or, still worse, fails to hear the familiar dial tone. Were this to happen as a regular occurrence, we subscribers would complain bitterly to the telephone company customer service representatives, and, if the poor service persisted, to our congressmen.

To increase the number of phone calls that the phone system can handle, there must necessarily be more circuit capacity. Using an earlier analogy, if the number of calls outgrows the circuit equivalent of a secondary highway, then a multilane highway has to be built as a replacement. Up until World War II, all the circuits interconnecting the telephones of the nation were wirelines, with various clever techniques for increasing the number of circuits a piece of cable could carry. But there were limits both to the capacity of these cables and to the amount of real estate available for installing more of them. The technology that helped solve this problem of capacity at mid-century turned out to be the old wireless. It seems ironic that after RCA had turned most of its attention from the wireless to broadcast radio, AT&T went back to the wireless to find the technology that made its continued growth possible at mid-century. But this wireless was far different from RCA's radio telegraphy of the 1920s, or even the radio telephony that was still the only way of carrying telephone conversations across the ocean. It depended on technology that was developed during the war for an innovation called *radar*.

Ask the man or woman in the street to name the single piece of technology most responsible for the Allied victory in World War II, and the answer, more than likely, will be the atomic bomb. Indeed, the atomic bomb shortened the war. It also saved thousands of American lives. But it did not change the outcome. By the time the first bomb was dropped on Hiroshima, the outcome was no longer in doubt. The only question was when and at what price.

Several years earlier, the outcome *was* in doubt. The Nazi armies had overrun Europe. Britain was next on the list. Had Britain been invaded and defeated, it is by no means clear what would have happened. But Britain was not invaded because the preinvasion air war resulted in a resounding defeat for the Germans. The British won this war in the air because of a new technology called radar.

Radar is an offspring of communication. In normal communication you send signals containing information to someone in another location. With radar, you send signals into space and these signals return with information impressed on them, information such as the location of objects—airplanes, ships, tanks, rain clouds—that get in the path of the radio wave. The reason it works is quite simple conceptually: An electro-magnetic wave travels in a straight line until it strikes something that absorbs, reflects, or bends it. When it strikes a reflecting object, some of the reflected energy will find its way back to the original source of the wave. Just as the time taken by an automobile to traverse a given distance is obtained by dividing the distance by the speed of the vehicle, so the time taken by a radio wave to reach a reflector is the distance to the reflector divided by the speed of light. And the time to return is that same time again. A radar is simply a device that sends out radio waves, observes reflections from whatever they strike, and measures the time the reflec-tion arrives back to determine how far away the object is. The word *radar* is an acronym for radio detection and ranging, which describes the process.

It would make a nice story if there were a single person who invented radar and then exploited it in the business world as did Bell for the telephone. That this was not the case is due to many things. For one, radar was not the kind of thing that one did in one's garage or on the grounds of one's father's estate. To make it work required sophisticated technology found only in research establishments. For another thing, the market for radars was specialized, especially in the 1930s. It was not a device like the telephone that every consumer would want to use. It had obvious applications to the military, to navigation at sea and in the air, and to scientific research, not the broad kind of market from which entrepreneurs in the mold of Marconi or De Forest might hope to make their fortunes.

The whole idea of using radio waves to determine the location of objects in the path of a radio beam turned out to be both obvious and not. The germ of the idea extends back as far as Hertz who observed reflections in his original experiments on electromagnetic radiation. As early as 1904, a German engineer named Christian Huelsmeyer patented a device that used radio reflections or echoes to prevent ship collisions, but there was little interest in the invention. In the mid-1920s, scientists in both Britain and the United States were using radio echoes to investigate the height and composition of the ionosphere that had been postulated two decades earlier by Kennelly and Heaviside to explain why radio waves could propagate beyond the horizon.

With all this background in the use of radio waves for the location of objects, it is difficult to credit any one person with the invention of radar. Nevertheless the person who comes closest is a Scottish scientist, Robert Watson-Watt, who led the British radar development activities before and during World War II. In his autobiography, Sir Robert—he was knighted after the war in recognition of his accomplishments—tells an amusing anecdote demonstrating that, in his wife's eyes, there was no ambiguity at all regarding the identity of the inventor of radar.[68] It seems that while driving in Canada after the war, Sir Robert was stopped by a policeman for speeding. "Did you do it by radar?" asked Sir Robert, to which the technically naive policeman replied, "It was not by radar; it was by an electronic speed-meter." This prompted Lady Watson-Watt to comment indignantly: "You may be interested to know that King George VI knighted my husband for inventing radar." "I don't know who invented anything," replied the policeman. "I know you were driving at an excessive speed."

The way Watson-Watt came to the idea of radar is an interesting case study of the processes of invention. He began his distinguished career as a meteorologist using radio techniques to investigate atmospheric effects. By the time Adolf Hitler took power and a second war within a generation began to look like a real possibility, he had achieved the distinction of being the leading radio meteorologist in Britain. As an indication of the government's concern over the events on the continent, Watson-Watt recalls in his autobiography how he was summoned by the Air Ministry in January of 1935 and asked whether radio waves might be used as "damaging radiation" to defend against attacking aircraft. He responded shortly thereafter with a paper saying that the requested "death ray" was not possible, but that even if it were, the attackers would have to be located before they could be destroyed. That the germ of an idea was there was confirmed in the paper's conclusion: "Meanwhile attention is being turned to the still difficult but less unpromising problem of radio-detection as opposed to radio-destruction, and numerical considerations on the method of detection by reflected radio waves will be submitted when required." Within a month these numerical calculations were incorporated in a second paper showing that the idea of radar was feasible in a theoretical sense. An experiment followed in short order that confirmed this feasibility. Radar as we know it was born.

Why was it that Watson-Watt had the idea when others had also been given the opportunity and had missed the idea? For example, in 1925 King George V had personally asked the director of scientific research at the Admiralty if there was some way of detecting aircraft analogous to acoustic underwater detection. The answer was negative. A more imaginative person might have reacted otherwise, especially since the ionospheric experiments with radio were going on at that time. Later, British Post Office engineers had noted that radio reception was disturbed whenever an airplane passed in the vicinity. But again no one had the imagination to put two and two together. Of course, we cannot know whether Watson-Watt would have made the connection had he been in those situations, but that is not really relevant. Watson-Watt came through when it counted in the situation that confronted him.

As the decade of the 1930s was coming to an end, war looked increasingly possible. The British suffered during the World War I, but, unlike the French, were spared the horrors of an enemy on its soil. But now, unlike twenty years earlier, the airplane was a mature weapon of war, and potentially devastating to the British Isles. It was essential to investigate some kind of protection from air attack. The first job given to Watson-Watt and his team was to construct an electronic fence that would provide warning of an attack. By the end of that year the first radars were constructed along the Thames Estuary. Additional stations of this kind were installed along the borders of Great Britain in the next few years. It was this chain of stations that was to work to the advantage of the British during the war, from the Battle of Britain in the early days to the attacks by the V1 and V2 missiles near the end.

While all radio waves are reflected by ships and aircraft, there are significant technical and operational advantages in using very high frequencies, especially if the radar is to be installed on a ship or aircraft. The principal reason for this superiority of the higher frequencies has to do with the antenna that converts an electrical signal into an electromagnetic wave and vice-versa. If you are a radio broadcaster, then you want your signals to radiate out from the transmitter in all directions. But when target location is your objective, the more the radio signal can be confined within a narrow cone, the more precisely you can pinpoint the direction of the target. As it turns out, the higher the frequency or the shorter the wavelength, the smaller the physical size of the antenna needed to achieve a given degree of directivity. The British radar chain used former BBC television transmitters operating at frequencies only slightly higher than those used for shortwave communication. But since these frequencies were much too low to permit practical airborne antennas, British researchers pursued the technology of the higher frequencies with vigor and determination.

Their great breakthrough came in 1940 with the development of a novel vacuum tube called the *magnetron* that permitted operation at frequencies 100 times higher, the so-called microwave range. The original idea came from the General Electric Company in its Schenectady research laboratories in 1921, but it was the British who converted the idea into a practical radar transmitter after an intensive investigation of several alternate approaches. Modern radar can be said to date from that invention. Since that time, many other vacuum tube and solid-state devices have been developed with properties superior to those of the magnetron, but this venerable pioneer led the way. Today magnetrons are so cheap that they are ideal power sources for the ubiquitous microwave oven.

Late in the same year, the United States began a massive research effort to develop radars for the army and navy, establishing the Radiation Laboratory at MIT for this purpose. One of the first visitors to this laboratory was Sir Henry Tizard, the chairman of the British committee on air defense research, who had been most instrumental in giving Watson-Watt the go-ahead to construct the chain of coastal radars. The purpose of his visit was to invoke a spirit of full cooperation between the scientific efforts of the United States and Britain. To this end, he brought the highly secret magnetron with him and demonstrated it to his American colleagues. From then on, both the British and the Americans pursued advanced radar technology with vigor and achieved the remarkable results that were so instrumental in winning the war.

It is interesting to note that the Germans contributed very little to the technology of radar, probably bedcause of Hitler's continued obsession with winning the war in blitzkrieg fashion, which impelled him to pursue offensive technology to the neglect of technology such as radar that is essentially defensive in nature. There is an even more graphic example of this fixation with the offensive. Late in the war when its outcome was no longer in doubt, the Germans developed the jet aircraft engine, and test aircraft so equipped easily outclassed anything available to the Allies. Hitler's generals recommended applying this technology to developing fighter aircraft that could put an end to the devastating daytime raids of the American Flying Fortresses. Hitler refused, commanding the development instead of jet bombers to attack the Allied forces.

By the time the war ended, radar had become a mature technology. All during the war the Bell Laboratories, the research arm of AT&T, were devoted almost exclusively to the war effort, but once the war was over, they could once again turn their attention to the telephone networks. It did not take long for microwave communication to come into being.

While these very high frequencies were important to radar, because with them highly directive antenna beams could be obtained with small physical structures, their primary value to communication was in the potentially high capacities derived from the inherently wide bandwidths obtainable at high frequencies. Recall that the bandwidth of a propagation medium is the extent of the band of frequencies that the medium can pass. The entire short-wave band is less than thirty megahertz wide. Since a single U.S. television channel is six megahertz wide, the short-wave band cannot support more than four TV channels. When we use frequencies 100 times as high, then the bandwidth increases by 100 times, but this characteristic leads to a dilemma: These very high frequencies that are necessary for very wide bandwidths are unaffected by the ionosphere. They travel in straight lines, limited in range by the horizon. How can they be harnessed to achieve long distances?

This dilemma was easy to solve on land in a straightforward way. A distance of 500 miles could be spanned by fifteen to twenty such line-of-sight links in tandem-relay fashion. There was a precedent for a relay of this sort in the optical semaphore systems of the early eighteenth century. But there was an important difference in that the new radio relays were automatic as opposed to their manual predecessors.

Why was a radio relay preferable to copper cable? It turns out that a copper cable attenuates high frequencies more than low frequencies, and that the longer the cable, the more bothersome this effect becomes. The result is that a long copper cable has a lower bandwidth than a short one. Until the microwave relay made its appearance, AT&T had no choice but to use cables to span long distances breaking up the long distances with amplifiers to sustain the bandwidth. But once the microwave radio became available, its advantages became evident, so much so that AT&T replaced most of its long-distance cables with these so-called microwave relays beginning in the late 1940s to meet the needs of the rapidly expanding postwar economy. Relay stations can be implemented relatively cheaply mounted on towers to increase the line-of-sight range of each link using relatively small antennas to concentrate the transmitted beam in the direction of the next tower in the chain. And to do this you do not have to own or lease all the real estate in between the towers. I show later how it was this factor that later enabled companies such as MCI and Sprint to build their own microwave links in competition with AT&T and that made the breakup of AT&T in the 1980s inevitable (see Chapter 27).

The concept of the microwave relay revolutionized overland communication. AT&T successfully built a complete microwave relay system between Boston and New York in 1947 with six channels in each direction, each channel having the capacity of 600 telephone circuits or a single TV channel. From this beginning, microwave towers began to spring up throughout the nation and the world. In 1951, the AT&T network made nationwide network television possible when it extended wideband service from coast to coast with a *golden spike* ceremony that linked its eastern and western microwave systems together.

But, as important as the microwave relay was to overland communication, it did nothing at all for the really constraining problem of crossing the ocean. It seems hard to believe that as recently as 1950, the only way of carrying telephone conversations across the ocean was by shortwave radio. Its bandwidth was so low that the amount of communication was severely constrained, and its quality and reliability were so poor due to the vagaries of the ionosphere that a transatlantic phone call was something not to be relished.

The first change in this situation occurred in 1956. AT&T had finally developed an amplifier with the power, ruggedness, and reliability to make an underwater telephone cable practical. And so, almost 100 years after the first transatlantic telegraph cable was laid, intercontinental telephony was at last freed from the limitations of the ionosphere. As important as this development was for international telephony, it was so long in coming that the human voice was not the only form of information requiring transoceanic transport. Thus, the new cable was indeed a great boon to international telephony, but it did nothing at all for television whose bandwidth far exceeded the capability of an underwater cable.

But, true to form, along came another surprise. While it was quite ludicrous to conceive of the equivalent of a string of microwave towers stretching across the ocean, might it not be possible to put the equivalent in the sky? This was precisely what the science fiction writer, Arthur C. Clarke, had the imagination to suggest in 1945.[69] He predicted that it might be possible to build an artificial satellite that would orbit the Earth and serve as a relay point to direct microwaves between distantly located places. Clarke's visionary prediction became true within about fifteen years. Again it was wartime developments—rocket technology along with the microwave technology—that provided the basis for these remarkable advances.

17

Communication via Space

Orbiting satellites have become so commonplace in our day that some of the associated esoteric language has become almost commonplace. Thus words like *apogee* and *perigee* have entered the vernacular. The most important of these orbital attributes, indeed, the thing that has been the greatest contributor to the practicality of communications satellites is the word *geostationary*—at rest with respect to a point on the Earth—that describes most of today's communications satellites.

Sir Isaac Newton's laws of motion describe the motion of the Earth about the sun, that of the moon about the Earth, and all other examples of planetary motion. According to these laws, the speed of an orbiting body depends on its distance from the celestial body around which it orbits; the greater the distance, the longer the time to make a complete circuit. Since the Earth also spins about its own axis once a day, might it not be possible, Clarke suggested in that pioneering paper, to place a microwave repeater in an orbit about the equator in which its orbiting speed would be exactly the same as the Earth's rotation speed, thereby making it appear stationary to an observer on the Earth—a veritable microwave tower in the sky? It was easy to calculate that the height of this orbit was about 22,500 miles above the Earth, the altitude that has come to be called, appropriately, the *geostationary altitude*.

A communications satellite, if it could be built as Clarke predicted, would add a degree of flexibility to communications networks undreamed of in the past. Just imagine its potential. Now, for the first time, wide bandwidths would be available over long distances in a single link. Television could be sent across the ocean. It could also be sent from coast to coast in one hop without the need to run cables or microwave relays.

The satellite would also provide a perhaps preferable alternative to these other methods for voice communication as well. Commercial organizations might install their own satellite-based domestic or international communications systems bypassing AT&T. And just imagine the potential of the satellite for military communication with its ability to span over-the-horizon distances with communication terminals that the troops could carry with them and set up rapidly.

With potential applications such as these it is no wonder that so much feverish activity began to take place beginning in the 1950s. The venerable National Advisory Committee on Aeronautics (NACA) was given a new mission and a liberal infusion of dollars to include space technology. Along with the new mission came a new name, the National Aeronautics and Space Administration, one chosen to yield the modified acronym, NASA. Its program was, from the beginning, oriented toward civil objectives. Not to be outdone, the Department of Defense began a program of its own pursuing military objectives in space.

The first to succeed was none of the above.[70] Rather, it was the former Soviet Union that shocked the world when it orbited its first *sputnik*. The specter of its cold-war enemy dominating space gave further impetus to the American space program, and it finally succeeded with Telstar, a joint effort of NASA and AT&T. This accomplishment was celebrated on July 10, 1962 with the first transatlantic television broadcast when Vice President Lyndon Johnson and several AT&T officials gathered at the Carnegie Institution in Washington and sent video greetings to France. On the following evening, a seven-minute taped program was sent in the other direction hosted by Jacques Marette, the French minister of postal services and telecommunications.

Telstar was not a geostationary satellite. Rather its orbit was elliptical with apogee and perigee (high and low points) about 3,500 and 600 miles respectively above the Earth. The rocket and guidance technology necessary to boost a satellite to the high geostationary altitude and maintain it in one spot in space was not ready. However, by the next year, Hughes Aircraft Co., under contract to NASA, succeeded with SYNCOM, the world's first geostationary satellite.

Since the first commercial applications were likely to be in the international domain, an organization called INTELSAT was chartered to field a system of Earth terminals with a worldwide system of geostationary satellites. INTELSAT was to be a *carrier's carrier* from which the standard communications carriers of the world, whether they be private companies as in the United States or governmental organizations as in most other countries, would obtain their satellite-based international connectivity for telephone or television services. The U.S. Congress chartered an organization in 1962 that became known formally as the

Communications Satellite Corporation and informally as COMSAT to represent the United States in INTELSAT matters and also to provide technical assistance to the international carrier in its early years. INTEL-SAT did not waste any time in carrying out its mission, orbiting its first geostationary satellite called EARLYBIRD in 1965. Since that time several generations of INTELSATS have been providing service to the international community.

The satellite communications zealots of the 1960s—and I count myself one of these—looked upon this method of communication as the potential cure for all the communications ills of the world, both commercial and military. Of course, this did not turn out to be the case. It never does. But this does not detract from the great contribution that it has made, the most obvious of which is in international television, something that until relatively recently could not be done in any other way. Until the first satellites, news and sporting events occurring overseas would be televised and recorded on tape. The tape would then be rushed to the United States by the fastest available aircraft.

The communications satellite changed all that. Events such as the funeral of President Kennedy in 1963, the Olympic Games of 1964, and the Ecumenical Conference held in Rome in 1965 were among the first great world events that became available to the television viewers of the world as they happened. At last a technology existed that placed our international expectations at the same level as those that we held domestically since the early 1950s.

But that was only part of the impact of the satellite on television. The domestic satellites that began to make their appearance in the 1970s revolutionized the way television programming was distributed. No longer were the television networks dependent on AT&T to carry their programs to their member stations as they had been since the 1920s. Television networks could now distribute programming themselves by buying or leasing satellite capacity and installing simple receive-only Earth terminals at the member locations. These domestic satellites were also to lead to the concept of *superstations*, such as WTBS in Atlanta, that would feed programming to cable networks in direct competition with the established networks.

Cable television had started well before the satellite became a practical reality. Its original name, *Community Antenna Television* (abbreviated CATV) describes its original function fairly well. Television signals propagate in straight lines over distances related to the local horizon. This property means that rural areas with highly dispersed residences may have too few subscribers to justify their own television broadcasting stations. It also can mean that even in densely populated urban areas with plenty of subscribers, the propagation path between the broadcasting stations and the customers may be disturbed by natural and man-made structures that block the signals. One answer to these problems that is sometimes helpful is to install large powerful antennas on rooftops to capture the weak signals from the distant or obstructed stations. But a more satisfactory and flexible solution is to bring the programming from several stations to a single point in a community and then distribute the signals to the subscribers via a cable that goes from house to house rather than by direct through-the-air transmission.

The first such CATV systems began in the 1940s in Oregon and Pennsylvania in the earliest days of television. The number of cable systems grew modestly until the 1970s when, with the aid of the domestic communications satellites, cable began a spurt in growth that now threatens the domination of the traditional networks. Because what started as simply a practical way to bring television to some communities and to improve the transmission to others had turned into something a great deal more, aided in no small measure by the facility with which programming could be brought to a cable head. The same cable that had, in the past, brought a handful of stations to the subscriber could carry dozens of channels, including specialized channels with such things as news, sports, congressional activities, courtroom proceedings, and movies galore. Ted Turner's Cable News Network (CNN), in just a few years, has become the standard for television news broadcasting with a larger staff of reporters throughout the world than any other network. Perhaps the greatest tribute to CNN came in 1991 when Defense Secretary Dick Cheney in a news conference found himself unable to remember whether a particular piece of information about Iraq came from an intelligence source or CNN.

If the satellite is so effective at carrying television signals to cable distribution points, why not go all the way and carry the signals directly to the home, creating, in effect, a *cable in the sky*? Such an approach has enticed communicators for a long time. In the earliest days, the technology was not up to the job of bringing television signals into satellite receivers economical enough for home installations. But by the mid-1980s there were many who thought the day of so-called direct broadcast satellite had come. The idea has penetrated the European market and Japan to some small extent, but even by the mid-1990s its impact in the United States has been negligible. The newest variation of this notion has been to convert the television signals to digital form. It remains an open question as to whether the improved quality of these digital transmissions will be sufficient to make direct broadcast television a success in the marketplace since we are likely to see digital television on cable in the same time frame. (See Chapter 30 for more on digital television.)

The beautiful marriage between television and the satellite resulted from many factors, chief among them the ability of the satellite to carry wideband signals in a very flexible way to almost any place on the globe. It was a different story with telephonic communication. Whether over land or sea, the satellite was not a unique way of carrying the narrowband voice signals. It always had to compete with other terrestrial means of doing the same thing. In overseas applications, the sheer capacity of the satellite gave it an advantage over the limited capacities of undersea cables. But over land where the microwave relays were providing huge capacities, the capacity battle was much closer. And it was precisely in this area that the satellite's major disadvantage quickly became evident.

You can always tell when you are talking over a satellite by the fact that there is a small delay between the time you end your sentence and when you hear the person on the other end of the line begin speaking. This delay is due to the fact that your signal takes a quarter of a second to reach the other end simply because the signal has to travel a total distance of 45,000 miles up to the satellite and back down at the speed of light. Similarly, your correspondent's signal requires another quarter of a second to get back to you. This round-trip delay of a half second is what is responsible for the delay that intrudes upon voice conversations. Now, to be sure, this small delay is, at most, an annoyance; once you have lived with it for a short while, you get used to it and you can carry on a conversation with hardly an impediment. In fact, in the early days of satellite communication when there were very few satellites in the sky, my colleagues and I built a system that could use the moon as a communications reflector. Since the moon is ten times as far from the Earth as is a geostationary satellite, the delays are ten times as great or five seconds for the round trip. Even with this enormous delay, we found that voice communications were possible, if a little peculiar.

But as acceptable as the half-second satellite delay may be to most people, it is still slightly less natural than the almost unnoticeable delay imposed by a terrestrial path. And it is primarily for this reason that the satellite was never used to any great extent for voice transmission by the telephone networks. In fact, in the small fraction of the cases in which AT&T did use satellites, it insisted on using them in only one direction with a cable or terrestrial microwave path in the other direction so as to cut the delay in half. Once the long-distance carriers began to install optical cable in the 1980s, some industry observers were predicting the end of satellite transmission by the major networks. Such comments were misleading. The transmission systems that were rendered obsolete by this new technology were the long-distance microwave relays, not the satellites, which were never much of a factor for these networks.

The military greeted the communications satellite with enthusiasm, and for good reason. Military communication is not neat and tidy as is its civil counterpart, because wars, even victorious, one-sided ones, contain an element of unpredictability, a quality not associated with commercial telephone or television systems. One fundamental distinction between military and commercial communication that contributes to this unpredictability is related to the fact that military forces are often in motion: ships at all times, land forces, in the heat of battle, and aircraft whenever in the air during peace or war. This necessity to communicate either when in motion or after moving to some unpredictable place means that the standard terrestrial methods of commercial communication are of value to military forces only when they are in one place for an extended period of time. It is radio communication of one kind or another that is the backbone of communication to mobile forces.

The virtue of satellites to the military was the fact that the satellite terminals could be installed on mobile vehicles or could be set up rapidly on any terrain to provide the equivalent of fixed-plant communication on a temporary basis. This mobility requirement means that if there are no other reasonable ways of communicating in some location, the satellite provides the mechanism. In most commercial applications, there is a telephone network to provide connectivity. But not so for ships at sea, tanks in the field, or aircraft in the sky. In fact, the most spectacular commercial triumphs of satellite transmission occur when the television networks fly a portable satellite terminal to cover fast-breaking news in some isolated part of the world where there is little or no commercial communication, in essence, a very militarylike application.

I described earlier how the navy struggled to use the peculiarities of the ionosphere in propagating both long- and shortwaves over long distances to maintain communication with its ships at sea, and how the erratic behavior of the ionosphere was a constant source of unreliability for shortwave communication. It is understandable, then, that the navy and the air force with similar needs greeted the arrival of the satellite with great enthusiasm as a replacement for its short-wave radio systems, with the satellite playing the role of a stable ionosphere, one that remained constant from day to night and year to year.

Not only does the satellite provide reliable long-distance connectivity, but also—and this is very difficult with short-wave radio—communication just over the horizon. With these characteristics, a fleet task group commander can stay in touch with his forces dispersed over hundreds of square miles, and at the same time maintain contact with his superiors no matter where they are located. It may seem incongruous to send radio signals over 20,000 miles into space to reach someone 100 miles away, until you realize that the less incongruous alternatives are awkward and unsatisfactory.

An even more extreme example of this use of satellite communications occurs with ground forces where the horizon limits line-of-sight communication to tens of miles. Until the advent of the satellite, the army used various strategies to overcome the fundamental range limitation, including the stringing of field wire, establishing special relays, and a form of atmospheric reflection known as tropospheric scatter that works over medium distances but requires high power or large antennas. Today's ground forces intercommunicate by voice service similar to the cellular radio service that has become so popular for automobile telephony in urban locations. The radios themselves are line-of-sight. They will therefore provide connectivity by relay over whatever distance the vehicle spacing allows. But when some vehicles outrun the others and get beyond line-of-sight, they are cut off without auxiliary systems, especially satellite systems.

But no individual radio technique, even the satellite, is a universal remedy that will cure all the communication ills of the armed forces. No single system ever seems to be able to satisfy the ever-increasing demands of its users. Telephone companies have the ability to install as much capacity as the demand requires, but not so with military communicators. Recall how during the World War I the radio made little impact because the capacity that could be reasonably furnished was so small compared to the demand that the technique was virtually useless. Now, decades later, with technology so different that it is barely recognizable, we see similar phenomena, of course on a different scale. As remarkable as the satellite is, its capacity is limited particularly when used for mobile applications. The capacities of practical numbers of satellites are well below the almost insatiable demand of modern command and control. Thus the older techniques are still used to help fill this capacity gap.

This attitude that "whatever you give me is never enough" may seem like ingratitude on the part of the users of military communications. But it also reflects the fact that military users are just like everyone else, accustomed to thinking of communications as a public utility with plenty to go around. Unfortunately the circumstances in which wars are fought are enough different so that this situation is not always applicable. The closest the rest of us come to understanding the military environment is the fortunately rare natural disaster—earthquake, flood, tornado—that can disturb our utilities and place us in an environment of scarcity for a short time. But a war can have lengthy episodes of unpredictable demand and equally unpredictable damage to communications along with everything else. It is almost never possible to plan adequately for these unpredictable circumstances. This observation appears to be time-invariant, and it is extremely unlikely that technological advances will ever change this situation. This is not an area in which to expect the surprises that technological developments have spun off elsewhere.

Plate 1. Morse's 1837 telegraph
instrument: receiver (above);
transmitter (below).
(Courtesy: Western Union)

Plate 2. Samuel F. B. Morse.
(Courtesy: Western Union)

The Telephone.

The proprietors of the Telephone, the invention of Alexander Graham Bell, for which patents have been issued by the United States and Great Britain, are now prepared to furnish Telephones for the transmission of articulate speech through instruments not more than twenty miles apart. Conversation can be easily carried on after slight practice and with the occasional repetition of a word or sentence. On first listening to the Telephone, though the sound is perfectly audible, the articulation seems to be indistinct; but after a few trials the ear becomes accustomed to the peculiar sound and finds little difficulty in understanding the words.

The Telephone should be set in a quiet place, where there is no noise which would interrupt ordinary conversation.

The advantages of the Telephone over the Telegraph for local business are

1st. That no skilled operator is required, but direct communication may be had by speech without the intervention of a third person.

2d. That the communication is much more rapid, the average number of words transmitted a minute by Morse Sounder being from fifteen to twenty, by Telephone from one to two hundred.

3d. That no expense is required either for its operation, maintenance, or repair. It needs no battery, and has no complicated machinery. It is unsurpassed for economy and simplicity.

The Terms for leasing two Telephones for social purposes connecting a dwelling-house with any other building will be $20 a year, for business purposes $40 a year, payable semiannually in advance, with the cost of expressage from Boston, New York, Cincinnati, Chicago, St. Louis, or San Francisco. The instruments will be kept in good working order by the lessors, free of expense, except from injuries resulting from great carelessness.

Several Telephones can be placed on the same line at an additional rental of $10 for each instrument; but the use of more than two on the same line where privacy is required is not advised. Any person within ordinary hearing distance can hear the voice calling through the Telephone. If a louder call is required one can be furnished for $5.

Telegraph lines will be constructed by the proprietors if desired. The price will vary from $100 to $150 a mile; any good mechanic can construct a line; No. 9 wire costs 8½ cents a pound, 320 pounds to the mile; 34 insulators at 25 cents each; the price of poles and setting varies in every locality; stringing wire $5 per mile; sundries $10 per mile.

Parties leasing the Telephones incur no expense beyond the annual rental and the repair of the line wire. On the following pages are extracts from the Press and other sources relating to the Telephone.

GARDINER G. HUBBARD.

Cambridge, Mass., May, 1877.

For further information and orders address

THOS. A. WATSON, 109 Court St., Boston.

Plate 6. Announcement of telephone service, 1877.
(Courtesy: IEEE Center for the History of Electrical Engineering)

Plate 5. Reproduced from *Scientific American*,
March 31, 1877, woodcut that shows Bell lecturing to an
audience in Salem, MA and demonstrating the telephone
by communicating with his laboratory in Boston.
*(Courtesy: IEEE Center for the History of Electrical
Engineering)*

The Telephone.

THE proprietors of the Telephone, the invention of Alexander Graham Bell, for which patents have been issued by the United States and Great Britain, are now prepared to furnish Telephones for the transmission of articulate speech through instruments not more than twenty miles apart. Conversation can be easily carried on after slight practice and with the occasional repetition of a word or sentence. On first listening to the Telephone, though the sound is perfectly audible, the articulation seems to be indistinct; but after a few trials the ear becomes accustomed to the peculiar sound and finds little difficulty in understanding the words.

The Telephone should be set in a quiet place, where there is no noise which would interrupt ordinary conversation.

The advantages of the Telephone over the Telegraph for local business are

1st. That no skilled operator is required, but direct communication may be had by speech without the intervention of a third person.

2d. That the communication is much more rapid, the average number of words transmitted a minute by Morse Sounder being from fifteen to twenty, by Telephone from one to two hundred.

3d. That no expense is required either for its operation, maintenance, or repair. It needs no battery, and has no complicated machinery. It is unsurpassed for economy and simplicity.

The Terms for leasing two Telephones for social purposes connecting a dwelling-house with any other building will be $20 a year, for business purposes $40 a year, payable semiannually in advance, with the cost of expressage from Boston, New York, Cincinnati, Chicago, St. Louis, or San Francisco. The instruments will be kept in good working order by the lessors, free of expense, except from injuries resulting from great carelessness.

Several Telephones can be placed on the same line at an additional rental of $10 for each instrument; but the use of more than two on the same line where privacy is required is not advised. Any person within ordinary hearing distance can hear the voice calling through the Telephone. If a louder call is required one can be furnished for $5.

Telegraph lines will be constructed by the proprietors if desired. The price will vary from $100 to $150 a mile; any good mechanic can construct a line; No. 9 wire costs 8½ cents a pound, 320 pounds to the mile; 34 insulators at 25 cents each; the price of poles and setting varies in every locality; stringing wire $5 per mile; sundries $10 per mile.

Parties leasing the Telephones incur no expense beyond the annual rental and the repair of the line wire. On the following pages are extracts from the Press and other sources relating to the Telephone.

GARDINER G. HUBBARD.

CAMBRIDGE, MASS., May, 1877.

For further information and orders address

THOS. A. WATSON, 109 COURT ST., BOSTON.

Plate 6. Announcement of telephone service, 1877.
(Courtesy: IEEE Center for the History of Electrical Engineering)

Plate 1. Morse's 1837 telegraph
instrument: receiver (above);
transmitter (below).
(Courtesy: Western Union)

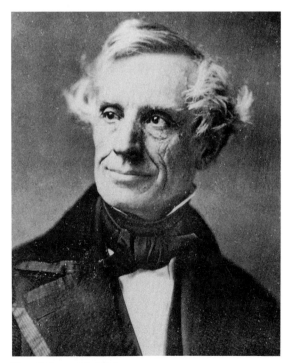

Plate 2. Samuel F. B. Morse.
(Courtesy: Western Union)

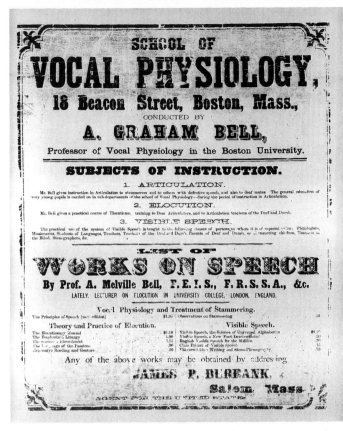

Plate 3. The announcement of Bell's *School of Vocal Physiology*. *(Courtesy: Library of Congress, Prints and Photographs Division)*

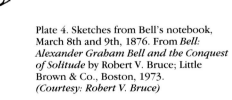

Plate 4. Sketches from Bell's notebook, March 8th and 9th, 1876. From *Bell: Alexander Graham Bell and the Conquest of Solitude* by Robert V. Bruce; Little Brown & Co., Boston, 1973. *(Courtesy: Robert V. Bruce)*

Plate 7. Theodore Vail, president of AT&T, talking to San Francisco and Hawaii from New York, 1915. *(Permission of AT&T Archives)*

Plate 8. John J. Carty, an early chief engineer of AT&T and commanding officer of the *Bell Batallions* of World War I. *(Courtesy: IEEE Center for the History of Electrical Engineering)*

Plate 9. James Clerk Maxwell.
*(Courtesy: IEEE Center for the
History of Electrical Engineering)*

Plate 10. Heinrich Hertz.
*(Courtesy: Burndy Library of the
Dibner Institute, Cambridge, MA)*

Plate 11. Hertz's original apparatus, photographed at the Bavarian Academy of Science, Munich, Germany, 1913. The gentleman is unidentified. (Courtesy: *The Museum of Science and Industry, Chicago, IL*)

Plate 12. Guglielmo Marconi with apparatus at Signal Hill, Newfoundland, 1901. (*Courtesy: The Smithsonian Institution*)

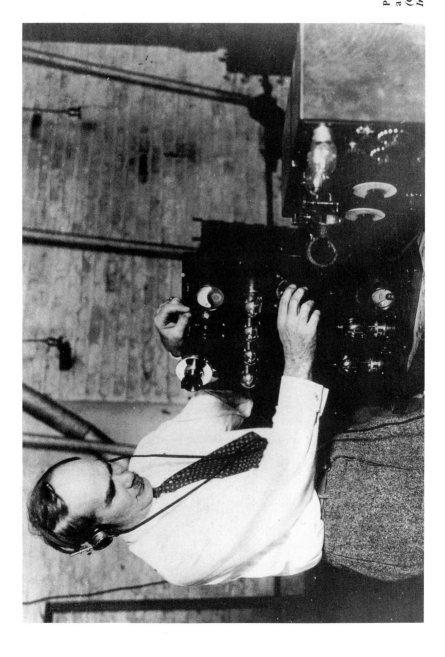

Plate 13. Lee De Forest operating a radio receiver, 1921. (*Courtesy: The Smithsonian Institution*)

Plate 14. Banquet of the Institute of Radio Engineers, New York City, 1915. Among the radio pioneers present were David Sarnoff, John Stone, Lee De Forest, Nicola Tesla, and E. F. W. Alexanderson.
(Courtesy: IEEE Center for the History of Electrical Engineering)

Plate 15. David Sarnoff with Marconi at RCA
long-distance communications station, Rocky
Point, Long Island, 1933.
*(Courtesy: The David Sarnoff Research Center,
Princeton, NJ)*

Inventor of FM

Armstrong Writes Note To Wife, Dies in Plunge

Maj. Edwin H. Armstrong, sixty-three, inventor of frequency modulation (FM) and one of the nation's leading radio pioneers, plunged to death yesterday from his thirteenth-floor apartment at River House, 435 E. 52d St.

Maj. Armstrong was found, fully clothed to overcoat, hat and gloves, on a third-floor extension at 10:30 a. m. by Alfred Henrichs, building maintenance man. He had apparently been dead several hours.

Police found a two-page note to his wife, Mrs. Marion Armstrong, signed "Ed," in which he said it was "heartbreaking" that he could not see her again and continued: "How deep and bitterly I regret what has happened to us."

The note, written in pencil on yellow legal paper, said he would give his life to be able to turn back to the time "when we were so happy and free" and ended: "God keep you and the Lord have mercy on my soul."

Maj. Armstrong, who began his brilliant career in electronics when just a boy, was a professor of electrical engineering at

Maj. Armstrong

Columbia University and the winner of a score of awards including the Medal of Merit and a Presidential citation for his contribution to military communications. He was a major in the Signal Corps in World War I and preferred that title to "doctor" or "professor."

Columbia University called Maj. Armstrong "the most important of all radio inventors, including Marconi." Besides his invention of FM in 1935, which

Plate 16. Front page article from the February 2, 1954 *New York Herald Tribune* that reports the suicide of Edwin Armstrong. *(Courtesy: Tom Lewis, author of* Empire of the Air)

Plate 17. Vladimir Zworykin.
*(Courtesy: The David Sarnoff
Research Center, Princeton, NJ)*

Plate 18. Philo Farnsworth.
(Courtesy: The Smithsonian Institution)

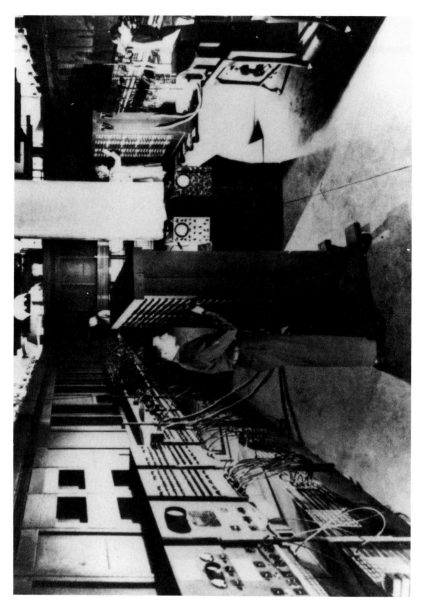

Plate 19. The ENIAC, invented at the University of Pennsylvania's Moore School of Engineering, is the ancestor of all present-day computers.
(Courtesy: The University of Pennsylvania)

Plate 20. John Mauchley, the leader
of the team that built the ENIAC.
*(Courtesy: IEEE Center for the History
of Electrical Engineering)*

Plate 21. John von Neumann and the Institute
for Advanced Study Computer, circa 1955.
Photograph by Alan Richards.
*(Courtesy: The Institute for Advanced Study,
Princeton, NJ, and the estate of Alan Richards)*

Plate 22. The inventors of the transistor:
(from left) William Shockley, Walter Brattain, and
John Bardeen, at Bell Telephone Laboratories, 1947.
*(Courtesy: The Emilio Segre Visual Archives,
Center for History of Physics, American Institute
of Physics, College Park, MD)*

Plate 23. The first integrated
circuit, invented by Jack S. Kilby
of Texas Instruments, 1958.
(Courtesy: Texas Instruments)

Plate 24. The first ARPANET packet switch at Bolt Beranek and Newman, Cambridge, MA, 1969. Robert Kahn is located far right. Frank Heart, project leader, is located center back row, with tie. *(Courtesy: Frank Heart)*

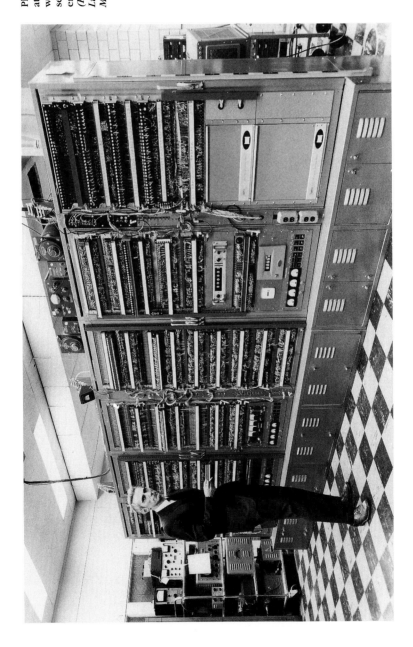

Plate 25. Claude Shannon at MIT Lincoln Laboratory with the first implementation of sequential decoding—a powerful error-correction technique, 1962. (Reprinted with permission of MIT Lincoln Laboratory, Lexington, MA, USA)

Plate 26. John deButts, flanked by top members of his management team, as he assumed leadership of AT&T, 1972. *(Permission of AT&T Archives)*

Plate 27. William McGowan, chairman of MCI, who challenged the AT&T monopoly. *(Courtesy: MCI)*

Plate 28. Charles Brown (on right), deButts's successor at
AT&T, and William Baxter, Assistant Attorney General,
at the press conference that announced the divestiture agreement,
January 8, 1982.
(Permission of AT&T Archives)

The Communication/ Computing Symbiosis

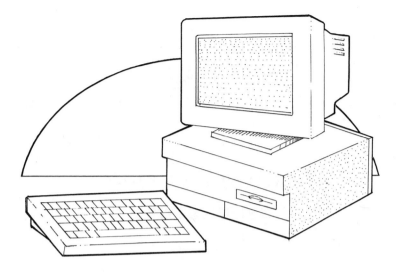

On the face of it, computing and communication would seem to be entirely different disciplines—the one concerned with the manipulation of information and the other with the transport of information from one place to another. Yet the histories of the two have been mutually dependent almost since the computer first made its appearance, and this interdependence has increased over time until the fusion of the two has become the foundation of what we call the *information age*.

This interdependence all started with the vacuum tube, the offspring of the wireless. This piece of technology, which made its parent practical and then gave birth to radio and television broadcasting, radar, and the communication satellite, was also the foundation stone of the computer. But here is a case where the grandparent and grandchild were seemingly so disparate in their nature that it appeared each would go its own way unaffected by the existence of the other. Of course, this was not to be the case for very long.

There are many reasons for this interdependence, spanning the whole range from basic technology to applications. Indeed, the story of the computer impinges on the story of communication in the latter half of the century in a complex pattern of plots and subplots of the kind that we would expect in a Victorian novel but not in the story of a scientific field.

As we look back to the origins of the computer, it is easy to see the first signs of this symbiosis, but they were surely not apparent to the founders of the field. Sometimes first impressions are deceiving!

Chapter

18

The Computer Makes Its Appearance

On November 4, 1952, the eyes of much of the nation were glued to the television screen to see whether the next president of the United States would be Dwight Eisenhower, the distinguished general and hero of the recent victory over the Nazis, or the governor of Illinois, Adlai Stevenson, the choice of the incumbent, Harry Truman. All of the preelection polls indicated that the race was very close. The TV viewers were expecting to settle in for a long night of vote counting and tabulation.

This was the first national election in which television was playing a significant role. The election of 1948, occurring only three years after the war, had come too soon for the postwar television boom to have had much of an effect. But the four years that followed saw television cover the landscape. It was only then that we could see clearly the impact that the new communications medium was to have on public affairs, and the 1952 campaign and election were to confirm these expectations.

But who could have foreseen that other great technological innovation that was first revealed to the public on that election eve? Because along with its usual array of news reporters, politicians, and political analysts, CBS television introduced a new player, a computer named UNIVAC from Remington Rand, a once-distinguished corporate name that has been all but forgotten, a casualty of the generations of mergers and acquisitions that led to the present-day Unisys Corporation. The idea was to feed the early returns from certain key precincts into UNIVAC where they would be compared with results of previous elections, and out would come a prediction of the election result. The only problem was that UNIVAC worked so well and so rapidly that the human experts did not trust its results. For, very early in the evening, the computer was predicting a landslide victory for Eisenhower, in contrast to the preelection predictions of a close race. And so CBS, reluctant to appear in public with egg on its face, withheld UNIVAC's prediction until much later in the evening.

The theory behind predicting elections is well known to statisticians. It is the same kind of mathematics that permits pollsters to judge the public response to anything, political or otherwise, by observing the response of a small percentage of the population. All it takes is some arithmetical manipulation of the data obtained from the small sample. In principle, the calculations required are very simple and anyone can perform them. But in any practical case, there are so many additions, subtractions, multiplications, and divisions to be performed that a small army of people would be required to complete the calculations quickly enough to do any good. And that is where a computer enters the picture, because, in essence, the computer does arithmetic so rapidly that it provides that small army in one box.

The UNIVAC was the world's first commercial computer. It was the product of two brilliant scientists, John Mauchly and J. Presper Eckert, who had embarked on an entrepreneurial venture after having built the computer that sired them all, a machine called the ENIAC, at the Moore School of the University of Pennsylvania shortly after the war ended. They had their troubles getting started as independent entrepreneurs and finally had to sell out to Remington Rand.

One is always on dangerous ground calling something the first, or some one individual the father of some invention—witness Marconi, Watson-Watt, or Zworykin. There were indeed computers of various kinds before ENIAC. The basic idea of automatic digital computation dates back to Charles Babbage, an English mathematician who lived in the first part of the nineteenth century. His machines, called the Analytical Engine and Difference Engine, were, of course, mechanical. Babbage was a man whose fertile imagination exceeded his ability to reduce his ideas to practice. As a result, neither of his machines was ever finished, although machines patterned after his were built by others and put to some practical use. It is an interesting historical sidelight that Babbage's assistant was Ada Byron Lovelace, the daughter of the celebrated poet, Lord Byron. She has gone down in history as the world's first computer programmer and for this was honored by having the computer language, *Ada*, developed by the Defense Department, named after her.

But in the mid-1930s, it was conceivable that mechanical computing mechanisms—gears, cams, shafts, and the like—could be replaced by electronic circuits using vacuum tubes, and researchers were beginning to experiment along these lines. Just a few years earlier, other groups of less adventurous researchers set their sights a bit lower and devised a class of computers similar to the older mechanical ones but that worked electromechanically. Instead of vacuum tubes, they used devices called *relays* that open and close contacts depending on whether an electric current is present or not, a particular application of the electromagnet that Morse and Bell had used to great advantage in an earlier day. But these had very little influence on the subsequent turn of events, becoming quickly eclipsed by the vastly superior electronic machines. The team led by Mauchly at the Moore School was the most successful of these electronic computer pioneers, leading to the almost universal recognition of the ENIAC as the first electronic digital computer. In 1947 Eckert and Mauchly applied for a patent that said as much and which was finally awarded in 1964. Shortly thereafter a complex suit and countersuit took place between Sperry Rand, a new company that resulted from the merger in 1955 of Sperry Gyroscope and Remington Rand, the owner of the patent, and Honeywell, another major player in the computer industry at that time.[71] On the face of it, there was nothing unusual about a suit over an invention, witness Bell and Gray, Bell and Western Union, De Forest and Armstrong, RCA and Farnsworth, and so many others. But this suit had a flavor all its own.

It seemed that the Eckert-Mauchly patent was exceedingly broad, so much so that Sperry felt that it had the license to collect substantial royalties from all the major computer manufacturers, because every computer in existence was a conceptual descendent of the ENIAC. To protect itself, IBM, which was emerging as the industry giant, entered into a cross-licensing agreement with Sperry. Honeywell took a different tack and contested the patent in court. After several years, the court ruled that the patent was invalid, in part because the ENIAC owed much of its conception to the prior work of an obscure researcher at Iowa State University named John V. Atanasoff. Sperry did not appeal the decision.

This was a monumental decision, not only because of its financial implications, but also because it appeared to rewrite the history of the computer that was apparently so well known by that time. Despite its consequence, the ruling was virtually ignored by the press. One of the reasons had to be in its coincidence with the Watergate scandal: the judgment was handed down on October 19, 1973, nine days after the resignation of Richard Nixon's vice president, Spiro Agnew, and one day before the "Saturday night massacre", when President Nixon fired the Justice Department's leaders. In another interesting coincidence, the suit was originally filed in Washington before Judge Sirica of Watergate fame who transferred it to Minneapolis.

In the earlier patent wrangles, the contest was between one inventor and another. This case was unique in that Atanasoff never patented his inventions. He and Mauchly had discussed the subject often. They had met in 1940, and, a few months later, Atanasoff had invited Mauchly to visit him at Iowa State to see his machine and freely discussed his ideas at those meetings. Atanasoff also visited the Moore School in 1945 where he saw the almost completed ENIAC. Apparently he did not realize the extent to which the ENIAC built on his work because the two machines looked so different. For whatever reason, Eckert and Mauchly never acknowledged any indebtedness of their design to Atanasoff. Chances are that had Sperry not been so greedy—it was trying to collect large royalties even before the patent was awarded, the suit would never have arisen and Atanasoff's role in the history of the computer would have remained obscured. Nevertheless, however much this bitter dispute may have damaged Mauchly's reputation, the fact remains that his creation, the ENIAC, whatever its indebtedness to Atanasoff, was still a remarkable feat.

The digital computer is so commonplace today that most people are not aware that there ever was any other kind. In fact, while Mauchly and his colleagues were building the ENIAC during the war, the armed services were making good use of the *analog* computer for a variety of functions. What's the difference? The digital computer is conceptually the most natural to us because it performs its arithmetic just the way we have been doing it since the first man who learned to add and subtract with the aid of the *digits* on his hands and feet.[72] All the information is in the form of whole numbers. Atanasoff used the binary number system in which numbers are all combinations of the two digits 0 and 1, rather than the decimal number system with the ten digits, 0–9. He made his choice to allow a vacuum tube to represent a binary digit by its state of conduction: if current flowed, it represented a 1; if no current flowed, it represented a 0. In using the tube in this way, he was emphasizing its switchlike characteristics, the property that led to the term *valve* rather than *tube* as the preferred terminology in Britain. To be sure, he could have established ten levels of current flow in the tube so as to represent a decimal digit, but he chose the binary case as a way of insuring reliability in the face of tubes with varying characteristics. This very practical reasoning established the pattern for all the computers that followed. The choice of a number system was important practically, but conceptually it was just a detail. Computers add, subtract, multiply, and divide these numbers just the way we do them by hand, only much faster.

But performing computations digitally is only natural when the data to be manipulated are derived from counting things. Money is in this category; so are the numbers of people who vote for one candidate or another. But how about the numbers that stand for physical quantities that have to be measured rather than simply counted, for example, the speed of a rocket, the distance between one place and another, or the strength of an audio signal? In these situations, a measurement has to be made with some degree of accuracy, and this measurement has to be converted into a number before a digital computer can go into action.

Sometimes it is easier just to take the electrical signal corresponding to the measurement and manipulate it directly without converting it into digits. This is exactly what an analog computer does—the designation *analog* indicating that the electrical signals are proportional to the quantities being manipulated. A radio receiver is a form of analog computer. It takes a signal from the air and ultimately converts it into a sound of intensity proportional to that of the audio signal impressed on the radio wave. A common use of analog computers during the war was to point radar antennas at hostile aircraft from the deck of a ship tossed about by heavy seas. The computers derived an electrical signal from a gyroscope that provided a fixed reference direction, compared this signal with another one proportional to the slope of the deck relative to the ocean surface, and used the result of this comparison to maintain the antenna pointing in a given direction regardless of the ship's motion.

Today this kind of job and, indeed, almost all computation is performed digitally rather than by analog techniques, because, for one thing, digital computers are now so cheap. But another reason that goes to the heart of digital computing is its ability to perform its calculations with as much accuracy as desired. When you perform a numerical calculation by hand, you know that your calculation is as accurate as the data that are being manipulated. The arithmetic itself does nothing to degrade the accuracy. For example, you know that, in principle, you can multiply twenty-digit numbers as easily as three-digit numbers; it is just more tedious, takes longer, and is, of course, subject to human error. The same thing holds true in a digital computer, only the computer does not mind the tedium and rarely makes errors (aside from roundoff inaccuracies under some circumstances). In contrast, the manipulations that comprise the analog computation processes have inherent accuracy limitations. The now obsolete slide rule, for example, is a form of analog computer, accurate to about one part in a thousand, limited by how accurately a person can read the engraved scale. While most electronic analog computers are considerably more accurate than manual slide rules, each improvement in accuracy is successively more difficult to achieve, and it may be very expensive to do so.

You might ask, then, why analog computers were ever used. The reason is that, in the early days, the manipulations required to convert a measurement into a digital number and then to perform the necessary arithmetic operations were too slow to keep up with the rocking of a ship or the equivalent. And even if they could, the cost of doing so was prohibitively high. But with time, the inherent advantage of digital computation has been accessible in more and more contexts by the high performance obtainable with ever faster and cheaper components. Thus the once important analog computer has become a relic of the past.

Even in World War II there were certain jobs that were not amenable to analog computation. One of these was to create tables that artillery officers used to guide the aiming of their guns. These tables took into account the various atmospheric conditions, such as wind direction and speed and humidity, that affected the trajectories of the projectiles. The calculations that went into creating those tables were so laborious that it was hopeless to even think of generating them by hand for all the conditions that might exist in a realistic battlefield situation. They were being calculated in a mechanical computer at the Moore School and in one of the army's computers at the Aberdeen Proving Grounds in Maryland. Mauchly had an idea for an electronic computer that would perform these calculations automatically, following in the footsteps of Babbage whose machine had been motivated by the similar problem of calculating navigational tables. He incorporated these ideas in a proposal, and, in 1943, the army gave him a $400,000 contract to build the machine. Its name, ENIAC, was an acronym for Electronic Numerical Integrator And Computer, describing its method of operation. The machine solved its first problem at the end of 1945, too late to influence the war effort, but early enough to influence virtually everything else in the latter half of the century.

Even though the ENIAC was built to solve a particular class of laborious mathematical problems, Mauchly and Eckert had the foresight to develop a computer structure that was general purpose to allow it to be used for other problems as well. To be sure, programming the computer to perform a problem was a formidable task, but once done, the computer would go through all its routines automatically. In this respect, the ENIAC and Mauchly's and Eckert's next efforts were far in advance of Atanasoff both conceptually and practically.

Once Eckert and Mauchly showed the way, it did not take long for others to get into the act. The fact that by the late 1950s IBM had become the leading computer manufacturer was itself a curiosity that demonstrated that technology alone does not make for commercial success. In the early days, the technological leader of the industry was Remington Rand, as the inheritor of Mauchly's and Eckert's pioneering technology. IBM as a business machine maker rooted in the technology of punched cards was a Johnny-come-lately to the business. Yet, by the end of the decade, Sperry Rand, despite its technological lead, had been surpassed by IBM, largely on the basis of superior marketing and, above all, superb customer service. The computer of those early days was not easy to use. While the general-purpose computer could, in principle, be programmed to solve a wide variety of problems, doing it turned out to be more complex than originally imagined, a fact that the early users soon came to to appreciate. IBM had neither the best hardware nor the best software to offer its customers. What it did have was an attitude that selling the computer was the beginning and not the end of its relationship with its customers, and it was this attitude that was primarily responsible for its enormous commercial success.

Many companies and research laboratories were experimenting with computers during the decade of the 1950s. You can just imagine the excitement in the field. Here was a new system, the computer, that was being used to solve all kinds of new problems on an almost daily basis, problems that ranged from business applications, to industrial process control, to military problems associated with defending the nation against hostile aircraft and missile attack. The more successful these applications, the greater the increasingly voracious appetites of its users for computers with ever higher capabilities. But as the decade proceeded, it was becoming increasingly clear that a limit was being reached. The expectations of the users were seemingly higher than the technology could meet.

The essential reason for this apparent limit was the inadequacy of the vacuum tube itself, the very technology that made the electronic computer conceivable to begin with. The most severe of the problems facing Eckert and Mauchly as they built first the ENIAC and later its successor, the first UNIVAC, was the fact that the computer had to use so many tubes to be able to perform useful functions. I described previously how the vacuum tube made possible the radio receivers that fueled the broadcast phenomenon of the 1920s and 1930s. These radios would use a handful of tubes. Those old enough to remember those days may perhaps recall the advertising of the manufacturers who claimed superior performance by virtue of using, say, six rather than five tubes. But you may also remember that the performance of a radio and, later, a television set, would degrade after a while, or even stop altogether. The repairman would peer into the back of the set, replace a tube or two, and the radio or TV would be as good as new.

But the early computer was far different. Its tube count was not four or five or even the dozen or two in the early TV sets; rather, it was measured in the thousands. One of the reasons for this is speed. For example, when you or I perform, say, an addition operation, we do it methodically one column at a time beginning at the right and proceed to the left until the addition is complete. The time it takes to do this for ten-digit numbers is about ten times that for single-digit numbers providing we do not get tired and make a mistake. A computer can also do it one digit at a time, hopefully without error. But it can also add all the columns at once, thereby performing the ten-digit arithmetic about as fast as single-digit arithmetic. The price it pays for this additional speed is the need for ten times as many electronic circuits and, therefore, ten times as many vacuum tubes. It is not fundamentally more complex to add this extra equipment. It just takes more of the same vacuum tube amplifier elements.

A computer also has a need for electronic elements that simply store numbers. The common name for computer storage is the anthropomorphic term *memory*. Even the cheapest of modern computers have memory elements that number in the millions. This was far from the case in the early days. The most straightforward way to build a memory element to store a single binary digit requires two vacuum tubes. The early computers could not afford very many memory elements built this way and had to use other less-satisfactory mechanisms to reduce the need for tubes. And, over the years, many different physical phenomena have been used to increase the quantity and speed of memory elements at an acceptable level of cost.

What is the problem with using a large number of tubes? Certainly cost has to be one of them. But if cost were the only issue, some of the early pioneers, particularly those funded by the Defense Department, would have found ways to build ever larger machines. A more fundamental reason was reliability.

The vacuum tube is a fragile device. It depends crucially on its vacuum. If the seal between the envelope of the tube and its base should spring a leak, even a very tiny one, eventually enough air seeps in to degrade the tube's performance. The basic functioning of the tube depends on a wire being heated to a high enough temperature to boil off electrons. After a while, the efficiency of this electron emission process decreases as the wire ages, and the performance of the tube begins to degrade accordingly.

As long as we are dealing with something like a radio receiver with a few tubes, an occasional malfunction is not too much of an annoyance. But when dealing with a computer that uses thousands of tubes, the situation is quite different. Just suppose a tube of a given type can be expected to perform satisfactorily for an average of 10,000 hours, approximately one year. Then a computer system with 1,000 tubes can expect the average failure rate to be one every ten hours. If the computer were to contain ten times as many tubes, then failures would be expected to occur ten times as often. The lifetime of 10,000 hours was typical for the more reliable tube types—many were less reliable. But even if the reliability were ten times as high, the size of the computer would ultimately be limited at some value. In fact, the reliability degrades as the temperature increases, and any computer that uses thousands of tubes generates a huge amount of heat that has to be removed by an extensive cooling system if it is not to degrade still further. ENIAC used some 18,000 tubes and consumed 140 kilowatts of power. It was nothing short of a minor miracle that it could be kept working long enough between tube changes to yield useful results.

Thus, the situation facing the fledgling computer companies of the early 1950s was one of an increasing demand for computing power with the inability of the technology to keep up with the demand. What was needed was either a vastly more reliable vacuum tube or else some other device that would do the same thing with more reliability.

As it turned out, that device was the transistor.

Chapter

19

The Transistor

The way Jane Bardeen recalls the incident, her husband John, a research physicist at the Bell Laboratories, came home one afternoon at the usual time, parked his car in the back of the house, walked into the kitchen and said very quietly: "We discovered something today." That something was the transistor.[73]

This quiet unemotional demeanor was typical of John Bardeen, one of the most brilliant physicists of the century, the only person ever to have won two Nobel prizes in the same field. After receiving his doctorate in 1936, he continued his research at Princeton and Harvard, and contributed to the war effort at the Naval Ordinance Laboratory. In his brief career he had already earned the great respect of his colleagues, and once the war was over, he had to decide which of many offers to accept. He chose to go to the Bell Laboratories to work on a class of new materials called *semiconductors*.

The Bell Laboratories had made it a policy to support research in fundamental science in the hope that it might yield results that could benefit the telephone system in the future. One of these areas of research was solid-state physics, and, within this broad area, the field of semiconductors was of particular interest. Semiconductors are materials with properties intermediate between good conductors of electricity, such as copper and silver, and very poor conductors or insulators, such as rubber and glass. The semiconductor material most widely used today is silicon, the oxide of which is the principal ingredient of common sand. One of the first to work in this new field for the Bell Laboratories was a young physicist named William Shockley, who came to Bell in 1936 shortly after obtaining his Ph.D. from MIT. Shockley, who had once worked with

Bardeen, is the man who induced his former colleague to come to Bell to collaborate in the work that ultimately led to the invention of the transistor. In a retrospective article published in 1976, Shockley recalled that he wrote the following in his laboratory notebook in December, 1939: "It has today occurred to me that an amplifier using semiconductors rather than vacuum is in principle possible."[74]

Recall that a vacuum tube amplifies because a small signal impressed on a wire mesh or grid in the path of a stream of electrons from a hot wire can modify the electron stream to produce an amplified signal. Shockley's idea was to do something analogous within semiconductors. Key to this notion was the fact that while a pure semiconductor is a poor conductor of electricity, the introduction of controlled amounts of the right kinds of impurities can introduce behavior similar to that of the vacuum tube. If the ideas worked out, there would be no vacuum, no hot wire, and no fragile grid structure. Here was the potential for a much more reliable device that would be capable of operating at much lower temperatures and at lower power levels, the answer to the dreams of a computer designer.

It would be nice and logical if the sequence of events that led to the invention of the transistor, the device that replaced the vacuum tube, followed from this pressing need of the computer industry as did the invention of the tube by De Forest's need for an improved radio receiver. But the fact of the matter is that the invention of the transistor had nothing at all to do with computers per se—the research that led to the transistor occurred at the same time as Mauchly's and Eckert's struggles with the ENIAC. Rather it sprang from communications, as did the vacuum tube. The difference is that this time it was the telephone giant AT&T and not an eccentric entrepreneur in the image of De Forest that was responsible for the invention.

There were, in fact, several reasons why the telephone company should want a substitute for the vacuum tube. For one thing, the telephone was approaching its seventieth birthday and a transatlantic cable was still beyond grasp because there was no way of building long-lived amplifiers with the ruggedness to withstand the underwater environment. Eckert and Mauchly may have had a lot of tubes to change but at least they were not located under water. However, the primary reason was a computerlike application, electronic switching.

The automatic switches that were being installed in the telephone systems were based on relays, the same devices that the electromechanical computers of the 1930s had used. The relay contacts opening and closing are what connect one circuit to and disconnect it from another. A practical switch requires thousands of relays to make the necessary connections. There were good reasons for desiring to replace this electromechanical switching by electronic switching in which the current in vacuum tubes would be switched on or off. But this goal leads to exactly the same problem as in computers: A useful switch containing thousands of tubes constitutes a problem in maintenance and reliability. The close kinship of communications switching systems and computers was to become increasingly evident in the decades that followed.

It was the reliability problem inherent in the use of large numbers of tubes that led to AT&T's interest in finding another way of amplifying, one that did not require the vacuum devices. The result of these labors, the transistor, came into existence in a far different way than did the vacuum tube. De Forest, in seeking a new radio receiver, came up with the idea of building a vacuum tube triode out of the diode that had been already been developed. His invention was, therefore, an inspired modification of existing technology. In contrast, invention of the transistor required not only entirely new technology, but also the understanding of the basic science behind the technology.

The way this revolutionary device came into being is a prime example of how the enlightened management of the Bell Laboratories was willing to invest in fundamental science that had some chance of impacting the telephone industry at some unknown time in the future. But it was not an accident that the Bell system alone in the industrial community would engage in such fundamental research. The transistor was a product of a program of breadth and depth that was only possible in a public utility that could pay for its research through the regulated rate-making process. (It was, in fact, this public support of the research program that led some to quip that the old Bell Laboratories was the finest *government* laboratory in the nation. There were many industry observers who viewed the breakup of the old AT&T with alarm for a variety of reasons related to the quality of service that divided management would provide to the public. Most of these pessimistic predictions have not materialized. However, in the opinion of many, the most significant change brought about by the divestiture was in the necessarily changed character of the Bell Laboratories, which no longer operates under conditions so favorable to the pursuit of fundamental research, the effects of which will not be evident for some time in the future.)

Once the war ended, the scientists of the Bell Laboratories were able to turn their attention to the new field in earnest. Shockley, Bardeen, and Walter Brattain formed the team that pursued the semiconductor amplifier with great intensity. Brattain, the oldest of the group, had gone to work for Bell in 1929 just after receiving his Ph.D., working first on vacuum tube research before transferring to the semiconductor group. By the end of 1947 they had fabricated a laboratory device that produced a measurable amount of amplification. Then they set up a demonstration for their colleagues and the Bell Laboratories management in which they hooked up a microphone to the amplifier input and a loudspeaker to its output. Each, in turn, whispered "hello" into the microphone and were greeted by a loud "hello" from the speaker. The vacuum tube had a competitor at last.

In recognition of the potential importance of this development, the next goal at the Laboratories was the development of practical devices. Almost as important was finding a name for the new device. The inventors enlisted the aid of their Bell coworkers in this search. The important property of both the vacuum tube and its new solid-state cousin was the ability to modify the current flowing between a pair of electrodes by impressing a signal on a third electrode. In the theory of the vacuum tube, the term used to describe this property was *transconductance*. The corresponding name for the transistor was *transresistance*, which prompted John Pierce, one of these colleagues, to suggest the name *transistor* combining the prefix *trans* with the suffix *istor* from the resistor. When Brattain heard Pierce's musings, he was quoted as saying, "Pierce, that is it!"[75]

This first transistor was related to the crystal diode used as a radio receiver in the early days. The semiconductor crystal was firmly connected to one electrode, and the other two were *catwhiskers* placed close to each other on the opposite side of the crystal, and, for this reason, it was called a *point-contact transistor*. It resulted from a felicitous collaboration between Brattain, the master experimentalist who had the appropriate feel for manipulating the whiskers to obtain the best results, and Bardeen, the superb theorist who was always ready with an explanation of Brattain's sometimes peculiar results. But it was a finicky device, not the kind of thing that would replace the vacuum tube for reasons of reliability. Shockley himself was only an indirect participant in this work on the point-contact transistor. But shortly thereafter he developed the device that was to be of far greater impact, one that did not depend on the ideosyncracies of catwhisker contacts. This device, called the *junction transistor*, became the ancestor of all the transistors in use today.

No three persons have been more influential on the way our modern technological society has developed than Shockley, Bardeen, and Brattain. The three were justly rewarded with the Nobel Prize for their work in 1956. Yet who outside of the scientific community is even aware of them today? The most famous—perhaps *infamous* is a more accurate word—is Shockley, but for reasons having nothing to do with his scientific abilities. There is a disease that inflicts some people who, having achieved greatness and recognition in one field, feel impelled to express themselves in unrelated fields and expect the same respect and recognition. It seems that later in life Shockley became an exponent of a theory that he called *dysgenics* in which he claimed that blacks were genetically inferior to others and, if allowed to propagate at will, would, over time, cause a general degradation of the nation's "human quality." We are fortunate that since his death there have been few if any respectable adherents to his racial theories.

The transistor took the world by storm, aided by AT&T's seemingly altruistic policy with respect to its application. The telephone monopoly took the unusual step—attributed by some to a public relations act motivated by a pending antitrust action by the Justice Department—of offering to license one and all to manufacture transistors for the low price of $25,000 in lieu of charging royalties on its inventions. And, in keeping with its Alexander Graham Bell heritage, it waived all royalties in the application of the transistor to the hearing aid, the first commercial product to benefit from the small size and low power consumption of the transistor as compared to the vacuum tube. The antitrust action initiated in 1949 still dragged on in the 1950s with the Justice Department and AT&T trying to agree on the provisions of a consent decree that would settle the issue out of court. During these negotiations AT&T dropped its licensing fee for all American companies. By 1955 more than twenty American companies—most of them funded by the Defense Department—had obtained these licenses. Among the foreign licensees were Masaru Ibuka and Akio Morita, the founders of The Tokyo Telecommunications Engineering Corporation, which later became famous as Sony. They applied for a license in 1953 but the Japanese government held up the application for a year, concerned about such a large amount of money leaving the country. Scarcely a year after receiving its license, Sony produced Japan's first transistor radio.[76]

AT&T held an information-sharing symposium for its licensees in 1952. This modus operandi featuring complete openness was a new experience for the telephone monopoly. A Bell Laboratories' official, Jack Morton, described it this way sixteen years later: "But it was a departure for us to tell our licensees everything we knew. We realized that if this thing was as big as we thought, we couldn't keep it to ourselves and we couldn't make all the technical contributions. It was to our interest to spread it around. If you cast your bread on the water, sometimes it comes back angel food cake."[77]

Of course, the consumer product that made the transistor a household word was the portable radio powered by a flashlight battery that began to appear everywhere in novel lightweight versions previously out of the question as long as they depended on vacuum tubes. The pioneer manufacturer was Regency, a small company located in Dallas, that responded to the challenge of Patrick Haggerty, the head of Texas

Instruments Company, a small electronics parts company also in Dallas and one of the first of AT&T's transistor licensees. Haggerty, in seeking a market for his transistors, had first tried unsuccessfully to convince his own engineers at Texas Instruments that such a project was worthwhile. He met similar responses when he approached the major radio manufacturers, none of whom was willing to gamble on the commercial success of a portable radio. With the benefit of hindsight, we can observe how foolish and unimaginative they were, especially in view of the fact that more than ten years earlier the comic strip character, Dick Tracy, had made the idea of a wristwatch radio an image of what would be possible in the future. However, electronics manufacturers were beginning to understand the difference between the technical feasibility of a product and its commercial acceptability. The former is something quantifiable and predictable; the latter is anything but.

The Regency pocket radio made its appearance in time for the Christmas season of 1954, and it made a big splash. So closely did the transistor become associated with the pocket radio that in the popular vernacular its name was shortened from transistorized radio or even transistor radio to simply transistor, just as the microwave oven is popularly called a microwave after the technology that makes it possible. There is an interesting story about how Hagerty turned this success into another. It seems that Thomas J. Watson, Jr., the head of IBM, bought 100 Regency radios and distributed them among his engineers to see if he could inspire them to apply the new transistor technology to the computer.[78] Apparently this ploy worked, because in 1957 Texas Industries became a major supplier to the country's largest computer company.

It did not take too long for the transistor to eclipse the vacuum tube as the dominant component of the computer. The decade of the 1950s saw the proliferation of computers small and large by many competing manufacturers, all using vacuum tubes and all becoming obsolete as the computer companies began experimenting with transistorized versions of their machines. By the end of the decade, all the commercial computer manufacturers were replacing their vacuum tube machines with transistor-based versions. Thus began the phenomenon that has continued to our day in which one generation of computers has been succeeded by another generation using the components developed during the lifetime of the preceding generation. The vacuum tube that was once so influential was fast disappearing except in certain specialized applications unsuitable for transistors. And so it remains to this day.

Chapter

20

The Chip

With the relatively reliable transistor replacing its less reliable predecessor and with advances in the semiconductor art, the many computer manufacturers continued to build larger and more powerful machines. The more powerful these computers became, however, the greater the appetite of their users for still more powerful machines, capable of solving more problems more rapidly than ever. Could the capability of computers grow indefinitely? As important a step as the transistor was in this quest for more computing power, it too had its limitations. It was not that the transistor was insufficiently reliable to use in very large numbers. Rather, it was the inability of computer designers to make effective of very large numbers of transistors in their computers. There appeared to be a limit to the power of transistor computers, just as for vacuum tube computers, but for a different reason.

The problem that was beginning to manifest itself in the computer world of the late 1950s was what Jack Morton called "the tyranny of numbers." Just consider the fact that a computer of that era, the CDC 1604, manufactured by the Control Data Corporation, a spin-off of Remington Rand, contained some 25,000 transistors, 100,000 semiconductor diodes, and hundreds of thousands of resistors and capacitors. Each transistor had three wires to be connected in some way, while each of the other components had two. The transistor solved the problem of reliability, but it was little better than the tube when one considered the problem of mounting and interconnecting this huge number of electronic elements. Unless something new were to materialize, the increases in these numbers by a factor of at least ten that the new applications seemed to demand looked beyond the capability of the existing technology.

Many approaches were being investigated to the escalating interconnection problem facing the computer industry. The common method of construction depended on what was called a *printed circuit board*, a plastic card on which the components would be mounted with interconnections between components provided by thin copper ribbons plated on the top and bottom of the board to which each wire from each component had to be soldered. If the board contained many components, it was often not possible to fit all the necessary wires on top and bottom; other layers in between were necessary. Each board would be fitted with a connector at its end from which wires would be run to make the board-to-board connections. While this was a more manageable way to interconnect large numbers of components than to run pieces of wire between every component, it had its limitations. Something drastically different was needed.

That something was the *integrated circuit*. This invention came about in a manner more like that of the vacuum tube than of the transistor. No new science was required. In contrast to the invention of the transistor that had required a research laboratory in which the fundamental properties of semiconductors could be investigated, the invention of the integrated circuit was much more in the nature of an ingenious engineering solution to a seemingly intractable engineering problem, within the capability of many people in many organizations. It is, therefore, not surprising that the principal of the integrated circuit was, in fact, discovered independently by two people, Jack Kilby at Texas Instruments in mid-1958, and Robert Noyce, one of the founders of a new company called Fairchild Semiconductors, some six months later. There was the inevitable patent fight between the two companies, but this one was different from the others that had characterized the communications industry from its very beginning. It was settled amicably by the two companies agreeing to colicense others to use their inventions.[79]

The integrated circuit is, in essence, the equivalent of the printed circuit board constructed out of a single semiconductor crystal. How is such a thing possible? An electronic circuit such as an amplifier is constructed out of several components. While the key component is the active component—the vacuum tube or transistor, other so-called passive components are needed. One such component is the *resistor*, a device that impedes the flow of current by a controllable amount. Resistors are customarily manufactured in a wide range of sizes so that the circuit designer can tailor the amount of current flowing in each part of the circuit in just the right way. Another passive component is called a *capacitor* or *condenser*, a device that can store up an electrical charge.

It is also fabricated in a range of sizes. The art of electronic circuit design is to devise combinations of transistors, resistors, and capacitors that perform the various functions required by the system. These are the components that would be mounted on the computer printed circuit boards and wired together by the plated copper wires.

The observation, made independently by Kilby and Noyce, was that if resistors and capacitors could be manufactured out of a slice of a semiconductor crystal along with the transistors, and if the conducting wires could also be printed on the same slice as on plastic boards, then an entire circuit could be fabricated out of that single piece of semiconductor. Imagine what this would mean. Since a single electronic circuit usually contains several passive components for every transistor, a printed circuit board filled with such integrated circuits instead of the individual components would contain several times the processing power of the older boards in the same space and with the same wiring complexity. But that is only the beginning. If one amplifier can be fabricated on a single chip, then why not two amplifiers, or ten, or one hundred, or a million? This was the way that computers of the level of complexity that the applications seemed to demand could be fabricated.

The two inventors, Kilby and Noyce, who came up with the same idea arrived at their solutions in different ways. Both understood semiconductor technology in a very deep way, and both were aware of the significance of the connections problem. Kilby, a large, quiet, kindly, introverted man came to work for Texas Instruments in the spring of 1958 from a small company in Milwaukee. He may not have known a correct solution to the connections problem, but he knew the wrong solution when he saw it, and that was what he saw his new colleagues at Texas Instruments about to embark upon under Defense Department sponsorship. Fortuitously, the company was about to close for its annual vacation. But since, as a new employee, he did not have any vacation time, he remained back in the laboratory, desperately seeking an alternative to being forced to work on what he knew was an unproductive approach.

Texas Instruments had committed itself to manufacturing its semiconductor devices out of silicon rather than germanium. From the beginning, the semiconductor community recognized that silicon was superior to germanium because of its ability to withstand high temperatures, but the problem of obtaining silicon with the requisite purity was an obstacle in the early days of the transistor. Kilby knew, therefore, that because of his employer's large financial commitment, anything he did had to exploit the properties of silicon. He asked himself what else silicon might be used for in addition to transistors. It was in response to this question that he concluded that resistors and capacitors might also be made out of silicon, perhaps not as good as the discrete devices that were conventionally used, but good enough to do the job. He convinced his boss that his idea had enough merit to warrant some initial experiments, and the integrated circuit was born.

Noyce was a very different kind of person from Kilby, a highly charged, extroverted type, and the sequence of events that led him to the integrated circuit was a little different. He and several colleagues had started Fairchild after a brief stint with the first of the Silicon Valley establishments, Shockley Transistor, founded by the Bell Laboratories' pioneer himself. Noyce and the others found themselves unhappy enough with Shockley's management capabilities to strike out for themselves as independent transistor manufacturers. One of his colleagues had the idea of embedding the transistors in a cocoon of silicon dioxide to protect them from external contamination. The idea was original and potentially of great value. When Noyce spoke to his lawyer about patenting the idea, the latter suggested that the patent would be the more valuable the more all-inclusive it could be. Accordingly he asked what else might be done with the idea. It was thinking about this problem that gave Noyce the idea of the integrated circuit, completely unaware of Kilby's work some six months earlier.

The first integrated circuits were available for the marketplace in the early 1960s and, by the midpoint of the decade, it was a common component used by computer designers. These first circuits contained tens of circuits on a single chip of silicon, something that later became known as *small-scale integration* to contrast it with the *large* and *very-large-scale integration* that followed. The process by which they were manufactured was one that required several successive steps of silicon processing in which layers of controlled amounts of impurities, oxide, and metallic conducting layers would be laid down on the chip in a geometric pattern determined by a set of masks placed over the chip for successive processing operations. It was these masks that defined the design of a chip. Once a set of masks was produced, then multiple copies could be fabricated with little trouble. If the raw silicon crystals were pure enough, and if there were good quality control in the manufacturing process, then most of the copies would be satisfactory and the manufacturing yield would be high. Thus, while it might be very expensive to produce any particular set of masks, if the production yield was high enough, then this cost would be amortized over a large number, and the resulting cost per unit would be very low.

While this first generation of integrated circuits was being gobbled up by computer manufacturers, the semiconductor manufacturers were increasing the number of circuits on a chip at a rapid rate, from tens to hundreds to thousands and more. Gordon Moore, a colleague of Noyce's at Fairchild and later at Intel, predicted in 1964 that the number of circuits on a chip would double each year.[80] This statement, which became known in the industry as Moore's law, has turned out to be a reliable guide. The remarkable thing about the process was that highly complex chips cost hardly more than simpler ones. The silicon itself costs almost nothing, and a complex set of masks costs more than a simple one, but not a great deal more. The final cost of the finished product is largely determined by the yield, the fraction of chips that work reliably. The yield will be smaller, the more complex the circuit, and so the cost will be larger but not proportionally.

This last point is important. It means that to build a computer of a given capacity, the larger the chips become, the fewer are required and the lower the cost and physical size of the resulting computer. Or, turning the problem around, for the same physical size and cost, the higher the integration level, the more powerful the computer. It is easy to see how this integration phenomenon has led to the vast inroads made by the computer into our society during the 1980s.

But it took more than integration in general to make this happen. There are many ways in which a large number of elementary electronic circuits on a chip can be interconnected, and many of these are potentially useful. But most influential of all in fueling the computer revolution was a configuration that crammed the guts of a general-purpose computer on a single piece of silicon, the chip that became known as the *microprocessor.* The most obvious result of this development was the ubiquitous desktop computer.

But the desktop computer was just the tip of the iceberg.

Chapter

21

A *"Computer on a Chip"*

The thing that made the microprocessor stand out among all the other applications of very-large-scale integration was the way it found its way into just about everything electronic and some products that had never made use of electronics previously. John Naisbitt put it nicely in his book *Megatrends*, written in the early 1980s when the microprocessor was first coming into prominence: "Earlier computer technology could be applied to some products, electronics and large-scale office information equipment, but not others. Microprocessors can improve almost anything, anywhere, and are consequently far more threatening [to the established order]."[81] And the years that have followed have borne out this comment in the way in which the microprocessor has brought the computer into virtually every aspect of society and has transformed it irreversibly, sometimes in ways that have had profound implications.

The microprocessor is the name given to the single-chip version of what is called the *central processing unit* or CPU of a general-purpose computer. It is that part of a computer that performs the arithmetic and orchestrates all the events occurring everywhere in the computer. Combine a CPU with some memory chips, a keyboard, and a display monitor, and you have a complete computer. That the microprocessor is often referred to popularly as a *computer-on-a-chip* is therefore something of an overstatement, but considering the remarkable technology that this CPU on a chip represents, a little exaggeration is understandable.

The general-purpose computer structure that the microprocessor implemented on a single chip began with the ENIAC. Mauchly and Eckert could have taken a special-purpose approach to solve their problems as did Atanasoff; that is, they could have devised a structure that had the capability of doing little else but solve the particular problem at hand. Had they done that, then they would have had to modify the guts of the machine whenever they wanted to make a change in the calculation. The choice of the general-purpose structure was an indication of their wisdom in recognizing that problems change sometimes rapidly, and that a computer that could solve only a single class of problems had limited utility. The ENIAC's generality was more theoretical than practical, but it did not take long before the ENIAC's structure was extended in a most elegant fashion by John von Neumann, one of the great mathematicians of the century.

The Hungarian Phenomenon is the name used by physicists of World War II vintage to describe the extraordinary contributions of American scientists of Hungarian origin at that time. In the days preceding the outbreak of hostilities, the United States was a haven for refugees, scientific and otherwise, from all countries under, or potentially under, the domination of the Germans. That was hardly a surprise. What was surprising was the fact that the number of outstanding Hungarians was far out of proportion to the size of that small country, including many who made important contributions to the development of the atomic bomb. Perhaps the best known to the general public is Edward Teller, the father of the hydrogen bomb and, in more recent years, a strong proponent of the Strategic Defense Initiative.

John von Neumann was another of the Hungarian emigrés. He differed from most of his fellow mathematicians in the breadth of his interests. During the war he made important contributions to the research that led to the atomic bomb. Once the war was over he joined the faculty of the Institute for Advanced Studies at Princeton where his interests turned to computers, leading him to become associated with the ENIAC team at the Moore School as a consultant.

While the ENIAC was the first general-purpose electronic digital computer, it was not easy to take advantage of its generality. Changing the program that defined the problem that the ENIAC was to solve required modifying a large configuration of plugboards and switches. In principle, a wide variety of problems could be set up in this way, but doing so was laborious and very time-consuming. Von Neumann's variation was what became known as the *stored-program machine*, in which the program defining the task of the computer was stored not mechanically in switches and plugboards but, rather, in the memory of the computer where it could easily be changed by the programmer or by the program itself.

This concept was embodied in the next effort by the Moore School called the EDVAC, an acronym for Electronic Discrete Variable Computer. The concept was advanced still further in another seminal paper coauthored by von Neumann.[82] It was the computer structure described in this paper that became known as the *von Neumann machine*, perhaps a little unfair to the other members of the ENIAC group, especially Eckert, who contributed to the thought processes out of which von Neumann's concepts grew. The Institute for Advanced Studies undertook the construction of a computer based on these principles that was called simply the IAS computer, but is better known by its nickname, Johnniac.

The term von Neumann machine is used to describe the basic structure of the computer, independent of the nature of the components used to construct it. It is just as applicable to today's microprocessor-based machines as it was to Johnniac and all the others in between. It is only since the late 1980s that some advanced computers are beginning to stray from this structure. Among its features are the fact that it is general purpose, stored-program, and sequential in the way it solves its problems.

When you perform a complex calculation by hand or with the help of a pocket calculator, you divide the problem into elementary steps and proceed to carry out each step in turn until the calculation is complete. For instance, if you want to perform the computation: $16 \times (43 + 75 + 87)$, you first add together the three numbers within the parentheses and write down the result. Then you multiply the sum by 16 and write down the answer. Or for a different problem, say: $(125 + 57 + 32 - 65)/(345 + 14)$, you again take one step at a time with the appropriate combination of similar operations. Each of us has learned the elementary steps of arithmetic, and we can perform any calculation no matter how intricate with a sequence of these steps.

A von Neumann computer does much the same thing. It has the built-in ability to carry out a number of elementary operations, such as addition, multiplication, storing, printing, displaying, interpreting a keyboard stroke, and so on. The computer solves a particular problem by executing a *program* defined as a sequence of these elementary operations, proceeding methodically and automatically from step to step. The characteristic that gives it its great power is its ability to store the program in its memory as a sequence of instructions to the computer telling it what to do. If an ENIAC program consisted of, say, 1,000 instructions, then 1,000 sets of wired connections had to be changed—a task not to be taken lightly. In contrast, a new program could be inserted into a stored-program machine from a tape of some kind, just as in today's personal computers a new program is inserted from a floppy disk. With the correct sequence of elementary operations, such a computer can, in principle, compute anything at all, even though some calculations may not be practical. Von Neumann's structure was truly general purpose.

Generality is one of the attributes of today's computer that makes it so versatile and useful not only in the workplace but in a substantial number of homes. The home computer might be used by the children to help with their homework, or, more likely, to play games. The adults in the family might use it to maintain their financial records, to prepare income tax returns, to maintain files of recipes, or write letters. Once you buy a computer, you are deluged with advertising literature promoting this or that program easily inserted from a floppy disk to enhance its utility.

The generality of the computer is a feature of great beauty and elegance. It is also deceptive, because writing a program to do almost anything does not necessarily imply that the program so prepared will function correctly. It is easy to imagine that a complex program—perhaps a word processor—might require many thousands of these elementary instructions. It is also easy to appreciate the fact that the person or team of people who writes such a program might make errors in the process. The only way to assure that the program works perfectly is to test all possible configurations, and this is often not a feasible thing to do. Indeed, the computer pioneers vastly underestimated the problem of writing programs that do what they are supposed to do without error. Today's greatest computer challenges are in the software much more than they are in the hardware.

With such a general-purpose structure, it is not surprising that the uses to which computers were applied strayed far from the kinds of problems that originally motivated their construction—I would suspect that a word processor was far removed from the thoughts of Eckert and Mauchly. The computer's ability to store large amounts of information is key to the practicality of this general-purpose structure. A von Neumann machine has to store both its program and its data. Without a goodly amount of storage capacity, its ability to execute programs would be severely limited. These days when the computer is found almost everywhere, the sales literature touts the size of the computer's storage in *mega* units, illustrating how common millions of units of storage are for a relatively small amount of money. It is not at all surprising that the ENIAC and its early successors had far less storage than today's inexpensive desktop computers. Nevertheless, whatever storage was available was put to use in a variety of innovative ways.

The consequence of the microprocessor that Naisbitt was emphasizing in the earlier quotation was the fact that its small size and low price allowed the general-purpose computer to be used in applications that had heretofore been unthinkable. Before the microprocessor, special industrial and military applications required what are called special-purpose computers. These computers are made of the same kinds of elementary components as the von Neumann machines but configured to solve particular problems. A special-purpose computer can have a design optimized for the particular problem to which it is addressed and is, therefore, the most efficient way of performing the task. Such computers were found in military equipment, space vehicles, microwave ovens, washing machines and virtually countless other places. In the 1960s and early 1970s when the semiconductor industry was increasing the complexity of their chips according to Moore's law, computer designers were designing combinations of building blocks for chip implementation to build these special-purpose computers. As the complexity increased, the number of different special-purpose computers seemed to be increasing without bound.

Why build all these special-purpose computers? Why not use a general-purpose computer instead, programmed in software to perform all these various and sundry tasks? The answer was that the general-purpose computers of that vintage were far too large and expensive for these simple tasks. Could you imagine, for example, an IBM computer under the hood of your car? The situation changed abruptly in 1971 when Intel, a new semiconductor company started up by Bob Noyce, developed the central processing unit on a single chip. This microprocessor revolutionized computing in a way undreamed of by even the most visionary of the computer experts of the day. It was the versatility of the microprocessor that prompted Naisbitt to write what he did about its universality.

The way the computer-on-a-chip came about makes a fascinating story.[83] The prime mover was a Japanese company called Busicom, a manufacturer of desktop printer-calculators. Busicom did not have the expertise to build a new family of machines that they had designed, and they sought out the help of Noyce, who had just founded his new company. The Japanese company sent a team of engineers to Intel to provide the necessary liaison.

The Busicom design was a special-purpose one calling for twelve interconnected chips. When Ted Hoff, the engineer Noyce had assigned to the job, examined the design, he noted the gross inefficiencies in sharing the processing among twelve chips. A single chip that might solve the problem was much less complex than twelve times the complexity of a single Busicom chip. It was at this point that Intel proposed the approach of building a general-purpose processor on a single chip and actually succeeded in doing it.

The next chapter of the story brings in Intel's arch rival, Texas Instruments. By this time TI had brought out a handheld calculator that revolutionized the calculator business and, in so doing, rendered the proposed Busicom product line obsolete. The Japanese manufacturer thereupon found itself unable to fulfill its contractual obligations to

Intel. Negotiations between the two companies led to an agreement in which Intel reduced Busicom's financial obligations under the contract and received in return the rights to the microprocessor design. It then had the right to sell the chips to all comers.

The rest is now history. The microprocessor called the 4004 went on sale for $200 late in 1971. TI followed with one of its own some time later. With these chips, small inexpensive computers could be inserted everywhere without the need to design special-purpose chips. Intel soon replaced the 4004 with the 8008 having twice the power. A redesigned 8008 called the 8080 led to a new world of computing as IBM adopted it late in the decade as the heart of its personal computer. And the host of companies that followed in IBM's footsteps with *clones* of IBM's computers accelerated the process still further. It did not take long for the 8080 to become obsolete as Intel introduced a series of still more powerful microprocessors, designated by the numbers 80286, 80386, 80486, and 80586 (renamed Pentium), that have become part of the vernacular as the desk-top computer has been proliferated throughout the world. This brief story of the progression from the Intel developments to the IBM-style personal computer masks the ferment in the industry before IBM's entry. In fact, IBM had many predecessors in the desktop computer parade using various designs. But it was difficult to withstand the market power of IBM. The only competitive approach that persisted beyond the mid-1980s came from a company with the improbable name of Apple, which was able to hold its own by virtue of its very user-friendly design.

But the desktop computer is only the most visible aspect of the chip explosion. Much less evident to the general public are the host of jobs once performed by special-purpose computers that now could be programmed on a common hardware base. While these computers began to appear almost everywhere, nowhere did they have a greater impact than on the communications industry—not only on the way we build communications systems but also on the way we regard them.

On the surface, no two technology-based fields could be more unlike than computing and communication. What do the telephone, the radio, or the television have to do with computers? But probe just a bit beneath the surface and the multiple connections become clearer. It does not take too much stretching of the imagination to understand how the microprocessor that has influenced everything electronic might also influence the electronics used in communications systems. Nor is it hard to believe that the computers of the world might have something to say to one another just as people do, and that, consequently, computers located remotely from one another would require communications networks just as people do for their telephone instruments.

The need for computers to exchange information is far older than the microprocessor. The first such interchanges began in the earliest years of the computer when the general-purpose structure of the von Neumann machine was spawning novel applications at a rapid rate. But it was the microprocessor that increased the sheer number of computers to such an extent that intercomputer communications moved from the exceptional to the commonplace.

Chapter

22

The Gregarious Computer

In 1966 Bob Kahn, a young communications engineer at Bolt, Beranek and Newman, Inc. in Cambridge, Massachusetts, began to design a scheme for interconnecting computers. To Kahn the problem was an intellectual exercise. He had no idea that his intercomputer network would ever get built. And in the remote likelihood that it should get built, he was the last person in the world who would be involved in building it—or so he thought, because he was a communications theoretician, and everyone knew that theoreticians did not build things.

He had obtained his doctorate from Princeton two years earlier and had taken a job as a junior faculty member at MIT. A senior colleague there had urged him to take a leave of absence to obtain some practical engineering experience, and BBN looked like an interesting place in which to do this. The company, established after the war by three MIT professors, had made its reputation in the field of architectural acoustics and, later, had branched out into computer science.

Why did Kahn pick computer networking as the area in which to cut his "practical" teeth? It was not a *field* in any accepted sense. Yet he had a hunch that the problem was important enough for him to risk a budding career working in it for a while. He felt that the existing state of affairs in computer communications was not rational. It was under-standable in those days before the fax machine became widespread that when a person had a message to transfer somewhere, there was no choice but to send it by mail or some other form of transportation. But if the message were stored electronically in a computer, it was unreason-able to have to use physical transportation to move it by some mechanism such as transferring it to a tape. Why not run a communications link between the two computers and transfer the information electronically? Even more important, why should not a user of one computer be able to use another computer to augment his or her computing capability? If wires (or radio circuits) could eliminate the need for physical transportation in transmitting telegraph messages and the human voice, why not for computer data? Kahn simply had a hunch that the problem of interconnecting computers was of great significance and that his work would be useful to someone at some time.

While Kahn was probably the first to think about this problem in all its generality, others before him had tackled the problem for specific applications. Perhaps the first application dates back to the beginning of the cold war. Tensions between the United States and the former Soviet Union began to build up immediately after the war, reaching the point in the late 1940s that the U.S. government was fearful that a Soviet bomber attack was a real possibility. A study effort was undertaken by the air force to see how best to build a defense against such an attack. The system concept that developed out of these studies, which came to be known as SAGE, the acronym for Semiautomatic Ground Environment, depended on the use of the computer, which had only been in existence for a few years. In this concept, the country was divided into sectors, each of which would be scanned by a system of radars. These radars would detect incoming aircraft and automatically feed their positions to a central computer that would combine the radar targets, determine which planes were hostile, and then direct fighter aircraft against the attackers.

To mechanize this process, each radar would incorporate a special-purpose computer to automatically detect targets and convert their locations into digits that would be sent over a telephone line to the central computer. This whole ambitious concept depended on both the new technology of computers and the even newer technology of sending digits from one computer to another. While the project was a technical success, by the time it could be partially installed, the threat had turned from manned bombers to ballistic missiles and SAGE was eventually dismantled. Although SAGE was only a limited success, its technology had a far reaching effect on its many successor systems, both military and civil. It was the grandfather of all the computer based *real-time* systems— systems in which a computer has to keep up with a constant flow of input data. Clearly, all the schemes for coping with missile attacks from the 1960s up to the various approaches under the Strategic Defense Initiative are ideological descendants of SAGE. So also are the air traffic control systems that manage the heavy air traffic over and between airports throughout the world.

Another pioneering effort also involved airplanes but in a very different way. It was not a real-time system, and it was commercial not military, being concerned with the way in which airlines manage their entire flight reservation process. It was a system that made use of the ability of a computer to manage a large store of data and make this data available to a large number of people scattered over a wide area. Without it, our vast airline network would have groaned to a crawl many years ago.

In the early days of commercial aviation, flight scheduling and booking was all done manually. An airline would keep track of its seats sold using giant lazy Susans containing a card file for each flight, and bookings were called in by telephone from all over the country and manually entered into the card file. This system may have been adequate in those early days when the planes were small and the number of scheduled flights was limited, but as commercial aviation burgeoned with the arrival of the jet aircraft, manual processing became progressively more unwieldy. Recognizing that the time had come to begin automation, American Airlines contracted with IBM in 1959 to develop an automated reservation system that came to be known as SABRE, the acronym for SemiAutomated Business Research Environment.[84]

One thing that SABRE did, of course, was automate the lazy Susan. This was not unusual—Many companies in many industries were doing the same or similar things—but this was only part of the job. Because the SABRE team recognized that simply automating the records without facilitating automatic access to the records from agents anywhere in the country was futile. Without the automatic communication, a person would have to phone in to a computer operator who would retrieve the information rapidly from the computer and then read it off to the distant inquirer. For the automation to be really useful, there had to be a way for anyone to access the data personally without other human intervention. Otherwise one bottleneck would simply be exchanged for another.

SABRE made it possible for a travel agent to respond rapidly to a travel request from a customer by accessing the computer records on the time, status, and costs of the flights to the requested locations from a terminal in the agent's office. Once the customer made a selection, the agent would make the reservation from the same terminal and charge it to the customer's credit card, while, at the same time, potentially thousands of other agents were doing the same thing for other customers all over the world. And today, in a still more modern version, you can even do the same thing by yourself from your home computer without the intervention of a travel agent.

SABRE was the first of several similar automatic reservation systems instituted by the larger airlines.[85] Initially the airlines competed with one another to place their particular systems in the hands of the thousands of travel agents throughout the country and later throughout the world. While each of these systems included all flights by all airlines in addition to their own, the systems initially gave the travel agents a biased look at the schedules favoring their own airlines. By direction of the Federal Aviation Administration, these biases were later removed. Each system established its own communications network to connect its reservation terminals to its computer.

The way in which computer networks such as SABRE came into being within a few years of the invention of the computer is, in reality, a tribute to the general-purpose nature of the computer. The computer may have been conceived simply to perform laborious mathematical calculations rapidly, but its general-purpose structure made many completely different applications feasible. It is unlikely that Mauchly and his contemporaries in the 1940s ever thought about linking computers together, but it soon became a necessity for some of their followers.

The airline reservations system is just one of the most obvious examples of the ability of a computer to store huge amounts of data— data bases in computer jargon—organized in such a way as to make the individual pieces of data easily retrievable in any of a number of convenient ways. Banks were among the first institutions to computerize their records. The Internal Revenue Service computers, for example, store everyone's income tax returns organized by the taxpayer's name, social security number, and other distinguishing characteristics, so that any particular return can be retrieved with a few key strokes. Similarly, the card catalog of the public library can be stored in a computer so that any entry can be retrieved by author, title, or subject. We do not know who was the first to have the bright idea of using a computer to store databases in this way. After the fact, it is a most logical application of the computer, given its general-purpose structure, even though far removed from the number crunching jobs that motivated the computer to begin with.

All these database retrieval applications require many users to interact with the database computer simultaneously. This mode of operation would have been completely out of the question with the early computing machines that had all they could do to manage one user at a time. But after a few years, hardware and software that could be time-shared among a number of users began to appear. These computers were still ENIAC-type machines with a single central processing unit that could only perform one task at a time. However, this CPU was so much faster than the mechanisms for entering information into and extracting results from the computer, that it could service the slow in–out processes in sequence and still give the practical illusion of serving several users at the same time.

It is clear that information is of no use unless it is readily available to those who need it. And it is equally clear that those who need it are not always colocated with the computers storing the data. Thus the airline reservation systems are not unique in their dependence on computer communications to maximize their usefulness. With bank records on computers it was inevitable that banks found ways to transfer funds among one another electronically, and it was only a matter of time before the automatic teller machine (ATM) networks made their appearances. Similarly, it became convenient for organizations such as the Federal Bureau of Investigation to allow their agents access to centralized databases from all over the country. Public libraries could maintain centralized records accessible from branch libraries and, today, from ordinary subscribers with home computers. There are many such applications running from those that simply increase convenience to those, such as the airline reservation systems, where the computer networks are the difference between success and failure.

The airline reservation and ATM systems are a particular kind of remote time-sharing system. These have the advantage of being homogeneous, that is, all the hardware on both ends of the telephone lines is the same or almost the same and all the users of the system are dedicated to one specific set of tasks, such as the business of making and maintaining airline reservations. The more general and more difficult case occurs when a computer has to be shared among many disparate users doing a variety of problems. This more general case also requires more general communications to serve remote users than does the homogeneous airline reservation system. This more general case was the problem that Bob Kahn tackled, and, unbeknownst to him when he started his project, a subject that was beginning to interest a few people in the government's computer science research community.

This interest in networking was motivated by the fact that by the 1960s computers were becoming powerful enough to support many users in a time-shared mode, but the software technology to do this efficiently was in its infancy. Many government departments shared this interest, but the one that played the leading role was the Defense Department. Within the Defense Department, the organization that supported much of this research was an unusual one called the Advanced Research Products Agency, known familiarly as ARPA.[86] One of its most important achievements was a computer network named after the agency, the ARPANET.[87]

J. C. R. "Lick" Licklider was the first person at ARPA to consider such a network. Lick was a professor of psychology at MIT, also associated with BBN, who had become interested in computers early in the game.

So strongly did he identify with the field that he took a leave of absence in the early 1960s to come to Washington and run the information processing program at ARPA. Computer networking was at the top of his agenda.

Why should the Department of Defense be concerned with such a problem? The fact of the matter is that most of the government's support of information technology over the years has come through the path of national defense, and much of this through ARPA. Carrying out a good and useful research and development program is not easy, particularly for a large bureaucracy. The standard development process within the military services is for their operational forces to state "requirements" and for their laboratories and acquisition agencies to develop the systems that meet these requirements.

The weaknesses of this approach are not limited to the military environment. For example, it is highly unlikely that in the 1830s anyone in the newspaper business, if asked, would have stated a requirement for a telegraph system to speed up long-distance news gathering. While many must have desired it, most would have considered it too preposterous to state as a requirement. Recognizing the problem as early as the late 1950s, the Defense Department endeavored to augment this normal process by establishing ARPA, an organization that would be more adventurous. In theory, ARPA would direct advanced research in areas in which specific military requirements were hard to formulate or that did not naturally fall in the province of the existing research organizations. Once a project showed promise to meet a military need, it would be handed over by ARPA to a one of the military services for continued development in the normal way. It is easy to see that with this kind of charter, ARPA, if in the hands of imaginative people, would develop innovative technology useful in commercial as well as military applications.

The frame of mind that led the Defense Department to seek new ways of doing its research stemmed from the shock felt around the world when the former Soviet Union orbited its first *Sputnik* satellite in the late 1950s, well ahead of similar American efforts. The most famous reaction to the Soviet technological successes was President John F. Kennedy's establishment of the Apollo moon-landing program early in his administration. While ARPA and its undertakings did not have anything approaching the fame and glamor of the space program, its long-term impact is undeniably greater.

ARPA is not your run-of-the-mill Defense Department agency. Except at the very beginning of its existence, it has not been located in the Pentagon or in any of the other government buildings that house most Defense Department organizations. Rather, for most of its life, it was housed in a tall office building in the Roslyn section of Arlington, Virginia, just across the Potomac from the District of Columbia, until its expansion in the early 1990s necessitated a move a few miles down the road. Before World War II, Roslyn was a rundown area primarily noted for its pawn-shops. But after the war, its proximity both to the Pentagon and the District of Columbia made it a convenient location for the many companies that were springing up to perform services of various kinds for the rapidly expanding government. The pawn shops were torn down and in their place appeared a miniature Manhattan of unsightly high-rise buildings to house the new industry. Some of the occupants of these buildings have the fringe benefit of a magnificent view of the monuments of Washington. The view from the other side of the river is unfortunate, to say the least.

The people who staff ARPA are not run-of-the-mill government bureaucrats or technocrats. Most of them are scientists and engineers who leave their laboratories or universities to join the government for a limited period of time and then go back to being researchers at their old laboratories or elsewhere. It is a "revolving door" in the very best sense. Some of the information-processing people, in particular, are computer hackers at heart who sometimes look uncomfortable when forced to wear the Washington buttoned-down uniform instead of their more customary academic blue jeans. Given ARPA's mission, its employees must have a deep understanding of what advanced technology can do as well as an understanding of the military applications. Sometimes their efforts are not successful, usually because they attempt to achieve something that is too ambitious for the time frame. But this mixed success is one of the perils of doing research. If one succeeds in everything, then the sights have been set too low, by definition. On the other hand, if nothing is successful, then the sights have likely been set too high. The secret of successful research management is achieving the right level of aspiration.

ARPA's mode of operation was to identify areas of research in partnership with the research community and then to establish specific programs of relevance to the Defense Department's goals at several industrial, university, and governmental laboratories. One of ARPA's principal areas of concentration was and still is information processing, and, in the early 1960s, it was Licklider's job to lead the efforts in this area. The program was broadly based, but one of the things common to all elements of the program was its dependence on relatively expensive mainframe-type computers located at the contractors' laboratories, but paid for by ARPA. ARPA's work on time-sharing, therefore, had two motivations: It was an important research area in its own right, but it was also central to the economic viability of much of the rest of the program.

One way to hold down the cost of these computers was to facilitate the ability of the researchers involved in the programs to share them dynamically. And since these researchers were distributed throughout the country, meaningful and useful computer sharing meant a convenient communications network tying the computers and their users together. Since the applications varied and the computers themselves were not all of the same type, this meant that the communications network had to be general enough to allow for the ideosyncracies of a variety of computers and tasks. Thus was born the motivation for the ARPANET.

But Licklider had another objective that was harder to formulate. ARPA's mode of operation was to throw the best people it could at each problem regardless of where the people happened to be located. How better to foster this spirit than through a convenient communication system that helped bridge the geographical separations? Many years later Kahn expressed the feeling that Lick would have found some excuse for building the ARPANET even if resource sharing were not an issue because of his interest as a psychologist in the social aspects of research conducted in this way. This kind of motivation was similar to Bell's early notions of universal connectivity. Clearly, the ARPANET was not universal in the sense that the telephone system is—the users were restricted to be those in research organizations under ARPA sponsorship. Nevertheless, it had the generality that was theoretically extendible to a much larger set of users under the right set of circumstances. It was a start on the road to universality.

Why was it that ARPA had to build a special network for computer-to-computer communication? Why was the ubiquitous telephone network inadequate for the job? It could, in fact, have done the job, but at a price either of diminished performance or excessive cost. The reason for this is fundamental to the differences between computer and voice communication and relates to the kind of switching employed in the telephone system.

The switching that Bell first introduced was the essence of simplicity. To connect two parties to each other, an operator made an electrical connection from the telephone line connected to the calling party's telephone to that of the called party. The automatic switches, beginning with Strowger's, that replaced the operators and their manual plugboards worked in the same way, of course with the added complication of having to recognize the number that the caller dialed so as to know which wires to connect. This kind of switching is known as *circuit switching* because, whether manual or automatic, its function is to connect circuits together.

Think of the switch characteristics desirable for a voice conversation. Once you dial the number, you would like your connection to be made rapidly, preferably within one or two seconds; any connection time very much faster than that would hardly be noticed. You would also like to reach your party every time you call unless he or she is already using the phone. In other words, you are willing to accept a busy signal if the person you are calling is already using the telephone, but not if the network is overloaded. Then, once the connection is made, you expect the circuit to be totally dedicated to your conversation as long as it lasts.

Today's telephone networks generally meet these characteristics. Connection times are not quite down to the one or two second range, but they generally run under eight seconds, fast enough for most of us. The capacities of the long-distance networks are sized to provide good service without overloading during the peak daytime business hours. That is why home rates are reduced at night and on weekends to derive revenue from an otherwise underused telephone plant. For the same reason, the system can become overloaded on a few extraordinary occasions; Mothers' Day is the most predictable of these. Less predictable are natural disasters such as floods and hurricanes when seemingly everybody wants to call their loved ones. In these circumstances the attempted traffic can rise precipitously, often above the normal business-day levels.

A long-distance path between two subscribers consists of several shorter circuits connected in tandem with switches in between. When a call is established, all the circuits in the path from the calling telephone to the first switch all the way to the destination telephone are reserved for that one conversation until one of the parties hangs up. It does not matter whether any words are spoken; there can be long silent periods during which nothing is spoken by either party. The circuit is still reserved and charges are being made, even though no information is being transferred in either direction. It is the nature of human conversation that long gaps in speech are rare. A shocking statement by one might leave the other one temporarily speechless, but after a few seconds or so, someone will say something if only to assure that the connection is still there.

But computers are different from people. They do not interact in the same way, and they are not at all embarrassed by long gaps in the conversation. A typical dialog between a person sitting at one computer and a data base at another computer might last several hours, during which time the person occasionally sends a few characters to the data-base computer, that then responds with larger bursts of data, enough to refresh the monitor on the user's screen. Typically there are long periods of time during which no communication at all occurs in either direction, either because the computer is computing or the user is thinking about what to do next given the computer's response. A telephone connection that holds the line during all this time would meet the needs of the user but would be very wasteful and unnecessarily expensive. If the times to connect and disconnect were low enough, say well under a second, then the connection could be opened whenever either party had something to send and closed when the transmission was concluded. But until such time as these connection times become very low, the telephone oriented networks are very inefficient for the interactive traffic likely to be seen when computers are at the ends of the line.

The solution to this problem is to assign circuits in a way that is matched to the way computers rather than people intercommunicate. The new technique came to be called *packet switching* to distinguish it from the conventional circuit switching, and one of the great contributions of the ARPANET project was to develop this new way of allocating network resources. In this scheme, the information coming from a computer is divided into relatively small chunks called *packets*. Packet switches direct these packets throughout the network from source to destination on an individual basis. Circuits between switches are assigned on a packet-by-packet basis rather than to the entire session. Once the packet has been received on any link of the total path, the capacity that it used is free to be assigned to another packet either from the same source or from a different source. In this way, the network capacity is assigned in bursts only when there is information to be sent, quite unlike the conventional telephone network that assigns capacity on a continuous basis as long as the session lasts. If there is enough traffic in the network, the circuits between the switches will be at or close to capacity most of the time, making the scheme very cost effective. Of course, there will be some occasions in which a circuit will be filled with packets so that the next packet arriving at the switch will have to be delayed to await the completion of the transmission of previous packets. But if the capacity of these circuit is high enough, such delays should be short enough so as not to interfere with the response time as seen by the users.

Packet switching as a concept did not begin with the ARPANET. One of its antecedents was a scheme called *message switching* that had been developed earlier as a way of distributing telegrams. The Defense Department had developed such a system called the Automatic Digital Network (Autodin) in the early 1960s. There was one significant difference. In a message-switched system, each message, regardless of length, is transmitted in its entirety before another message can be sent. This means that a short message from one computer to another that happens to arrive at the switch after a long message would have to wait for the entire preceding message to be transmitted. This wait could introduce a delay into the process that might not affect telegram delivery appreciably but could be unacceptably long for a remote computer user. The notion of dividing a message into short chunks gets around this problem by sending the first packet of the second message directly after the first packet of the first message.

This idea of *packetization* was first conceived in the early 1960s by Paul Baran, then of the Rand Corporation, and published in a report sponsored by the Air Force.[88] The United States was then in the midst of the cold war. The Cuban missile crisis was fresh in our minds. The idea of a nuclear war in which the communications of the nation might be targeted was a real possibility. Baran was working on ideas for making message communication more survivable in the face of such attacks, and the idea of chopping transmissions into little chunks each of which might find its own way to its destination through a damaged network was appealing. His report included a proposal to build such a network, but the air force failed to act, and the report simply gathered dust.

In 1965, Donald Davies of the British National Physical Laboratory, unaware of Baran's work, proposed a similar capability but for a different application.[89] Davies was interested in linking computers together and came upon the notions of packet switching as a good way of doing this. He was the one who coined the term *packet* to describe the elementary grouping of bits that was being switched around. As it turned out, the British government was just as reluctant to proceed on Davies's application as was the American government on Baran's. Larry Roberts, a young computer scientist at the MIT Lincoln Laboratory who had been influenced by Licklider's ideas, also proposed some of the particulars of a packet-switched network at about the same time as Davies, although neither initially knew of the other's work.[90]

Licklider and ARPA had computer networking in mind even before Baran's work, but it took time before a specific practical project could be conceived and funded, and Licklider left ARPA before he could do this. A later succesor, Robert Taylor, picked up the ball, extended Licklider's conceptions, and focused them into the ARPANET program. He brought Roberts to Washington to head the project and eventually to succeed him in managing all the information programs at ARPA.

It is interesting that neither Licklider nor Roberts were initially aware of Kahn's work at BBN. The computer-oriented Licklider and Roberts did not know the communications theorist Kahn despite the fact that all three were MIT people. But Kahn's boss was involved in an ARPA contract and therefore had some knowledge of the agency's plans including the incipient computer network. When he saw the progress that Kahn had made, he arranged for Kahn to tell Taylor and Roberts of his work.

By this point in time, ARPA was already preparing a competitive solicitation to obtain a contractor to build the network. BBN established a strong team under Frank Heart to bid on the project, with Kahn responsible for system design, and succeeded in winning the contract. The project was begun in 1970, and, a year later, a pilot network with four switching nodes was placed in operation. Kahn demonstrated the full-fledged network in 1972. He went to work at ARPA shortly thereafter and, a few years later, moved up to head its information programs.

Although he was neither the inventor of packet switching nor the conceiver of the ARPANET, Kahn is the closest thing to a Mr. Computer Networking today because of his pioneering work at BBN, his long association with the field at ARPA, and his later interests in promoting very-high-speed data networks, about which I have a good deal to say in Chapter 31.

There is a fascinating cultural sidelight to the origins of the communications system called the ARPANET. Most of the people responsible for its development were computer-oriented rather than communication scientists and engineers. To be sure, Kahn's communications expertise enabled him to formulate a successful network approach. However, most of the others, whether at ARPA or at its family of contractors, were from the computer culture. They were the ones with the most to gain from a successful project, and the communication engineers and scientists were largely uninterested until the full impact of the fusion of the two fields into one began to make itself felt.

It is also both interesting and curious that the ARPANET originated in government rather than in industry and, within government, in the military rather than the civil sector. One might have expected a new communications capability of this kind to originate in industry without government support of any kind, perhaps in the Bell Laboratories, the source of so much communications innovation. It is not surprising that the operating arms of the old Bell System were uninterested since voice service was so dominant. However, one might have expected the forward-looking Bell Laboratories to be pioneers in this field. It may, in fact, have been that the Bell Laboratories were so dominated by communications- rather than computer-oriented people that the motivation escaped them. Baran invented packet switching as a way of improving the survivability of communications networks in the face of hostile enemy actions. Roberts, Taylor, and the others at ARPA were computer-oriented engineers within the military culture closely linked to the most advanced ideas in the research community with the foresight to see that universal computer networking using packet switching would be important both in the military and civil sectors.

It is clear from this chronology that the *real* reason for the ARPANET development was that fact that a few people had the foresight to recognize that computer networking was a research frontier of great promise and followed through to obtain the resources to act on their convictions. They knew that it had to have many potential uses, even though they could not pinpoint them. Computer resource sharing was just one of these, but it was sufficient to provide the official justification for a project that was to have far-reaching effects.

Chapter

23

The Aftermath of the ARPANET

By the mid 1970s, ARPA, in keeping with its charter, had relinquished its proprietorship of the ARPANET to the Defense Communications Agency where it came under the direct management of an operating arm of the department. In its few years directly under ARPA's control, the number of connected computers had grown to the hundreds including universities, government laboratories, and commercial organizations involved in some way with ARPA's research projects. By the mid 1980s this subscriber base grew to number in the thousands, as more and more organizations in the Defense Department found it to be useful. In assessing these numbers, however, it is important to remember that in those first years a computer was a mainframe varying in size from that of a single large refrigerator to a room full of such appliances. The lowcost microprocessor-based computer had yet to make its impact.

But even before the ARPANET became institutionalized in this way, the Defense Department found an important operational area to which the technology could be applied. For many years, the Defense Department had supported computing facilities installed at the headquarters of its major commands throughout the world, the so-called Worldwide Military Command and Control System, which, because of the awkwardness of this long and unwieldy name, is known by the acronym WWMCCS (pronounced "Wimex"). Each headquarters has a particular responsibility, and its computer software and databases are in support of these responsibilities. For example, The Strategic Air Command in Omaha is responsible for strategic weapons delivery, and the Transportation Command (formerly known as the Military Airlift Command) in southern Illinois just outside Saint Louis is responsible for all military transportation. Similarly, area commanders such as the European, Pacific, and the Central Commands each has its specific responsibilities and related computer capabilities. And, of course, the Joint Chiefs of Staff in the Pentagon are responsible for overall planning.

Having observed the success of the ARPANET, the Joint Chiefs of Staff recognized the potential benefits of netting together these WWMCCS computers. To do this, they built a clone of the ARPANET that became known as the WWMCCS Intercomputer Network or WIN, for short. The choice of building a separate network rather than using the existing ARPANET was necessary because the operations carried out by these major commands were so sensitive that, for reasons of security, they could not coexist on a network shared with the everyday traffic carried by the ARPANET.

The specific role played by these netted computers in the Desert Shield/Desert Storm operations in the Persian Gulf is something that could not have been perceived or formulated as a military requirement in the days when ARPA was doing the fundamental technology development. It is, therefore, extremely unlikely that computer networking would ever have been developed within the Defense Department if it had to be dependent on the normal requirements process.

An operation such as Desert Storm is an extreme example of the interplay between operational planning and logistics, an area in which the WIN proved invaluable. The process is simple in concept but highly complex when one gets down to nuts and bolts. It begins with a military plan to accomplish certain objectives, in this case to drive the Iraqis out of Kuwait with minimum loss of life on the Coalition side. Any plan requires a certain force structure together with the military hardware, ammunition, food, medical facilities, and countless other kinds of equipment and supplies that must accompany the forces. All this materiel must be transported into the combat area within tight time limits. The Desert Storm operation was particularly difficult in this regard because all the people and equipment had to be drawn from many places far removed from the Gulf and within a short time period. The best of military plans is worthless if the necessary troops and equipment cannot be brought into the area within the requisite time. If a plan cannot accomplish this that goal, it must be replaced by one that can.

How does the commander know whether a plan is sustainable? The planning staff has to list everything that is needed, determine where it is located, determine where all the transportation is located, assign transportation to all the forces and supplies, and then estimate how long it would take to bring everyone and everything to the specific area. The process is straightforward enough, but exceedingly complex for the scope of an operation such as Desert Storm. It would take weeks to complete a complex task such as this if it were done by an army of people without the aid of automation. The process, in fact, can be performed in time measured in hours rather than weeks by the judicious use of modern computation and communication, and this is where the WIN turned out to be a valuable asset in Desert Storm.

The operational program used to perform this task is called the Joint Operational Planning and Execution System, another of those unwieldy Pentagon names necessitating the use of the acronym JOPES. The planning portion of the program is resident in the Pentagon computer, and the transportation-related programs and data are located at the Transportation Command in the Saint Louis area. The Central Command in Tampa was given the responsibility for the Desert Storm operation. Its staff sitting at their screens in Tampa developed their plans by drawing on the programs and databases resident in Washington and Saint Louis using the WIN. Had the responsibility been given to the European Command, its personnel at their headquarters near Stuttgart would have made use of the same programs and data in the United States. Just consider what might have had to be done had this network not existed. All the computations could have been done in the Pentagon with the transportation database installed there. But databases are never static. Whenever a change occurred, the changes would have to be transported from Saint Louis to Washington in some other way, say by a dedicated communication link. Or perhaps both the Pentagon and Saint Louis databases could be connected to Tampa and Stuttgart by dedicated links, both examples of more expensive and less flexible alternatives than the WIN. Flexible computer networking is what enabled the Central Command to carry out its incredibly complex deployment in such a relatively short time.

Issues of security forced the WIN to be built as a completely independent network. This independence also became the pattern even when security was not an issue. Other communities of interest—government agencies, educational and commercial groups—followed the WIN model and built their own private networks. While this was happening in the late 1970s and early 1980s, it seemed the natural thing to do; it was simply following in the footsteps of the ARPANET. But when viewed from the perspective of more than a century and a quarter of communications history, it was a break with tradition. The telegraph and telephone were introduced by communications entrepreneurs who built systems and sold service to the public. It is not that private telephone systems did not exist. Both government agencies and private corporations often used these for economy. But it was usually AT&T that installed the system for the customer, and there was almost always a way of going *offnet*, the telephone jargon for allowing subscribers of the private network to communicate with those not on the private network through the public network. Even when an organization, whether commercial, government, or military built its own telephone network using leased lines from the telephone company, it had to conform to the standards of the large public network.

These voice systems were therefore built in a way that might be called *top down*. In contrast, computer communication systems were pure and simple *bottom up*. They were introduced, not by communications entrepreneurs foreseeing a need, but by the needers. And since it took AT&T a long time both to grasp the technology and its significance, the ARPANET pattern took hold. It is not that there were not attempts to introduce public computer networking services. Only a few years after the ARPANET became operational, there were efforts to build so-called Value Added Networks, the designation derived from the fact that the networks copied the private networks by leasing connectivity from AT&T and then adding their own packet switches in appropriate locations to interconnect the subscribing computers. Telenet (now known as Sprintnet) and Tymnet were the first of these in the United States. But it turned out that the prices that these carriers were forced to charge were economical only for small users. Anyone requiring substantial computer communication was better off building a dedicated network.

It is interesting to compare this situation in the United States with that in France, a country with a tradition of government ownership and control of communications. There it became government policy to build a universal data network and to use its monopolistic power to force its use, thereby making it economical. To this end, the government gave computer terminals to all its telephone subscribers free of charge. The government then stopped publishing its telephone directory, replacing it with an electronic directory, thereby forcing its subscribers to use their terminals to look up telephone numbers. In this way, the subscribers were induced to use other computer data that was made available to the public, though not free, through the network.

But such policies and tactics were not available to anyone in the United States. Since there was no centralized universal data network, computer networks were built by individual communities independent of all other networks. Their function was specific, not universal: to interchange computer information among themselves, without any concern as to whether the data was of use outside their own community. It was each community for itself. Even then, one would have thought that if all the networks were simply copies of the ARPANET, then it would be easy for a subscriber of one network to communicate with a subscriber of another network should the need arise. However, this was not the case. Despite their common ancestry, there were enough differences among these networks to make it difficult for a computer on one network to communicate with a computer on another network. When universality is not a goal from the start, free and easy interconnectivity is by no means assured.

With this laissez-faire start, was there any way to introduce interoperability among computers on different networks after the fact? In fact, there was, using a unique approach that also originated at ARPA, a product of Kahn and Vinton Cerf, then at Stanford, who subsequently joined Kahn at ARPA. Their reasoning was that if all networks were not destined to be identical, then the next best thing to achieving interoperability was to establish certain uniform interconnection rules or protocols that would enable networks to transcend their differences. These protocols would allow groups of subscribers to have their cake and eat it too, so to speak. A community of interest of some kind could form a private network of its own and at the same time permit its subscribers to communicate with subscribers of other networks, provided they all implemented the same protocol, which became known as the Transmission Control Protocol/Internet Protocol, better known by its abbreviation TCP/IP.

One of the factors that motivated ARPA to the importance of network interoperability was a very specific need within their own research program. ARPA had built a number of specialized experimental packet networks for military applications, one, for example, a tactical radio network and another a network using satellite interconnectivity. There were good operational reasons to find a way to permit the users of these very disparate networks to intercommunicate with one another as well as with ARPANET users, and this was the application in which the new protocols were first tested.

But Kahn and Cerf had forseen the need for more general interoperability from the beginning and had developed the TCP/IP protocols with this generality in mind. And so, once the protocols were checked out within the ARPA community, it was a straightforward matter to extend the concept of network interoperability more broadly. The obvious next step was to link the ARPANET to a few other research networks. Then came a less obvious concept: Why not establish an informal confederation of the many networks serving the worldwide government, research, and university communities, forming, in essence, a universal computer network for these communities? It was a unique approach to universality, born not out of the central planning of one organization but, rather, out of the anarchy of independently owned and managed networks. Thus was born in 1979 the idea of a network of networks named the Internet. Subsequent events were to show that this was an idea whose time had come.

The economic situation in which the Internet began the quest for universal computer communications was far different from that in the early days of the telephone. Bell was led to the concept of universal connectivity by the simplicity and low cost of the instrument he invented. Had the telephone been so expensive as to make the notion of every home having one implausible, he might not have come to the idea. Even with the revolution in computer hardware that brought us the microprocessor and with it the inexpensive desktop and laptop computers, the fact remains that as cheap as these computers might be, they are still many times as expensive as telephones. It is therefore understandable that in the early days of computer networking, when a computer was still a mainframe containing one or more free-standing cabinets, less thought was given to universality than would have been the case had the desktop computer been in existence. By 1991, roughly 30 percent of American homes had computers, a good start but still a long way from the ubiquity of the telephone.

Once the microprocessor took hold, and more and more people in industry could afford larger numbers of desktop computers, a new application for networking arose. Interconnect all the desktop computers in a given location with a *local-area network*, and the company had more than the equivalent of the mainframe in computing capacity with the convenience of simultaneous access by many workers. Calling these networks *local* distinguishes them from long-distance networks such as ARPANET, which have come to be called *wide-area* networks. In this way, the computer network has reached the point where it has become a major factor in the way in which computer systems themselves are built. A company with facilities in many locations will typically net its computers together in each location with local-area networks and then net its locations together with a wide-area network. With this kind of configuration someone in one location can have access, if he or she wishes, to data anywhere in the company.

Automatic computer communication allows unlimited amounts of information to be transferred from one location to another, either initiated by a person or according to some preplanned scheme. And it is this property that adds a new dimension to the whole concept of working at a distance. Having a computer at each end of a communications link removes many of the information transfer limitations of the telephone, making it feasible for people collaborating on a project or otherwise working together to be able to exchange as much information when separated as when together. In this way, an engineer in Seattle can exchange computations and drawings with a colleague in Philadelphia. A marketing manager at corporate headquarters in New York can discuss advertising copy with a manager in Chicago.

Perhaps the most publicized potential fallout of this newfound communications ability is the notion of allowing employees of a company to work at home rather than in an office. If the same information is available at home, why force everyone to be at a common location? Yet, despite this capability, working at home has not been as widespread as some thought it would be. Only part of the reason for this situation is the failure of management to trust its employees not to abuse their freedom. Another factor is that many individuals have been reluctant to depart from the old ways for reasons that are probably social. A person might not have to be in the company of his fellow workers to do his job, but, at the same time, he or she often prefers their companionship and the intangible communication that goes with it. The phenomenon is much like the one that impels us to take the time and spend the money to close business deals over lunch even though the same factual information can be transferred by telephone or some other form of communication. There is some indication that improving the remote connectivity to include video is facilitating this telecommuting, but how this will come out is not clear at the present time.

With the availability of vast stores of information from anywhere in the company, the CEO at company headquarters no longer has to depend on his or her subordinates for information about company operations; it can be obtained directly from the same databases no matter where they reside. Because information is so readily available, companies can structure their organizations in more efficient ways that are less dependent on geography than would be necessary without the ready availability of data wherever it is needed. Such access has, in fact, permitted some companies to streamline their organizations by eliminating layers of middle management.

But such information availability can be a mixed blessing. The negative side of this coin is the same one that worried some army officers in the days following the introduction of the telegraph in the Civil War and the seagoing navy after the invention of the wireless, when it appeared that information made available at a distance might tempt high echelon commanders to micromanage their subordinates. A CEO, like a general or admiral or the president of the United States, with information pertaining to low-level operations, might be inclined to interfere in low-level decisions that had best be left to lower levels of management. The human issues today with instant data availability are no different from those that faced industry and the military in the last century. Only the scale is different. One can only hope that individual managers in business as in the military have the good sense to use their new technology to best advantage.

Assessing the societal impact of computer communication is more akin to assessing that of the early telephone than that of the telegraph. I say this because it is easy to point out the several specific industries in which the telegraph had a first-order impact—newspapers, railroads, investments, and the like—but much harder to do the same for the telephone because the telephone soon became part of the infrastructure similar to electric lights, gas mains, roads, and bridges that contributed in small ways to every aspect of life. Even though access to computer networks is not yet universal, it seems evident that the day is not far when it will be, and that computer communication, widely available, will similarly become part of the infrastructure contributing to virtually every aspect of life.

Chapter

24

Speeding Up the Written Word

Once the idea of the Internet became a reality, the networks that existed at the time were eager to join up, even though each had been built for its own specific reasons having nothing to do with any of the others. The main reason for this collegiality was an application that sprang up almost as soon as the ARPANET went into operation. It caught on instantly and became the very paradigm of what could be done with a computer network. It was a new form of person-to-person communication that came to be known as *electronic mail* or, as it is usually abbreviated, E-mail.

If the history of communication teaches us anything, it is the fact that people will use a new communications capability in unpredictable ways. Typically, it is just as difficult to predict what applications a new technological development will spawn as it is to state a requirement for an application that depends on an unknown new technology. Thus, while it is hard to imagine a shipping company in the 1890s stating a requirement for a way to communicate from ship to shore by telegraph, it is equally hard to imagine anyone predicting that the newly invented wireless contained the seeds of a gigantic entertainment empire. Understanding this, Licklider, Roberts, Kahn, and the other ARPANET pioneers had the full expectation that their new network would spawn all kinds of unexpected applications once people began to use it. And, true to this expectation, E-mail became the most popular of these.

It occurred in the most natural way. Put yourself in the place of a researcher in Cambridge working on a computer in San Francisco in collaboration with researchers located there. During the session you might wish to discuss some results with one of your San Francisco colleagues. The conventional way of doing so would be to interrupt your computer session and place a telephone call. But look how much more convenient it would be to send a brief message to your colleague over the same ARPANET serving your research communication. It was this simple set of circumstances that gave rise to the notion of electronic mail.

With E-mail, the computer researchers could do such things as set up meetings by sending a single message to a distribution list requesting the recipients to reply also by E-mail. In addition, with the resources of the computers at their disposal, they could send large documents and even computer programs to one another all with the same network, since a computer at the end of a link can send small or large blocks of data on a moment's notice. The possibilities were endless. Electronic mail added the personal touch that was part of what Licklider must have had in mind when he envisioned a network fostering a spirit of collegiality among researchers separated by distance. Licklider was surely gratified by what he saw, although he probably had no inkling of how influential E-mail would ultimately be.

An electronic mail service shares some of the advantages of both the telephone and the traditional mail. Each subscriber is assigned an electronic *mailbox* in a computer somewhere on the network with a password that restricts access to the box to its owner. E-mail messages for the subscriber are addressed to the mailbox. The subscriber can read received mail whenever convenient. A sender can indicate whether the message is urgent, and, if so, a signal can be flashed on the computer screen so that the recipient can interrupt whatever he or she is doing to retrieve the piece of information. In some respects, electronic mail is more versatile than voice communication. An E-mail message is delivered to the mailbox whether or not the addressee is at home to receive the message. This capability makes E-mail a particularly useful way to communicate across time zones. So important did E-mail become, that special facilities were built into the ARPANET to allow people with simple keyboard terminals remote from computers to send and receive mail.

Electronic mail is not, strictly speaking, computer communication. Rather, it is a form of person-to-person communication that makes use of the ability of computers to exchange information. As its name implies, it has many of the characteristics of ordinary mail using electricity in place of physical transportation to deliver the information. At the same time, it is an informal version of the venerable telegram, with the big difference that the messages go from user to user without an intermediary, giving it some of the attributes of the telephone. The fact that it is user-to-user also gives it the potential of universality that the telegraph or its teletype successor never achieved. Of course, the original users of the ARPANET who conceived of the idea thought of it as a way of facilitating their work.

But it did not take long for many of them to perceive how powerful this new way of communicating might be in a future world that was filled with computers even though this was clearly not the case in the 1970s well before the full implications of the microprocessor had been felt.

So popular did E-mail become that it was not long before it became the tail that wagged the dog. People with access to computer networks used the E-mail services whether or not they used the network for resource sharing or anything else. Indeed, as time went on and the low-cost microprocessor-based computers began to proliferate, the whole notion of resource sharing became less and less cogent. E-mail became an important force in its own right, driving the construction of new computer networks and the expansion of those that existed.

Bell was led to the notions of universal connectivity because of his insight into the nature and potential of voice communication in contrast to the telephone's predecessor, the telegraph. It is not the fact that written communication is less universal than oral communication—the continued importance of the mail refutes that argument. It is more the fact that oral communication by telephone is so like the face-to-face communication with which we are all so familiar and that the telephone is so cheap and easy to use. Morse code was a giant hurdle that the average person was unwilling to leap. The teletypewriter, which became available around the turn of the century, did away with the Morse operator and, in so doing, represented a great advance over the telegraph. Gone was the trained hand tapping out Morse code with a manual key and the trained ear receiving it. In its place was a keyboard that anyone could use. When a key was depressed, out came five or six binary symbols that were sent out over the wire. The teletypewriter at the other end recognized the code and printed out the corresponding character.

Over the years, teletypewriters gradually replaced the Morse telegraph as the vehicle for sending telegrams. This teletypewriter, or Telex, service became the mainstay of the press just as its ancestor had been in the 1840s. Similarly it was the major vehicle for sending official State Department and Defense Department messages. Even switched systems such as the Defense Department's AUTODIN were introduced to facilitate the communication of these messages. And, as discussed earlier, it was this message switching that was the immediate precursor of packet switching. Clearly, there were so many common elements between this older message service and electronic mail that one might have expected telegraphy to have been the jumping-off point for the more modern service.

In fact, just the opposite was true. Electronic mail came to the military through the computer scientists who started the ARPANET, and it was no surprise that military personnel with access to computers became just as enthused about E-mail as everyone else. But should E-mail be used as a substitute for the traditional military message system already in place? I noted previously how important the formal message service with its built-in features of accountability and authority was to the way in which command is exercised. Electronic mail might be user-to-user, it might be fast, and it might be convenient, but, in the view of the traditionalists, it did not have the attributes that made it suitable for issuing official directives and delivering official reports. Because of this, the technically outmoded military message system descended from the telegraph has remained as a military mainstay, with E-mail used for informal transactions outside of the command structure, often as a substitute for the telephone. Ultimately, the older system will wither away as computer-based messaging is able to furnish the attributes essential to official messaging, but this evolution is taking a long time.

Despite its lack of acceptance by some of the traditionalists, there was a rapid growth of military users of the ARPANET all through the late 1970s continuing into the 1980s, mostly for electronic mail. As military users began to outnumber the research users of the ARPANET, the network was itself split into two networks, MILNET for the military users, and a residual ARPANET for the others with the ability of users on one to interconnect with those of the other via the TCP/IP protocols. Because of its highly classified traffic, WIN remained separate from MILNET.

With this division, the only thing military about the ARPANET was the fact that its users were primarily researchers supported by the Defense Department. It was inevitable, then, that researchers supported by other branches of the government should want to join, and the support of the National Science Foundation (NSF) made this possible in the early 1980s. Later in the decade, the NSF launched a program to build a new higher-speed network as the vehicle for making its very expensive ultra-high-speed computing centers available to users throughout the nation, and in 1988 the NSFNET came on-line as part of the Internet. By this time there was no longer a reason for the Defense Department to continue its sponsorship of a research network and the venerable ARPANET was retired in 1990.

E-Mail continued to dominate networking applications in the rapidly expanding array of new networks that appeared throughout the world in the latter half of the 1980s as the personal computer population continued to grow. Most of these new networks were joining the Internet primarily to extend the usefulness of E-mail. The year 1988 marked a watershed in the development of the Internet, for it was then that this network of networks first admitted commercial data networks to the fold—networks such as MCI-Mail, the first to join—which had been motivated largely by E-mail users. The Internet's subscriber list began to grow rapidly enough to astound even its biggest boosters. By 1993, it encompassed more than 10,000 networks in forty countries, more than 7,000 of which had joined in the preceding two years. This level of connectivity meant that for the first time businesses were using E-mail and even other forms of intercomputer data transfers to communicate with one another.

Even with this rapid growth, Internet was a name that rarely appeared in public. It did achieve some notoriety when a student hacker was able to infect this entire network of networks with a computer virus, a program that can be inserted into a computer unbeknownst to the computer's users. Once there, it can multiply and cause all sorts of mischief such as stealing or erasing data. This incident for the first time publicized the issue of computer security, one that is becoming more important the more computers become part of the infrastructure. There was some more favorable publicity in the general press beginning in 1992 commenting on the spectacular growth of the network and its potential role in the economic plans of the Clinton administration.

E-mail proved to be a remarkably versatile form of communication, something quite unlike any of its predecessors, with properties of both telephone and telegraph, an indispensable adjunct to anyone with access to a computer network. But even this remarkable new communications vehicle had its limitations. Most obviously, it was not an option for those without access to a computer network—and this meant most of us in the 1970s and 1980s, even into the 1990s. Even for those who did, it was of limited use to anyone who had a paper document of some kind to send and was impatient with the speed of the mail. Who would want to spend the time and effort rekeying a document into a computer that already existed in paper form so that it could be sent as an E-mail message?

It was just this impatience with the speed limitations of the mail in the age of information that gave rise to companies such as Federal Express and others that guaranteed overnight delivery of mail and packages. The cost of this special service was many times that of first-class mail, but there were many occasions in which this cost differential was worth paying not only to businesses but also individuals. The overnight delivery services began to boom in the late 1970s and early 1980s, during the same time that computer networks were beginning to proliferate. But as rapid as overnight delivery was, it was still not rapid enough for our increasingly impatient society. If the world was not yet ready for the paperless concept of E-mail, was not there a way of delivering paper electronically?

Indeed there was. Federal Express was one of the first to recognize that its burgeoning business was bound to lose some market share to electronic delivery of some kind. This foresight led it to introduce an electronic service of its own called Zapmail. Zapmail was nothing more than a particular form of facsimile service that Federal Express would furnish from its business offices, a combination of electronic and hand-delivery in which the airplane was replaced by the facsimile in carrying the message from one city to another. The corporate plan called for a later all-electronic version of Zapmail in which the company would provide its customers on-premises facsimile machines that would be internetted through a Federal Express-owned satellite communications system.

The concept was introduced in 1984 with much fanfare and then proceeded to disappear within two years. The thing that went wrong was the speed with which facsimile captured the business marketplace in its own right. Then nobody needed an intermediary like Federal Express to supply the machines, much less the specialized delivery system for which the universal telephone system was quite adequate.

Most people would agree that facsimile communication, best known by its nickname fax, is the most revolutionary communications instrument to hit the office since the telephone itself. It has made the average office worker conscious of the power of electrical communication as has nothing else in this century. This is true partly because of its relatively low cost, but especially because it is so flexible and easy to use, far easier than the computer or even E-mail. In fact, its ease of use is what contributed to the huge demand which, in turn, led to dramatic price reductions.

The fax mechanism is fundamentally different from E-mail or any of the forms of telegraphy. These latter systems all work by representing specific letters, numbers, and other keyboard characters by some kind of code. At the receiving end, a device recognizes the code and repro-duces the appropriate character. In contrast, fax reproduces at a remote location a copy of the pattern on a page regardless of what it is—key-board characters, handwriting, diagrams, or photographs. The fax trans-mitter scans a small spot across a piece of paper much like a television camera, converting the relative darkness of the paper under the spot to an electrical signal. At the destination end, these electrical signals are used to darken a piece of paper so as to create a facsimile or replica of the original. This versatility is another of its great assets. It allows an entire document containing text, figures, and signatures to be sent. Because there still remains some contention over the legality of signa-tures reproduced in this way, letters where the legality of the signature is important are often sent by fax for speed and followed up with the original sent by mail or some other delivery service.

So recently has the facsimile become popular, that it is hard to believe that it was actually invented in 1842, two years before Morse's Washington-to-Baltimore demonstration, by a Scottish clockmaker named Alexander Bain.[91] As ingenious as was Bain's idea, he was unable to capitalize on it in a practical way. The first to succeed in doing this was Giovanni Caselli, an Italian inventor priest, who established a commercial service between Paris and Lyons some twenty-five years later. Caselli's service was a remarkable novelty, but it lasted only a few years because it was truly an idea ahead of its time. Despite the ingenuity of the concept, the available technology was just too primitive. Light-sensitive material had yet to be discovered. Therefore, Caselli's facsimile system, like Bain's, had to be electromechanical. The text to be faxed was embossed on a metal plate that could support an electric current when scanned by a pendulumlike arm. The signal generated in this way was sent over a telegraph wire. At the other end another pendulum, synchronized to the first, directed the signals to electrically sensitive paper.

The same discovery of photosensitive materials that made Nipkow's early television idea conceivable also was the key to making the facsimile idea practical. The document could now be scanned by a fine light beam inducing a current flow through the new material in proportion to the relative lightness and darkness of the paper along the scan. With this technology, a German named Arthur Korn was able to develop a practical system early in this century, and, since that time, the facsimile has been in continuous use.

Why are so many people surprised to hear about this venerable history? The essential reason is that facsimile transmission was initially used only in very specific applications. But ask yourself how newspaper photographs are transferred rapidly from one place to another. This use, in fact, was one of the major early applications of Korn's device and of the improved versions that followed. Now pictures could be transmitted along with text in reporting a story. By the First World War, battlefield pictures were being faxed by the wire services. In a similar application, the fax was put to use by the weather bureau in distributing weather maps, and the military put the facsimile to similar applications.

Since the late 1970s, it has become common for newspapers with nationwide circulation such as the *New York Times*, *Wall Street Journal*, and *USA Today* (and, a little later, international newspapers) to deliver their papers simultaneously to all their readers wherever located from a few printing plants that receive the information by very high quality facsimile transmission. These fax machines are understandably expensive, but providing timely delivery to their customers makes them well worth the money. It is interesting to note that the notion of faxing newspapers dates back to the 1930s and 1940s when there were several attempts to fax papers not to a few printing plants but directly to homes to avoid the distribution problem completely. These turned out to be uniformly unsuccessful, originally because of the poor quality and cost, and later because television made the whole notion obsolete.

There were other attempts at various times during its evolution to generalize the application of the facsimile. The most notable of these occurred in the 1950s when Western Union sold some 50,000 units that gave its customers remote access to its telegraph offices. That this move failed is not surprising considering the fact that the old-fashioned telegraph service had already declined significantly. It is, perhaps, more surprising that neither Western Union nor anyone else thought seriously about broadening its application beyond that of the telegram.

The technology that converted the facsimile from a device used by a few specialists to more general application was the microprocessor. By the late 1970s, small and relatively inexpensive fax machines began to make their appearance, and they have since taken the world by storm. That the Japanese have been the world leaders in their manufacture is hardly surprising considering their success in the manufacture of similar equipment. But, unlike much of the other equipment, the use of fax became common in Japan before it did so in other countries. The Japanese language uses an alphabet of about 2,200 characters, some phonetic and some Chinese ideographs, making it considerably less suitable for telegraphy than the Western languages that use alphabets with a relatively small number of characters. Any system that reproduces a pattern on a page rather than the characters constituting that pattern has obvious advantages with such a language. In fact, Edison noted this fact many years ago to justify some research of his own on facsimile.

But even the digital revolution would not have been sufficient to create the huge demand that ultimately resulted had not standards been developed that guaranteed that the fax machine that one company bought would be able to talk to the fax that another company bought. The effect of these standard protocols can be compared to that of the computer network protocols developed around the same time that made the Internet possible.

With the proliferation of both fax machines and personal computers, it was only a matter of time before it was recognized that, with a little additional hardware and software, computers could send and receive fax messages. In this way you can compose a message in your computer and send it in fax format to someone's fax machine. However, if the message exists in paper form, it has to be entered into the computer with an optical scanner. A scanner adds enough to the expense that most have chosen to buy an independent fax machine.

Thus fax and E-mail stand as complementary capabilities in the long communications tradition. To be sure, they are competitors of sorts in that they both transmit the written word electronically. And yet, they are different enough to find uses that capitalize on their unique strengths. Fax is a paper system; E-mail is paperless. Fax can transmit pictorial information as easily as print; E-mail is primarily for text. Fax therefore functions as a very fast mail service. E-mail can do the equivalent in a paperless way, provided that you have the document in electronic form in your computer.

But recall that E-mail arose not as a mail substitute but rather as a telephone substitute. And this remains one of its most popular uses in a kind of cultist way. Led by the members of the research communities who were the first users, E-mail is now used as a way of communicating informally, that is, sending brief notes or even chatting. Business cards and letterheads typically include the E-mail addresses along with the telephone and fax numbers. To some of the researchers, E-mail was a free good, supplied by the network sponsor, giving it an economic advantage over long-distance telephoning, which was not. But others used E-mail to take advantage of its peculiar advantages over telephoning, with some going so far as to simulate the personal element in transmitting the human voice through the use of certain keyboard character combinations as a kind of shorthand language to indicate emotions, such as :-) for happiness and :-(for sadness.

E-mail as a popular method of discourse spawned another phenomenon: Why not address messages to a mailbox accessible to anyone on the network, the electronic analog of pinning a notice on a bulletin board. These electronic bulletin boards have become very popular wherever networks exist. They are used for buying and selling, informing, propagandizing, even slandering, so much so that questions of free speech have arisen. Of course, as the Internet grew, more and more ordinary people were admitted to the cult. And now that computer service companies such as Prodigy, America Online, and CompuServe have become so popular with computer users, their bulletin boards have become among their most used services. People seem to have a natural desire to express their opinions on any and all subjects. How else can we explain the propensity of the amateur radio hams of a previous generation to talk to any and all for hours on end, and of the popularity of call-in radio and television shows. Today's *computer nerds* in their affection for bulletin boards are cut from the same cloth. Technology may change, but people do not.

The fax's greatest strength in the short term is its major weakness when we look to the long term. The strong point is its ease of operation that requires the user simply to place a sheet of paper in the machine, dial a phone number, and push a button. But, when you consider that this is an essentially manual operation, you have the source of its greatest weakness. It is not that the fax machine will disappear over time. To the contrary, as long as we have paper, the fax process will be useful and important. Yet, in the long run, I would think that the essentially paperless nature of E-mail will make it the more influential technology.

Fax and E-mail have very different histories. The former is a late bloomer, the latter, a child prodigy. Yet the prominence and popularity of each is primarily due to the same thing: the computer and the digital revolution. It is because of the computer that, on the threshold of the twenty-first century, communication of the written word is assuming the societal importance that oral communication did a century ago.

Part

IV

On the Way to the Next Century

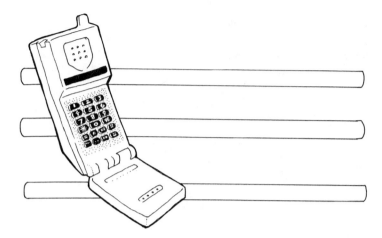

What could have been simpler than the world of communication in the immediate post-war years: Two giant industries, telephone and television, brought us everything that was to be brought, the first by wires and the second by wireless, the first by a monopoly and the second by an oligopoly. The telegraph was no longer much of a factor in the industry, and cable television was an economic solution in a few limited locations. The computer had not yet become a factor at all.

Now, in the closing years of the century, this neat picture of the 1950s has been torn asunder. The old telephone monopoly, the Bell system, is no more, and its residuum, the Baby Bells, are fighting to loosen the bonds of the divestiture decision. Moreover, the telephone is no longer confined to the home and office; it is common to people on the move, in their cars, in airplanes and trains, and even on the street. Cable television is eroding the influence of the networks, and high-definition TV is on the horizon. The computer has insinuated itself into all aspects of communication. And, perhaps most significant of all, the boundaries between the television and telephone industries are breaking down with the telephone systems struggling to carry video and the cable networks on the verge of becoming interactive.

When such fundamental change occurs, it is invariably the result of a complex combination of factors. It is always an oversimplification to ascribe such change to only one thing. Yet, if pressed to name the principal cause of all this ferment, one would have to say it was the computer and its intrusion into the world of communications.

The marriage of computers to communications is permitting instantaneous remote access to information of all kinds, for knowledge or entertainment, for business or pleasure. Morse's "one neighborhood" is becoming a reality in more ways than anyone could have guessed. The broad outlines of the path are clear, but a continued stream of technological and entrepreneurial surprises keep the details anything but so.

Observing how it all plays out will be an interesting pastime.

Chapter

25

Digitizing the Telephone System

No matter what is about to happen in the future of communication, there is no disagreement about one aspect of this future: The communication in the years to come will be digital. But to say that communication is digital does not necessarily imply that computer-to-computer traffic will dominate all other. Voice and video are here to stay whatever happens. What it does mean is that the information being communicated will be in the form of digits regardless of what they stand for.

The telephone system was built for communication by voice. It was Bell's vision of the universality of voice communication that led to his conception of the universal telephone system. Everything in today's network is optimized for this purpose. Yet, at the same time, these networks have enough versatility built into them to handle other kinds of information. The whole fax boom would not have been possible had not the telephone system been able to transport 0s and 1s as well as voice. The same thing is true for the digits that go from computer to computer, digits that are far different from the speech signals that the phone system was built to handle. The computers and fax machines essentially fool today's telephone lines into thinking they are carrying ordinary voice by using devices called *modems* that convert the digits into audio signals at the sending end and do the reverse at the receiving end.

Why is it still necessary to fool the telephone system into accommodating digits? It is as if the telephone company had never heard of the computer revolution, which is, of course, not true. To the contrary, the telephone companies have been in the vanguard of the computer revolution. How is it, then, that today's telephone systems appear to be so little different from their ancestors in the 1950s when long-distance dialing was first introduced?

Sometimes appearances are misleading. While to their subscribers these networks look much as they did at mid-century, internally they have been continually transformed by the computer since its advent, beginning with the mainframes of the 1950s and 1960s up to today's modern microprocessors. While much of this change is hidden from the subscriber, the carriers do, on occasion, give us a few glimpses into what has been happening. The most obvious sign lies in the data networks and especially the E-mail that most of the long-distance carriers provide separate from their telephone networks. Less obvious is the fact that specific telephone features such as call waiting, call forwarding, and caller ID that the telephone companies now furnish on a routine basis depend on computers in the telephone network interchanging information. But these are only surface effects. The surprising fact is that these telephone networks are in the process of evolving into computer networks. What is even more surprising is the fact that this evolution has been happening in a way that is almost invisible to most of us. Yes, we notice the new services, but to the ordinary subscriber, these are minor perturbations on our basic telephone service. How the telephone systems could change so much internally while making so small an impact on its subscribers is another interesting story.

Relatively few subscribers have availed themselves of the opportunity to buy the new features, and still fewer have taken advantage of the carriers' E-mail services. But every subscriber who ever makes a long-distance call enjoys far better voice quality than in previous years. Subscribers may have a vague notion that digitization might have something to do with this improvement from the way in which the long-distance carriers' advertising has suggested as they trumpeted their use of optical fiber as the transmission medium of choice. There was a time when the competitors in this area were trying to outdo one another in proclaiming how, with this new medium, they were providing their customers with connections as crystal clear as the thin glass fibers that carried the voice signals.

While these advertisements contain the usual hyperbole common in the advertising business, the essential truth of the statements is borne out by the fact that in recent years we have come to expect the quality of a connection between New York and London to be no different from one between upper and lower Manhattan—a situation far different from what it was in the early postwar years. Yet so accustomed are many of us to relatively poor long-distance connections that when the quality is good we are still often inclined to say in astonishment, "You sound like you are next door."

As the ads have implied, it is not the optical fibers themselves that have produced this great quality improvement in long-distance calling. It is, rather, the fact that with optical fibers, all the information is converted into a stream of digits before transmission, regardless of whether the information is computer data, voice, or television. Before the advent of the optical fiber, it remained economically preferable to maintain analog transmission throughout much of the telephone plant. With the optical fiber, the economic balance has swung to digital transmission.[92]

But not everywhere. The digits stop at the phone company's central office in your neighborhood. The circuits that the telephone company brings into your home from this office are analog not digital, very similar to the ones that have been used for the better part of a century. When you make a long-distance call, your voice signal is in analog form from your telephone instrument until it encounters a switch at this central office, just as it has been from the earliest days. In the old days, it would remain this way as it traversed the network to its destination. However, today it is most likely to be converted to digital form at this first central office and remain so until it reaches the last switch on its path, where it is converted back to analog form and put on a wire to the destination phone. Since the digital long-distance links have such high quality, it is these analog tails that contribute most of the degradation in a modern phone circuit, and this degradation is the same regardless of how long the path is. Moreover, it is the presence of the analog tail that gives the illusion that the network is still the same old network that has been in existence for decades. So instead of seeing, feeling, and touching the digits, the subscribers are forced to experience the effects of digitization as if wearing a blindfold and rubber gloves. And that is why, despite all the digital transmission within the network, your fax machine and computer have to use modems to fool the telephone line into thinking that it is carrying a voice signal.

It is easy to understand the point to this grand deception. The network is becoming digital in its internals because there are both performance and cost advantages to doing so. It remains analog in its appearance to its subscribers because by far the bulk of them are interested primarily in voice. All other services are of significantly less concern.

The signal, voice or otherwise, that comes out of a circuit is not exactly the same as the one that was placed on the circuit to begin with. Rather, it is corrupted by noise. You can think of noise as any extraneous signal interfering with the signal that you are trying to send. You can hear it in the form of a hissing sound on the radio and telephone, or a louder burst during a thunderstorm. You can see it in the form of snow on your television set. Noise at some level is unavoidable. Successful communication has to confront and overcome it one way or another.

We have learned to live with the telephone and its degrading effects. Most of the time the noise level is low enough to keep us satisfied. But these are the same phone lines that are used for sending digits from one computer to another through a pair of modems. If there were no noise present, the destination modem would always identify the signal correctly. However, noise can confuse the modem and cause a misidentification; the more noise, the more often this will happen, just as in ordinary voice communication, where the more noise on the telephone line, the more likely it is that the listener will mistake one word for another. While a noisy phone line may be annoying to talk over, it can be disastrous when it is carrying computer digits that represent bank balances or airline schedules.

Noise is cumulative. A transcontinental telephone connection passes through 3,000 miles of phone line, partly cable and partly microwave. When the circuit is analog from one end to the other, the noise introduced on each leg of the path all contributes to the noise that you hear along with the voice. It is only natural, then, that long analog connections will not sound as good as short ones. When a circuit is digitized, however, the signal is reconstituted each time it goes from one link to another. While this process does not remove all noise effects, it cuts down on the cumulative effects producing the long-distance quality that is now the rule rather than the exception.

But the high quality that you hear in a transcontinental phone conversation may still not be high enough for the Federal Reserve system when it transmits funds from one bank to another using the same circuit. Achieving this level of circuit quality demands special techniques that are only possible when the information to be transmitted is in digital form, using techniques that are derived from an esoteric branch of communication called *information theory*.

Information theory provides the very foundation of communication. It was first articulated in 1948 by Claude Shannon in his monumental work, *The Mathematical Theory of Communication*.[93] In his introduction, Shannon posed the issue he was addressing: "The fundamental problem of communication is that of reproducing at one point either exactly or approximately a message selected at another point." Loosely translated this statement asserts that when information is sent either by wire, microwave, or optical fiber, it is the job of the communicator to see to it that what is received is either identical to or at least a very close approximation of what was transmitted despite the noise that is always present. If the transmission is corrupted, then some of the information contained in the transmission is bound to be lost. Shannon's assertion is self-evident. The remainder of his work is anything but.

The nub of Shannon's work was his mathematical proof that it was possible to send data as accurately as desired regardless of the amount of offending noise. It is just that the greater the noise level, the longer it takes to transfer a given amount of information. This result was the very model of elegance. However, one problem turned out to be frustrating indeed. Shannon derived his result using a technique that mathematicians call an *existence proof*. That is, he was able to show that there are ways of achieving these ideal results without shedding any light on what those ways are. In the decades following Shannon's work, his disciples sought the Holy Grail of how to achieve these results in practice. While no one has found the grail except in a few very special cases, enough solid practical schemes have been found to make high accuracy digital communication of great practical utility.

It is no exaggeration to state that Shannon's information theory is among the most important technical contributions of this century. Nor is it an overstatement to say that Shannon's reputation among communications engineers is similar to Einstein's among physicists. Shannon is the man who had the breadth of vision to start a new field. As modern scientists go, he is well known even to people in fields other than his own. Nevertheless, in keeping with the modern tradition, scientists, technologists, and inventors, with the rare exception of someone like Einstein, are essentially unknown to the general population. And when one considers the significance of Shannon's contributions, his obscurity is unfortunate.

Shannon is not your typical scientist. He is an introverted man, very gracious and self-effacing, who, unlike most other outstanding scientists, has published little during his long career. He did his seminal work at the Bell Laboratories just after the war, in the same time frame and the same place that witnessed the invention of the transistor. He had come to Bell after studying at MIT as did Shockley—the former in mathematics and the latter in physics—and he returned to his alma mater in his later years just as Bardeen and Brattain left the Laboratories for the academic life not too long after their great discoveries.

Shannon's ideas, while developed solely for communications engineering, have been influential in other fields. To quote Jeremy Campbell in *Grammatical Man*: "Essentially [Shannon's] papers consisted of a set of theorems dealing with the problem of sending messages from one place to another quickly, economically and efficiently. But the wider and more exciting implications of Shannon's work lay in the fact that he had been able to make the concept of information so logical and precise that it could be placed in a formal framework of ideas."[94] And indeed,

Grammatical Man addresses itself to the insights provided by information theory and the thermodynamic concept of entropy to such fields as linguistics, genetics, and cognitive processing.

Not everyone agrees with such a broad interpretation. Even Shannon, who published seemingly only under duress throughout his career, suggested in an article in 1956 that "information theory has perhaps ballooned to an importance beyond its actual accomplishments."[95] But regardless of the breadth of applicability of Shannon's theory, its contribution to communications in the narrow sense is of the greatest significance both because of its intellectual stimulation and for the foundation it provides for the practical business of communications.

It took a frustratingly long time for practical applications of information theory to materialize. In the two decades following Shannon's work, mathematicians developed approaches that had great potential, only to find that the cost of implementing them was so great that their application was limited to a few areas where cost was not a primary consideration. Then came a major triumph not from the world of communications as we know it, but from the world of audio recording. It was the compact disc, now known to everyone as the CD.[96]

This link seems strange at first blush, until one recognizes that audio recording is also a communication process, one that begins in the recording studio and ends in your living room. Making the recording is analogous to transmitting a message; the playback process is analogous to the reception of the message; and the recording medium, disc or tape, whatever it may be, plays the role of the telephone line or radio circuit. A music system demands especially high accuracy of reproduction. What may be acceptable in a telephone conversation is far from acceptable for music transmission. The music that reaches your ears should be as close as possible to a replica of the music played by the recording artists. Even the highest quality phonograph needle riding in the record groove so that it barely touches the surface is the source of a slight hiss. Noise at some level is unavoidable. For this reason music professionals and amateur audio buffs have spared no expense in buying playback equipment to reduce the noise to a minimum and distort the sound as little as possible.

And that is why the digital compact disc has been such a spectacular success. The conversion of the recording business from analog to digital is similar to that in the telephone networks in many technical and economic ways, but far different in public perception. Digitizing the recording process with the compact disc has yielded the same kind of quality improvements as digitizing telephone circuits. But the record companies and the consumer electronics industry that manufactures the players have stressed the digital nature of the system in their advertising much more so than the long-distance telephone companies. The result is that most people know that the CD is digital, while the person who knows anything about the digitization of the telephone system is much rarer.

The CD is one of the smash technological hits of our time. It has captivated the public in much the same way as the other communication advances of the last century and the early part of this one. Many people were surprised at the astonishing speed with which the CD took over the recording industry. After all, it was not in the category of the telephone or the radio or any of the other earlier inventions because it does not provide a radically new capability that did not exist previously. The difference between its sound quality and that of the long-playing record is more quantitative than qualitative. (There remains a small, but vocal, minority of audiophiles who prefer the analog recording media to the digital.) And yet the CD sound has so captivated the public that within a few years of its first appearance on the market, the LP has become almost as extinct as a celluloid collar. The source of this quality lies in the adjective *digital* that describes its concept and to the microprocessor that made it possible in a practical sense.

The history of audio recording has seen other inventions that, on the face of it, were far more revolutionary in their impact on the industry. The original invention of the phonograph by Edison, at about the same time as Bell's invention of the telephone, was one of the principal contributors to the inventor's fame and fortune. A major breakthrough occurred in 1925 when the vacuum tube allowed the hitherto mechanical recording and playback to be replaced by electronic processes, allowing for a vast improvement in quality. But even more important was the fact that the recording artists were no longer required to position themselves directly in front of a mechanical recording horn. Using a microphone in place of a horn removed the limitation on the size of the musical ensemble that could be recorded. Now, for the first time, a full symphony orchestra or a large chorus could be recorded.

The LP itself that came along in 1948 introduced another large improvement in fidelity. Still more important was that by increasing the playing time of a record from four minutes to almost thirty minutes per side, it became practical for the first time to record very long works such as operas and Broadway musicals. The magnetic tape, first in reel-to-reel form and then in handy cassettes, allowed professionals and amateurs alike the flexibility of recording on this medium. By the 1970s, the LP and cassette tape had reached very high standards of audio fidelity, and almost every piece of music ever published had been recorded.

Then along came the CD. It introduced a number of improvements, none of them earthshaking, or so it seemed. It was smaller than the LP and stored about 25 percent more music on one side than the LP did on both sides. It was more rugged than the LP and did not require such gentle handling. The CD is compact because both the recording and playback mechanisms use very fine light beams generated by lasers. Since nothing actually touches the CD surface during playback, there is no obvious wear mechanism, making it the delight of radio stations that previously had to constantly replace their worn-out records. Even more important, this lack of contact eliminated record scratch as a source of noise that became increasingly annoying after each playing of an LP.

But just because there is no record scratch does not mean that there are no other sources of noise. In fact, the disc itself has imperfections that could make the music at least as unpleasant as a conversation over a very noisy phone line. Consequently, the recording and playback process uses an embodiment of Shannon's theory that counteracts these imperfections and enables the digits extracted from the disc by the player to be almost identical to those derived from the music in the recording studio. This accuracy, unmatched in analog systems, is what gives the CD such fidelity and has contributed so much to its success.

It was not necessary for the CD developers to invent their own information-theory scheme. They simply had to look back to all the work that was done in the aftermath of Shannon to find a technique. The one they chose dated back to the 1950s when it was conceived by two mathematicians, Irving Reed and Gustave Solomon, then at MIT's Lincoln Laboratory. The thing that made the difference between the 1950s and the 1970s was the microprocessor. A technique that was applicable in only a limited set of circumstances was now inexpensive enough for consumer electronics.

The microprocessor did not remove cost as an issue. Rather, it brought the cost down to the point where mass-production economies could be brought to bear. The early CD players cost well over $1,000, much more than the lower-end phonographs but less than the high-end precision-engineered turntables, tone arms, cartridges and needles used by professionals and amateur high-fidelity buffs. But despite these high prices, the crucial ingredient for success occurred: enough people began buying CD players that mass-production economies began to take effect, bringing the prices of the players down rapidly to less than $200. Higher priced deluxe models were far less expensive than the top-of-the line record players, and these differed from the low cost models more in convenience features than in basic fidelity. The avalanche effect of increased volume, lower player costs, and increased numbers of titles in the new medium led to the virtual disappearance of the LP in just a few years. The first CDs were between one and one-half and two times as expensive as LPs, a substantial increase considering the modest increase in music capacity. These prices have remained high, too high in the view of many industry observers. Yet, it is hard to sustain this argument in view of the enormous success of the medium.

Despite this success, the inventors of the CD remain shrouded in obscurity. We know the names of the organizations responsible for the development—Philips of the Netherlands and Sony of Japan—but not of the individuals who made the most significant contributions. Contrast this obscurity with the fame surrounding Edison some hundred years earlier upon his invention of the CD's predecessor many times removed. Ironically, one person whom we can cite as indirectly responsible for the success of the CD, is Claude Shannon, the theoretician, a man as different as one could imagine from Edison, the intuitive inventor who had no use for theoreticians. I suspect that Shannon has been both surprised and delighted at the influence he has had on the entertainment industry.

If the way in which digitization took over the audio recording industry can be characterized as a surge, its penetration of the telephone system is more properly characterized as seepage. AT&T introduced digital links into its long-distance network as early as the 1950s. Despite the quality advantages over analog links, the amount of digital transmission increased only modestly over the years. The reason for this was related to the properties of microwave radio, the workhorse transmission vehicle of the postwar years when the capacity of the network was increasing rapidly. The microwave radio minimized the need for real estate and greatly reduced the installation expenses relative to copper cable. But since it was a through-the-air system, its capacity was limited by the available bandwidth, the same kind of limitation that faces radio and television stations. And the fact was that there were certain analog transmission schemes that could cram more circuits into a given amount of bandwidth than the digital schemes. Thus, while AT&T digitized some of its long-distance microwave transmission, most of it remained analog to keep up with the demand for circuit capacity. It was deemed more important to satisfy this demand while leaving quality improvement for another day.

The development that was to change this situation and lead to the rapid digitization of long-distance transmission facilities was the optical fiber, a fine thread of glass, one-tenth the size of a human hair, that can pass light analogous to the way in which copper wires pass electricity. The advantage of light lies in its extremely high frequencies, some ten thousand times those in the microwave region—because along with the higher frequency goes a commensurately high bandwidth, implying that enormous capacity increases were potentially available if only the technology could be developed. And these huge capacities meant that at last the performance advantages of digital transmission were potentially achievable.

The notion of using guided light to send signals goes back to the 1870s when an American named William Wheeler had the idea of using mirrored pipes to channel light by a series of reflections. Not much later a British physicist, Charles Vernon Boys, came up with the more sophisticated notion of doing the same thing, not with physical mirrors, but by encasing the light pipe in an optical material of a lower refractive index that produced reflections at the interface between the two materials.[97] But these accomplishments were just curiosities. Serious development did not occur until the latter half of the twentieth century.

Why did it take so long? It was not simply a matter of perfecting the glass fabrication techniques. More important was the fact that before such a technique could be useful, there had to be a way of generating light waves analogous to the way in which radio waves are generated. Light is typically generated from heat, as in the electric light bulb in which a fine wire filament is heated to such a high temperature that it glows. While it is useful for lighting rooms or even for searchlights, it is impossible to impress intelligence on light of this kind except by the crude technique of turning it on and off at a relatively slow rate. The first wireless transmitters that generated a spark between two metallic contacts were much the same. They could only support the on/off Morse code; voice was out of the question. Then Fessenden's alternator and later De Forest's vacuum tube permitted the radio signals to be generated smoothly and continuously enough to carry audio signals.

The laser played the same role for light generation as did the vacuum tube for radio-wave generation. Once the laser made its appearance in the late 1950s, then optical communication became a possibility worth working for. These early lasers required extremely low temperatures that could only be obtained by sophisticated refrigeration techniques. The extension of the technology to work at ordinary room temperatures was a necessary step to making the devices practical.

Radio waves propagate through the atmosphere almost oblivious to its various constituents. It is this virtual transparency of the atmosphere that made radio and then television broadcasting feasible. But there are just too many impediments to light being used in this way. We could indeed focus a laser beam on a mirror and create, in this way, an extremely powerful beam of light that could be picked up by another mirror a distance away. But the propagation characteristics of such a link would be much worse during the day than at night because of the noise contributed by daylight. Also, what if it were a rainy or foggy day? The light signal would be severely degraded or, in the extreme, completely cut off. Even though the light sources were much stronger, the propagation problems were the same as those that made the optical semaphore of the nineteenth century impractical.

And that is where the optical fiber comes in.[98] By guiding the light through a pipe, all the effects of the atmosphere are eliminated. The freedom and simplicity of the radio link are given up, but in its place is a potentially reliable, extremely high capacity medium.

The first optical fibers were developed by the American Optical Co. in the early 1960s only a few years after the first lasers. Shortly thereafter the British Standard Telecommunications Laboratories were sufficiently successful to interest the British Post Office, the proprietors of the British telephone system. The Corning Glass Company and the Bell Laboratories were among the prime developers in the United States.

When these optical light pipes were first developed, the maximum distance the light beams could shine without excessive attenuation was just a few miles. For example, in the late 1970s, AT&T built the first prototype link in Atlanta about five miles long. With such "lossy fibers," spanning long distances required too many intermediate amplifiers to make it economical. But continued research extended those distances to tens of miles, now making truly long distances feasible.

AT&T first used these fiber cables in its urban telephone plants. In big cities, microwave relay is of limited utility because the obstruction of high-rise buildings constitutes too much of an impediment. The work-horse medium is thus the wideband cable laid under the ground. The telephone company was able to replace its relatively low-capacity copper cables with much higher-capacity optical cables to vastly increase its local transmission plants without the need for more real estate as early as the late 1970s.

By the early to mid-1980s, all the long-distance carriers were install-ing vast amounts of this cable. The first long-distance installation by AT&T generated an international incident that was to be the harbinger of things to come in other areas. In 1980 AT&T announced its intent to build a fiber network between Cambridge, Massachusetts, and Washing-ton, D.C., with the contruction to be in two phases, the first from Cambridge to New York and the second from New York to Washington. Western Electric, the wholly owned subsidiary of the company, was to supply all the fiber. When this choice of the in-house supplier was announced, the competitors, especially Corning, registered their com-plaints with the Federal Communications Commission. In a typical compromise, the FCC allowed the first phase to proceed as planned but required a competitive procurement of the fiber cables for the second phase. To everyone's surprise the winner was neither Western Electric nor Corning, but Fujitsu, the Japanese computer giant. Thereupon, the

FCC reversed itself, and Western Electric was allowed to supply the cable for the second half as it did for the first.

Fiber is most economical on the highest traffic routes between the large urban centers of the country. This stems from the fact that since much of the cost of any cable system—as opposed to a radio system—is in obtaining the real estate and installing the underground or pole-mounted cables, the incremental cost of installing a large number of fibers in each cable is relatively low. In the case of the newer carriers, such as MCI and Sprint, this was the principal way in which they built up their intercity connectivity to high volumes. AT&T already had large microwave capacities on these routes, and so it overbuilt with fiber to expand still more and keep up with the competition in the use of digital transmission. By the end of the decade, the technology was sufficiently advanced to permit the first transoceanic fiber cables to be installed. Before the first Atlantic optical cable, satellite dominated both the television and telephone markets between the United States and Europe; it was unique for television and its only competition for telephone was the low-capacity undersea copper cables. Once the optical cable was installed, the satellite had a competitor for both services.

Until something new is invented, the optical fiber cable will remain the workhorse transmission medium for the high-capacity links in the communications networks. From their very beginning, optical links have been digital, not only because it was the desirable thing to do, but, more importantly, because it was the *only* thing that could reasonably be done with the available technology. Since then, analog light systems have become feasible and there are special applications in which fiber is used this way. But it is hard to imagine that the bulk of the applications will be anything but digital in the future.

When will the telephone companies see fit to digitize the entire network, including the last mile of cable that enters your home? Will it be an explosion in data services that will demand it? Or will it have to wait until the pressure of video interests demand the installation of optical fiber into the home or the local telephone pole? These questions have been asked since the mid-1980s, and the answer has always seemed to be later in coming than anyone predicts.

But who knows? True to the history of communication, we should expect to be surprised at both the timing and rationale for the inevitable digitization.

26

Computers in the Network

It may take a little imagination to understand the benefits of digitizing the circuits in a telephone network. The whole notion of converting voice signals to a stream of 0s and 1s at one end of a wire or light pipe and then reconverting the digits back to voice signals at the other end strikes some people as counterintuitive. However, digitizing the other main element of communications networks, the switches, is anything but.

There is something intuitively digital about a switch. An electric light switch, for example, has two positions: on and off. The earliest manual switching behaved just like a light switch when an operator connected one wire to another (on) and then disconnected the wires after the call was over (off), and so did the first automatic switches. Over the years, research and development by the Bell system and others led to more sophisticated switches, but the basic operation remained the same: The switch responds to the numbers that the caller dials, makes the connection to the selected destination, and turns on the ringing. Then, when one of the parties hangs up, it breaks the connection.[99]

The process of interpreting the dialed numbers and making a switch connection based on this interpretation is also a computerlike operation. It is therefore no surprise that the switches in use today, whether the circuit switches in the telephone system or the packet switches in the data networks, are forms of digital computers. Of course, the first automatic switches, beginning with Strowger's, did not have the benefit of the vacuum tube, never mind the computer. The switching element itself was an electromagnetic device called a *stepping switch*, taking the place of the operator-actuated switch, used to locate an unused circuit and then make the connection. While this was going on, complex combinations of relays stored the incoming numbers as they were dialed.

As the telephone systems expanded in the 1920s and 1930s, the switches became more complex to keep up with the increasing numbers of subscribers. But they were still local devices, capable of automating local but not the more complex long-distance calling. The broadband circuits (called *trunks*) running between cities have the capacity to carry many individual phone calls. When a party in New York calls one in San Francisco, the call must be routed through a number of switching points in between. In order for a call to be put through, there has to be space available on each trunk of the route. With manual long-distance connections, an operator—AT&T invariably hired women for these tasks— makes this determination. If there is space, the operator puts the call through; if not, she looks for another route. If she can't find any way of getting the call through, she informs the caller to hang up and try again later. When she does put the call through, she has to time the call so that the caller can be billed the correct amount. An automatic long-distance switch has to be smart enough to do all these things. It is understandable, then, that switches smart enough to accomplish all these tasks and more took longer to develop, especially since the computer came along well after the perceived need for long-distance switching. By 1951, when the computer was still in its infancy, nationwide direct dialing had been introduced, and by 1967 the same was true for overseas dialing.

The electromechanical devices that were at the heart of the infant direct-dialing system were not altogether satisfactory. Chief among their problems was the limited reliability inherent in their electromechanical nature. As more and more were used in the more complex systems, failure became a serious problem of the same kind that plagued the early computers with their unreliable vacuum tubes. Another problem was their limited speed. A new generation of so-called crossbar switches (many of which continue in service in the 1990s) replaced the older Strowger-type switches, relieving the speed deficiencies to an extent. But ultimately something faster and more reliable had to be found. Thus AT&T became convinced that the switching of the future would be electronic and it prudently supported the semiconductor research in the 1940s that ultimately led to the transistor. It is unfortunately true that very few companies, even then, had the foresight and the resources to tackle hard problems with basic research. It is even less true today.

Help with these problems of complexity also came from an unlikely source. It seems that a young graduate student at MIT named Claude Shannon wrote a master's thesis in 1938 on the subject of switching theory (ten years before his seminal paper on information theory). In this thesis, Shannon made the brilliant observation that the abstract algebraic formulations of a nineteenth-century English mathematician named George Boole could be put to practical use in the design of switching systems. With this mathematical tool, there were systematic ways to design these systems to minimize the number of relays required to perform a given function and hence maximize its reliability. Bell Laboratory mathematicians took up where Shannon left off and developed the whole science of designing switching systems that would later become so important in the design of the early computers.

The first use of computers in switching gave the switches a dual personality. The actual switching was performed in roughly the same way as the switches earlier in the century: by an electromechanical switch closing a contact that made the connection. But all the decision making was performed by a closely associated computer. Switches of this type were the workhorses of the world's telephone systems beginning in the 1960s, and many have remained in use well into the 1990s.

Finally in the 1970s, the same time frame in which the ARPANET was using minicomputers for packet switching, the latest generation of circuit switches completed the process of computerization by performing all the operations including the switching itself in a computer. Gone was the mechanical closing and opening of switch contacts. Instead, a computer accepted a signal from an input line and directed it to an output line, analogous to the way a computer might accept a character from a keyboard and direct it to a monitor or printer. When several phone conversations were to be multiplexed onto a single trunk, the computer arranged the digits representing the conversations in time sequence, a few digits of one followed by a few digits of another, and so on. The motivation for this computerization was cost. The integrated circuit and microprocessor were driving down the cost of electronics of all kinds to such an extent that the telephone company could not afford not to convert its plant to the new technology. In addition, eliminating the physically large banks of relays with the small computer-based switches allowed large savings on the buildings that housed the switching systems and the land on which they were located.

That the information to be switched must be in digital form complicated the introduction of these computer-based switches. AT&T addressed this problem in what seemed to be a logical way. They would begin the digitization process with both switches and transmission in the high-density backbone of their network. Then they would extend this digital service to the periphery of the network. But AT&T was not the only switch manufacturer. Competitors began to manufacture smaller switches suitable for the periphery of the system as well as for local switches that customers would use on their premises. Most of the transmission was still analog. Yet so economical were these new switches compared to their predecessors that it paid to go through the complexity of converting the signals on the analog circuits entering the switch to digital form, and the digital signals leaving the switch back to analog form. The switches were, in fact, so economical that they were being introduced into the networks at a much faster rate than the transmission was being digitized. It was only the advent of optical fiber that allowed the digital transmission to catch up with the computerized switches.

By the 1980s the central backbone of the AT&T network used these completely computerized switches and digital transmission almost exclusively. Once the switch is a computer and the transmission is digital there are further economies. A single broadband trunk supports many circuits through a process called multiplexing. We only have to recall that both Bell and his competitor, Gray, came upon the idea of the telephone through the route of developing a harmonic telegraph that promised to multiplex several telegraph signals on a single wire. When the circuits carry analog signals, then the multiplexing technique is analog as was Bell's. But when the signals are digital, so is the multiplexing technique. In the latter case where the transmission, multiplexing, and switching are all digital, it is hard to tell where one begins and the other ends, because all the elements are constructed of the same integrated circuit elements and microprocessors. This backbone can be thought of as a large distributed computer system.

The computer has given the telephone companies the flexibility to use their networks in ways that would not have been possible in the past. For example, with these computerized switches, the telephone company can create special private networks for the internal communication of corporate customers. In the past, large telephone users such as the federal government, IBM, and General Motors found it more economical to acquire such private networks rather than to use the public networks. Such networks were usually not economical for medium-size companies with lower volumes of traffic. Now, with their computerized networks, the telephone companies can easily and economically dedicate a fraction of their public facilities to small companies by the simple act of reprogramming their switches. In fact, AT&T calls its version of this customization a *software-defined network,* emphasizing the fact that it is the computers in its network that make such services possible.

But using network computers in this way is just the tip of the iceberg. If these computers can be used to create specialized networks, and to provide such services as call-waiting and call forwarding, why can't they supply other information services as well? Or should the telephone companies simply transport services from third-party information vendors to their subscribers?

These are but a small sample of the many questions that can be raised about the future use of these communications networks. Others include: Will the increasing proliferation of computers lead eventually to computers competing with or even supplanting telephones as the principal users of the networks? If this should be the case, should packet switching supplant or supplement circuit switching in the networks of the future? And what about the role of video as more and more bandwidth is made readily available by optical fibers? And under these circumstances, will it continue to make sense to maintain analog tail circuits?

All these questions and more are consequences of the interrelationship of computers and communications, questions that were part of the day-to-day business of the great AT&T monopoly during the 1970s when the microprocessor was revolutionizing so much of industry. But AT&T had more than telephone service and technology on its mind during those years. The primary focus of its management during that time was a nontechnical revolution, one that was precipitated by the march of technology, but one that threatened the very existence of the Bell system as it had existed for one hundred years.

Chapter

27

A Natural Monopoly?

The time has come for a thinking-through of the future of telecommunications in this country, a thinking-through sufficiently objective as to at least admit the possibility that there may be sectors of our economy—and telecommunications [is] one of them—where the nation is better served by modes of cooperation than by modes of competition, by working together rather than by working at odds.

The time has come, then, for a moratorium on further experiments in economics, a moratorium sufficient to permit a systematic evaluation not merely of whether competition might be feasible in this or that sector of telecommunication but to the more basic question of the long-term impact on the public.

These words were spoken by John deButts, the chairman and CEO of AT&T in September 1973.[100] The occasion was the annual convention of the National Association of Regulatory Commissioners (NARUC) being held that year in Seattle. This speech was greeted with warm applause by the audience consisting mainly of the people associated with telephone regulation at the state level. These state public utilities commissions are responsible for the regulation of intrastate communication. It is only when the communication crosses state lines that the federal government regulators are involved, via the Federal Communications Commission. In the early years of the century, the Interstate Commerce Commission had served in this function along with its many other regulatory functions. But the Communications Act of 1934 established the FCC as the agency in which all communications activities would be regulated, succeeding the ICC for the common carriers and the Federal

Radio Commission, which had been established in 1927 to regulate the radio spectrum.

Bernard Strassburg, chief of the FCC's Common Carrier Bureau since 1963, was also in the audience that day. He was one of those principally responsible for the "experiments in economics" that were permitting competitors to invade the previously exclusive domain of the Bell system. DeButts was letting the world know that AT&T was about to institute new hard-line policies that would modify the stand of his predecessor at AT&T. As the economic historian Peter Temin put it, "Strassburg and deButts were as compatible as Luther and the Pope."[101] While deButts addressed his speech to many constituencies in the communications community, Strassburg's was one of the most important. Following the speech, deButts went over to Strassburg and said, "No hard feelings Bernie." The events that followed indicate that this comment of deButts to Strassburg may well have backfired.

The year 1973 did not mark the beginning of encroachments on the telephone company's *natural* monopoly, but with his speech in September of that year, deButts signaled the world that AT&T was finally taking a strong stand against such encroachments. Upon the conclusion of the NARUC convention, deButts put his money where his mouth was: AT&T began a calculated effort to impede and, it was hoped, break the symbol of telephone competition, a company called Microwave Communications, Inc., better known by its initials MCI. As it turned out, deButts's strategy failed. Just about one year after his speech, the Department of Justice initiated an antitrust suit against the telephone giant that was to lead to the now famous divestiture decision in 1982.[102]

But it was not simply the events relating to the struggles between AT&T and MCI in the early 1970s that led to this action. For virtually the entire postwar period, the Justice Department's antitrust division had been examining the complex issues surrounding the telephone monopoly. In the early postwar years, the main concern was Western Electric Company, AT&T's manufacturing arm, which supplied almost all the equipment used in the network. An antitrust suit was initiated in the Truman administration in 1949 seeking the divestiture of Western Electric with its division into three pieces as the mechanism for introducing competition into the equipment procured by the system. In this plan, Western Electric would be forced to divest itself of its 50 percent interest in the Bell Laboratories—AT&T held the other 50 percent interest.

The case languished for several years with virtually no external visibility. It appeared that the Eisenhower administration was much less inclined to pursue the case than the Truman administration. Finally the Justice Department and AT&T settled out of court in 1956 with the government capitulating on the issue of divestiture. In the resulting consent decree between Attorney General Herbert Brownell and AT&T, known as the Final Judgment, the telephone company was allowed to retain its monopoly over services regulated by either state or federal agencies. It was, however, forbidden to engage in nonregulated businesses, the most notable of these being the computer business. It had already become clear that the computer, then scarcely ten years old, would have significant impact on communications, although the enormous extent of this impact would not become apparent for several years.

AT&T was delighted with the outcome. Giving up competitive activities, even those related to the new computer, seemed like a small price to pay for recognition of its natural monopoly. There were those in Congress who were not so delighted. Many of the Justice Department's antitrust lawyers also shared this view, resenting the government's apparent cave-in. They continued to maintain files on AT&T waiting for the right moment to strike. It took close to two decades for that moment when the Watergate affair was over, Gerald Ford was president and William Saxbe, an aging former senator from Ohio and a holdover from the Nixon administration, was his attorney general. Those two decades saw changes in the communications scene that were to be irreversible.

No one would have thought that Jack Goeken, a down-to-earth entrepreneur from Joliet, Illinois, was the kind of man who would be the catalyst for much of this change. He had obtained a franchise from General Electric to sell mobile radios out of Springfield, the state capital. But to this man who had never gone to college came a brilliant flash of marketing insight. His customers were mostly Illinois farmers who liked to keep track of their merchandise on the way to market in Saint Louis and Chicago. The range of a portable radio was limited to a few miles. Once a truck driver exceeded that range, he had to stop his truck, get out of the cab and make a phone call. Goeken's insight was that if he built a chain of radio links—a microwave relay—between the two cities, then the truckers could keep in touch over the whole route and he might sell a few more radios.

This idea did not require brand new technology: AT&T had been installing microwave relay all over the country to increase the capacity of its network, enabling it to satisfy the pent-up telephone demand of the war years but especially to satisfy the needs of television distribution. Nor was it a novelty for a private company to install its own microwave link. The microwave technology that stemmed from the radar developments during the war made it relatively easy for anyone to do. To run cable required real estate rights of way and large construction expenses. In contrast, radio links required relatively little real estate and fairly modest outlays of money for a few radios and towers. Motorola found that it could sell private microwave links to large companies at prices well below that of AT&T's service, and the FCC allowed such activity over the objections of AT&T. After being overruled, the telephone company fought back with a new private-line tariff, called TELPAK (the first of many attempts to use the tariff to stem the tide of competition), that lowered rates by over 75 percent for bulk users. The suspicious FCC approved it after a three-month delay, but continued to fight it. The tariff was finally killed in 1981.

Goeken's insight was to recognize that his private microwave link could be used by businesses other than his farmers, companies that were too small to be able to afford their own private links but that were unhappy with AT&T's service and pricing. In other words, he could sell communications services over his link. In a very small way, he would be competing with the largest corporation in the world.

Goeken quickly came to realize that what he wanted to do was indeed a step beyond what the FCC had allowed Motorola to do. Not only was he trying to sell services, but he would have to interconnect his proposed customers to his long distance lines from their existing telephones, or, in other words, he would require connections into AT&T's local Saint Louis and Chicago telephone plants, something that was not apt to warm the cockles of the Bell system's heart. He applied to the FCC, and thereby began a process that lasted from 1963 to 1969, when the FCC finally authorized Goeken and MCI, the company he founded, to begin delivering this service.

These were very frustrating years for Jack Goeken. The FCC was not favorable to his request; the idea of competing with AT&T was just too radical. At first, Goeken was naive enough to believe that AT&T might even look with favor upon his notions since it would derive additional revenues for the local Bell companies. However, was soon disabused of this notion when AT&T opposed his application to the FCC with all the resources at its command just as it had opposed Motorola some years earlier. And Motorola's networks, while draining some revenue from the telephone company, did not compete for business on AT&T's turf. Jack Goeken was trying to infringe on the natural monopoly.

Many interests throughout the country were happy with the AT&T monopoly. During most of the company's first century, the system worked in accordance with Theodore Vail's principles articulated with the slogan "One policy—One system—Universal service." He convinced his subscribers, stockholders, and the government that the public was best served by monopoly telephone companies operating under government surveillance and semi-control, dedicated to the proposition that if the companies met their service obligations, they and their owners would prosper. The public received good service at comparatively low rates and the company and its stockholders received stable rewards, even in the years of the great depression. Vail's other guiding principle was that end-to-end service was essential. Customers paid for a user-to-user service, not for a set of equipment. True, there were still a number of independent local telephone companies scattered throughout the country that violated part of this principle. AT&T had tried to do away with these, but in its first encounter with the antitrust laws, it had been forced to stop such practices before World War I. Since that time the situation had been one of live and let live.

The way the telephone services were priced made many people feel comfortable. With one big interrelated network and no competition, it was not necessary to price services that used parts of the network solely in accordance with the costs to provide those specific services. Political ends could also be satisfied. For example, it was good politics for long-distance services to subsidize local services. Most voters used long-distance services only rarely, and the state regulators found it expedient to keep local rates low. Even long-distance pricing was kept uniform throughout the country (a practice begun during World War I when the government ran the phone company), to avoid the wrath of farmers and small-town America: The price for 100 miles of toll service was the same anywhere in the country. Since the cost to provide this service on a lightly loaded rural route was higher than on a heavily used route serving major metropolitan areas, the farmers and small-town citizens were being subsidized by the city folks, mostly business users. It was precisely the oddity of these pricing arrangements that paved the way for competitors. AT&T's rates for a high-density route such as between Chicago and Saint Louis were artificially high because they were subsidizing both rural and local area subscribers. The competitors, who were subsidizing no one, were able to step in and *skim the cream* by underpricing AT&T on high-traffic routes, avoiding the other less-lucrative routes. Business users might be more than inclined to leave the telephone company for dramatic rate reductions.

Whether or not a telephone monopoly was *natural* was something that one had to take as a matter of faith. It seemed intuitively obvious to most that having one company responsible from end to end was bound to yield superior service. But how much worse would it be if parts of the system were subject to competition? It was even harder to prove convincingly that the economies of scale achieved in a single large system made it necessarily cheaper than if parts of the system were competed— the Justice Department's lawyers thought otherwise when they attempted to divest Western Electric. If one could prove in some way that a regulated monopoly such as AT&T was actually both best and cheapest without competition, then there would be some factual basis to the claim of natural. But lacking such definitive proof, the claim of naturalness was reduced to one of theology: people believed it because they were brought up that way. It was as unthinkable to some to believe in competition in the telephone system as for a Christian to forsake his or her cherished beliefs in favor of those of Buddhism, or vice versa.

Goeken was innovative and entrepreneurial, and he had boundless energy. But he was not a good businessman, and, to compete with AT&T, more than an entrepreneurial spirit was necessary. His company acquired the necessary business skills in the person of Bill McGowan, the man who more than any other came to symbolize MCI and its struggle against the AT&T monopoly. McGowan came from the anthracite country around Scranton and Wilkes Barre in northeastern Pennsylvania. The son of a railroad engineer, he made it through the Harvard Business School in the top 5 percent of his class. A mutual friend introduced him to Goeken, and, after much soul searching, McGowan agreed to join the company as an equal partner with Goeken. At first the two got along well, with Jack doing marketing and Bill raising money. But it did not take too long for fundamental differences in approach to create a cleavage between the two that ultimately led to Goeken's withdrawal from the company's management.

McGowan recognized the economic facts of life regarding communications carriers that had escaped Goeken. The business is highly capital intensive. An initial layout of cash is required to purchase the equipment needed to establish service. This money is recovered gradually over an extended period of time after service begins. Any expansion of the system requires a new outlay of cash to be recovered still later through the revenues for this expanded system. And once capital equipment is in place, it is necessary to derive as much revenue as possible from this equipment to maintain a positive cash flow. The use of microwave radio rather than cable made it possible for an upstart to get into the business, but it still did not make it easy.

McGowan joined Goeken in 1968. The application to the FCC had been submitted five years earlier and still no permission had been granted. Goeken was in deep financial trouble. McGowan set about to raise money everywhere he could. He also recognized that a single link would never be very viable; he had to expand the system beyond the original Chicago to Saint Louis route that continued to occupy Goeken's attention. He set up the framework for these additions independent of the original link to avoid complicating that issue still pending at the FCC. The commission, as subscribers to the natural monopoly theory, had not taken Goeken seriously for several years. Finally in 1967 they at least gave him enough credibility to formalize the proceedings. The common carrier bureau was preparing to reject the application but, in the end, decided to recommend approval.

Strassburg described his change of heart as follows in his book:

Notwithstanding some personal misgivings [about Goeken's ability to run a common carrier service], it looked like here was a legitimate opportunity to factor in a new supplier. The conventional thinking was still that the Bell System was a natural monopoly, but some changes in the demand side of the environment were beginning to show themselves. We were starting to think about how to accommodate data transmission on the network, and we had started the computer inquiry which exposed some new dimensions of the communications infrastructure. . . .

Jack Goeken's . . . proposal looked like a sage and prudent guinea pig. I couldn't see any harm to be done by giving it a try to see what happened. We could find out whether there was a market for the specialized services he was proposing. So I issued instructions to rewrite the bureau's position, which had been drafted as a denial, to recommend a grant.[103]

The commissioners upheld the bureau in a four to three vote along party lines with the Democrats in the majority. Subsequently, one of the commissioners in the majority, Kenneth Cox, left the commission to join McGowan in a senior management role. None of the authors writing about the period indicate any collusion here. Cox was simply so very sympathetic to MCI's approach that he readily accepted the offer to join McGowan. (This occurrence is in marked contrast to AT&T's practice of never hiring former FCC officials.)

The FCC's decision came as something of a bombshell, but it was not the only one. The previous year, the FCC had decided another groundbreaking case that had come before it at about the same time as the MCI application. Tom Carter was a Dallas businessman. Like Jack Goeken he was involved in mobile radio communications, but in support of the drillers in the Texas oil fields. There would be occasions in which someone on the oil fields would want to call outside through the telephone company, and Carter rigged up a device—the Carterfone—that would couple his mobile radio acoustically to a telephone to make this connection. He was flabbergasted when the telephone company refused to allow this nonelectrical connection. The AT&T contention was that any foreign device could ultimately degrade the performance of the system to the other subscribers in some way.

The FCC had upheld this monolithic view of the system years before when, preposterous as it now sounds, it had forbidden the use of the Hush-A-Phone, a telephone mouthpiece shield that provided the talker with some degree of privacy when others were in the room. When Carter went to court, it referred the issue to the FCC for an opinion in 1967, at about the same time as the FCC was formalizing the MCI application. The common carrier bureau acted on the Carter case before the MCI case, recommending that "foreign" devices be allowed to connect to the telephone system providing that such devices did not adversely affect the behavior of the system. This was not nearly as divisive an issue as the

MCI case; the commissioners approved the common carrier bureau's recommendation unanimously. The fact that we are free today to buy our own telephones from any vendor who meets the proper specifications stems from this decision.

Strassburg and Henck provide an insider's view of these events. The fascinating thing is that at the time these two cases were not considered particularly important. In their words, they were "cats and dogs." Now from the perspective and wisdom derived from hindsight, we can see quite clearly that in the Carterfone and MCI decisions, the FCC was eroding the issue of the natural monopoly by permitting the notion of competition in two important aspects of telephone service. It did not take long to prove that these decisions marked the beginning of the end of the AT&T monopoly. The cats and dogs had become lions and tigers.

This "cats and dogs" attitude probably accounts for the FCC's approval of MCI's application while at the same time maintaining their theological beliefs about the natural monopoly. After all, MCI was not attempting to compete in normal switched long-distance service, the mainstream of the telephone business, but rather in the much less important business segment of private lines. A private line is a permanent connection between two telephones; pick up one of them and the other rings almost instantly. There is no switching in the route to allow the caller to select the telephone to which he or she wants to be connected. It is the kind of service that businesses often find useful in connecting together their remote offices. Sometimes the businesses provide their own switches on each end to permit any phone in one location to talk to any phone in the other location. But as useful as it may be to some commercial subscribers, private-line service constitutes only a very small fraction of the telephone company's traffic. It is the universal switched service pioneered by Bell and Vail that dominates the telephone system. This service is the heart and soul of the telephone system, and neither MCI nor anyone else could conceivably get into this business.

Or so the conventional wisdom held. But there was a loophole within the private-line category. Foreign Exchange, or FX, is the name given to a kind of service that permits a telephone in one city to be a subscriber of an exchange in another city. For example, it allows a person living in Detroit to be given a Chicago telephone number, so that any call to his number from a Chicago subscriber is treated as a local call. The way this feature is implemented is to run a private line from the subscriber's Detroit telephone exchange to a Chicago exchange. For this reason, the AT&T tariff for FX service was categorized as a subclass of private-line service. This service was to be MCI's wedge into the telephone business.

MCI, of course, recognized this loophole and claimed that FX service was included in its private-line authorization. AT&T took the contrary position that MCI would need specific authorization for FX service; the blanket private-line authorization was insufficient. But it was now the fall of 1973, after John deButts's hardball speech in Seattle. And so AT&T backed up its contention with aggressive action. Rather than filing a nationwide tariff with the FCC for the interconnection between its local plants and MCI's private long-distance lines, it would submit each request to the relevant local telephone company, which would then file a tariff with the local public utilities commission. The time taken for this process when coupled with the bias of the local regulators toward the Bell system meant that, for all practical purposes, MCI would not be able to provide service. It could even mean the financial strangulation of the upstart company. Strassburg's reaction to deButts in Seattle had to have influenced his actions in the events that were to transpire.

AT&T's tactics forced MCI to take the issue to the FCC in the form of a letter requesting an official ruling. Strassburg immediately sent the letter to AT&T requesting its views on the issue, with the reminder that for interstate services there was no requirement to go to the state regulatory authorities. AT&T generally denied MCI's charges but did admit that it was their intent to file local tariffs. It did not report that it had already instructed the local operating companies one month earlier to file tariffs with the state authorities. The commissioners came down formally on MCI's side, directing AT&T to file a nationwide tariff, and, shortly thereafter, Strassburg ruled that FX service was to be included in the general private-line authorization.

AT&T did not give up; it asked the commissioners to review this action by its bureau chief. To MCI these were delaying tactics that could only continue to erode its precarious financial position. As a measure of its dependence on these connections, MCI's revenues at the time were a mere $48,000 per month; the requested services would add $800,000 to that figure. MCI therefore had to take drastic action. It went to a federal court in Philadelphia court asking that AT&T be required to provide interconnect services for FX. AT&T's response was that this was all a subterfuge to get into the universal long-distance business.

The court granted the injunction that MCI had requested. Of course, AT&T appealed, and the appellate court granted a temporary stay of the injunction until a panel of the full court could consider the matter. While the appellate court was considering the issue, the telephone company had to comply with the injunction and it began interconnecting to the MCI routes. But as soon as the court granted its temporary stay, the injunction was no longer in force, and AT&T pulled the plug by disconnecting the MCI circuits. The panel of judges removed the stay, but its action was stayed until the full court could consider the issue. In mid-April the full court passed the buck to the FCC with the statement that the FCC's interconnect order had not specifically mentioned FX. The following spring, the FCC cleared up the apparent ambiguity and the appellate court removed its stay of the district court's injunction. MCI had won an important battle.

AT&T may have thought that its action in fighting MCI constituted an appropriate hardball tactic at the time, but it turned out to be strategically disastrous. All this litigation by MCI was short term; its purpose was to keep the company alive. But while the appeals and counterappeals were going on, MCI introduced additional litigation in another forum. In March of 1974, it brought a civil antitrust suit against AT&T in Chicago. As we shall see, this suit had much in common with the almost simultaneous criminal antitrust suit against AT&T by the federal government.

After the ruling by the appellate court, MCI was free to offer its services, FX included, unimpeded. But that ruling was only the beginning. The FCC had let the genie out of the bottle. MCI proceeded to file a new so-called modular tariff detailing a menu of services that its customers could choose. This approach was new to the commission. Even though they did not really understand the new approach and its implications, it appeared harmless enough and they approved it. But one of the items on the menu was a service called Execunet, and this simple filing led to the revolution that was to follow.

It did not take AT&T long to grasp the implications of Execunet. One day an AT&T representative appeared at the FCC in Washington and made a call to the weather report number in Chicago using MCI service. This, he exclaimed, was service from an arbitrary location in Washington to an arbitrary location in Chicago. It was *switched* service and MCI was providing it without authorization.

Execunet was a direct consequence of the FX decisions. FX is a private-line service *closed* on one end and *open* on the other. These terms are telephone jargon describing the fact that the private line allows a single phone on one end to access anyone on the other end. But what if a customer chooses two FX lines from the modular menu, open and closed on opposite ends. This choice provides effectively open-ended service on both ends. The service is not as good as normal long-distance service—the customer has to dial some twenty-four digits instead of the ten required by AT&T—but it is long-distance service, and its low price might be worth the inconvenience.

Of course AT&T objected and, for the first time in the long battle, the FCC came down on the side of the Bell system and rejected Execunet service. Once again MCI went to court, this time in Washington in July

1975. The judge returned the case to the FCC to hear new justifications from MCI. But now the FCC stuck to its guns, continuing to hold that universal long-distance service was a natural monopoly; it was trying to put the genie back in the bottle. After all the preceding events, however, this was a difficult contention to sustain, and, finally in 1977, the court ruled in MCI's favor and the Supreme Court refused to reconsider the issue. Long-distance service was no longer a monopoly, natural or otherwise. MCI had won the right to compete head-to-head with AT&T.

While all this activity was going on at the FCC and in the courts, the antitrust division of the Justice Department was methodically building its case against "Ma Bell," and the hardball tactics espoused by deButts played right into its hands. The action was finally taken in the fall of 1974 shortly after President Gerald Ford took office and just a few months after MCI filed its civil antitrust suit in Chicago. Among the complaints of the government were the old ones relating to the Western Electric monopoly and many new ones related to the interconnection issues surrounding the MCI case. In the suit, brought in the District of Columbia before Judge Joseph Waddy, the government demanded that AT&T be required to divest itself, at least in part, of both Western Electric and the local operating companies. For three years, Judge Waddy was occupied with settling jurisdictional issues relating to the roles of his court, the New Jersey court having jurisdiction over the old consent decree of 1956, and the FCC. Finally, at the end of 1977, AT&T having exhausted all the dilatory means at its disposal, the judge proposed that the lengthy process of discovery begin. The trial would begin at last.

But, in the end, Judge Waddy was not to be the trial judge. He was stricken with cancer, and, by mid-1978, all his cases were assigned to his colleagues. His successor in *U.S. v. AT&T* was Judge Harold H. Greene, a name that was to become well known throughout the nation through this landmark case. Harold Greene had immigrated to the United States from Nazi Germany in the days just before the outbreak of the war. After serving in the army in Europe, he went to law school and, upon graduation, went to work for the Justice Department in the Civil Rights division. It was there that, with the full encouragement and support of Attorney General Robert Kennedy, he authored both the Civil Rights Act of 1964 and the Voting Rights Act of 1965. So high in Kennedy's esteem was Greene, had Greene, at his side when he made his only personal appearance before the Supreme Court to argue a civil rights case. Steve Coll, who wrote eloquently about these events, quoted Kennedy as saying "Harold was the guy who had all the answers," at the Justice Department's going-away party for him after Kennedy's successor as attorney general, Ramsey Clark, appointed Greene to the District of Columbia Court of General Sessions, Washington's municipal court system.[104] Greene was later appointed to the federal bench in 1978 replacing John Sirica, the steel-willed Watergate judge, after the Democrats returned to the White House.

The events that followed in the next two years make a fascinating chapter in legal history, but an issue such as this one cannot be simply a legal issue. As it turned out, both the executive branch and the Congress were active players in the saga that unfolded. One element of AT&T's strategy involved the Congress. It attempted to bypass the judicial proceedings by working for a bill that would validate in law the de facto situation. Initially this Bell Bill picked up a great deal of support, but the legislation languished as the many opposing interests made their voices heard. Ultimately, it was Greene's expeditious handling of the case that doomed all the efforts to solve the problem legislatively.

Judge Greene's approach was to impose severe deadlines on the attorneys on both sides. He later was prepared to relax these deadlines when necessary, but even when he did so, his tactics forced the trial to proceed at a much faster pace than would have otherwise occurred. His timetable called for the completion of the discovery process and the start of the trial by September 1980, a truly heroic schedule considering the fact that AT&T was required to furnish Justice with 2.5 million documents. In fact, it took just a little longer, and the trial was set to begin in January, 1981, just as the new Reagan administration was about to take office.

During this discovery period, there were off-and-on discussions between the Justice Department and AT&T regarding an agreement that would settle the suit out of court with a consent decree as happened with the previous suit. But whereas in the earlier case the government was all too willing to let the telephone company off the hook, the situation now was substantially different. The attorney general's office now insisted that some sort of divestiture had to be included in the settlement. Late in 1980, AT&T was becoming more inclined to accept such a solution, for several reasons. One of these occurred in June of that year when MCI won its civil antitrust suit and was awarded the enormous sum of $1.8 billion (later reduced on appeal). Another significant change was the retirement of deButts and his replacement by the more pragmatic and less doctrinaire Charlie Brown. The basics of the deal being worked out involved a divestiture of half of Western Electric and three of the operating companies. An advantage of such a partial divestiture was the possibility of obtaining a measure of the economic gain or loss accrued that might help answer the theological question of natural monopoly.

But this agreement was not to be. When Sandy Litvack, the lame-duck assistant attorney general in charge of the antitrust division, and AT&T's chief counsel requested the judge to delay the opening statements to permit the two parties to flesh out this proposed agreement, the judge refused. By the time such an agreement might be consummated, a new administration with unknown views on the whole matter might have completely different ideas that could delay or even stop the whole proceeding. Nevertheless, the litigants returned to Judge Greene a few days later with more detail on the proposed deal, enough to lead the judge to postpone the trial for a short while to allow the deal to be finalized. But the deal never materialized. The trial was to begin, but now with a new government protagonist.

The most important reason for the failure of the deal was its unacceptability to Litvack's successor, Professor William Baxter of Stanford, who had strong ideological thoughts about the case. Baxter was not a politician; he had not been at all active in Ronald Reagan's bid for the presidency. He was appointed because of his strongly held conservative ideas, which many assumed would lead him to reject an activist position on antitrust issues. This evaluation indeed held true in many instances, but *U.S. v. AT&T* was not one of them, because of his cherished legal/economic point of view that it was improper for a single company to be in both the regulated and competitive domains. Local telephone service was a monopoly that had to be regulated, but long-distance service was already competitive. Therefore, it was clear to him that the operating companies had to be divested. In contrast, he had no problem with AT&T's ownership of Western Electric. Therefore, in his view, Litvack's proposed agreement with AT&T went too far with respect to Western Electric, but not far enough with respect to the operating companies. These principles of Baxter were to form the basis of the consent decree that was ultimately agreed upon.

But it was not easy to reach that agreement. There were strong voices in the new administration that pressed that the whole suit be dropped. The loudest of these belonged to Commerce Secretary Malcolm Baldrige and Defense Secretary Caspar Weinberger. The Defense Department's view is easy to understand. Much of the communications on which our national command and control depends is commercial, at the time all supplied by AT&T from *end to end*. If the department needed a new circuit, all it needed to do was to call the AT&T representative and the circuit was expeditiously installed, often without an explicit charge; the cost just went into the rate base (the cost basis on which tariffs are determined), ultimately to be paid by everyone. If the local companies were divested, then the department would have to deal with two local companies as well as the long-distance company for every installed circuit.

Baldrige's actions were more ideological, based on the old dictum "if it ain't broke, don't fix it." He preferred a legislative solution that would preserve the integrity of the Bell system while, at the same time, allowing competition. It is interesting to note that Baxter's superiors in the Justice Department, the attorney general and his deputy, both had to refrain from taking part in the proceedings to avoid a conflict of interest due to previous dealings with AT&T. Therefore, in all the discussions and intrigue that was to follow, Baxter was the senior Justice Department official to take part. Through sheer intellect and motivation, this nonpolitician managed to outmaneuver the others. In the end, the White House refused to overrule Baxter and dismiss the case. It chose instead to continue to seek a legislative solution that Baxter knew would not work. Baxter was to have his way.

The government did a thorough and professional job in presenting its case. Before the defense began its presentation, it submitted a routine request for dismissal. Some weeks later, during the defense presentation, Judge Greene delivered a lengthy written reply denying this request with language indicating that he felt that the government had proved its case unless the defense could refute it. It was now apparent that AT&T would have a difficult time winning this case. They might still win on appeal, but the case would take years to settle, years in which Bell would be in a condition of suspended animation while the whole communications world was in ferment. This prospect together with the failure of the White House maneuvering and the unlikelihood of a satisfactory bill making its way through Congress prompted Charlie Brown to think the unthinkable: He would end the apparently endless years of litigation and accede to Baxter's conditions. AT&T would divest itself of all the local telephone companies, but not Western Electric. In return it wanted the right, denied it in the old 1956 consent decree, to compete in the computer business and thereby to become a full participant in the information age.

To accomplish these goals required an innovative legal approach. Since the old 1956 consent decree, the Final Judgment, kept AT&T out of the computer business, the new consent decree would be a modification of the old one that removed this restriction explicitly. Then the government would propose that the New Jersey judge having jurisdiction over the old decree transfer the case to Judge Greene. The government would officially dismiss the current suit and the new consent decree, the Modification to the Final Judgment, would replace it within Judge Greene's jurisdiction.

Baxter's staff drew up the new consent decree during the Christmas season of 1981, just before the first anniversary of the antitrust trial. The participants worked at a feverish pace to consummate the agreement, which was announced to a stunned public on January 9, 1982. Most of the planned legal actions involving two federal courts moved along on schedule. There was a potential snag in the proceedings caused by Judge

Greene's absence from Washington. Greene's acquiescence was essential because of a law known as the Tunney Act that empowered the courts to approve out-of-court antitrust settlements to protect the public interest. It was not absolutely clear as to the applicability of the Tunney Act in this case because technically speaking the case was a modification of an old one. Nevertheless neither the government nor AT&T wanted any trouble from Greene and recognized that some sort of Tunney procedure was inevitable.

There was little doubt that the judge would approve this Modification to the Final Judgment, or MFJ. Henck and Strassburg quote Greene as saying,

> I have no doubt about the correctness of deregulation. The basic fact of the phone industry is it grew up when it was a natural monopoly: wooden poles and copper wires. Once it became possible to bypass this network through microwaves, AT&T's monopoly could not survive. What the Bell system did was illegal. It abused its monopoly in local service to keep out competitors in other areas. Competition will give this country the most advanced, best, cheapest telephone network.[105]

What was so obvious to Judge Greene was not obvious at all to his colleague Judge Charles Richey who presided in the civil antitrust trial of Southern Pacific, the owner of Sprint, against AT&T, patterned after the suit that MCI had won in Chicago. Just a few months after the MFJ, this judge found for the defendant with the comment: "The FCC's introduction of competition in the long-distance market has been and will be shown to be contrary to the best interests of millions of Americans."[106]

But by the roll of the dice, Harold Greene and not Charles Richey presided at *U.S. v. AT&T*. The outcome was now a fait accompli. AT&T would divest itself of 75 percent of its assets and 60 to 70 percent of its employees.

The Congress that had labored in vain during the many years of the antitrust action was now in a flurry of activity to modify the legal proceedings by law. Of sudden concern to the lawmakers was the realization that the separation of long-distance from local service would mean an increase in local telephone rates along with the realization that they could be blamed for the decision by a rebellious electorate. All the unsuccessful efforts of the past decade had been orchestrated by AT&T and its friends to solve a seemingly intractable legal problem by legislation. Against them were MCI and other competing interests together with certain elements of the executive branch. Now that a deal was closed, AT&T and the Justice Department were both opposed to any new tampering with their efforts. True to form, Congress failed once again.

Under the terms of the MFJ, the divestiture was to take place on January 1, 1984. There was precious little time for AT&T to take apart what had been so carefully crafted over the years. Because time was so short, the company took the calculated risk of proceeding with the complex problem even before Judge Greene had completed his job of examining the agreement in accordance with the Tunney law. In the end, the judge approved the deal with only a few changes. The divestiture plan worked out by AT&T with the concurrence of the court grouped the twenty-two Bell operating companies into seven so-called regional Bell operating companies (RBOCs) of approximately equal size. The name *Bell* was to be the property of the local companies with the single exception that the Bell Laboratories, which remained with AT&T, could be called the AT&T Bell Laboratories. It was only logical, then, for the RBOCs to be referred to in the popular press as the Baby Bells. In addition to being limited by certain specific restrictions, these new companies would have to apply to the court for a waiver whenever they wanted to enter a new line of business. In this action, the federal court became a regulatory agency in competition with the FCC. Judge Greene (Czar Harold, as he came to be called) was the final arbiter on what was and what was not to be allowed.

The fateful day of January 1, 1984 came and went. The sky did not fall down, as the Chicken Littles of the communications world had predicted. The nation's telephone service still worked. But the average subscriber was confused. Instead of the all-powerful Telephone Company, he or she had to deal with a local operating company and a long-distance carrier. To add to the confusion, the telephone instruments themselves, which most subscribers continued to lease from the old AT&T, remained with the new AT&T. While it had to be this way because the sale of telephone instruments had become highly competitive, it was nonetheless confusing.

One of the most important and problematic parts of the divestiture was how the operating companies would provide equal access to all the long-distance carriers. All the competitors of AT&T had inferior access provisions at lower costs. With equal access, all the carriers including the new AT&T would receive interconnection service of the same quality. Every local company would permit its subscribers to select any long distance carrier they chose. Of course, AT&T's competitors would have to pay more than before for the superior service, which would cut into the price differential between AT&T and the others. The court specified a schedule by which this *dial 1-service* would be implemented throughout the country.

The Defense Department, which had fought the antitrust suit with all the power at its disposal, now had to live with a disagreeable outcome.

To cope with its new facts of life, President Reagan established a committee consisting of the CEOs of the major long-distance carriers as well as the principal manufacturers of telecommunications equipment to develop processes and procedures to assure that the national defense requirements of the government would be satisfied in the new multiple-vendor environment.

Peter Temin points out clearly that, while the technology of the microwave radio made competition possible, it was the political process that made competition successful.[107] The antitrust legislation at the beginning of the century was written to protect the public from monopolies, but was not specific about how to do it. There are two ways: Break up the monopolies and allow competition, or leave them in place and regulate them. For the first half of the century, it was public policy to regulate AT&T; for the latter half, public policy leaned the other way, favoring competition and breakup. The entire AT&T corporate culture established by Vail was geared to universal service by a regulated monopoly. DeButts's hardball game in the 1970s was a reflection of his inability to think beyond this culture.

But, as Temin further points out, it is naive to blame the sequence of events entirely upon AT&T's rigidity in a changing world. The regulators did their share as well. If the prices of AT&T's long distance links had been based on their true costs, then we might have seen whether MCI and others could have competed successfully against the monopoly. But the politically expedient cross-subsidization that existed invited cream skimming, and when AT&T attempted to respond with reduced rates on the competitive links, the FCC interfered. These attitudes on the part of the FCC precluded a test of the naturalness of the monopoly. And so the camel's nose kept protruding further and further into the tent until finally the whole animal was inside.

Was divestiture inevitable? I conjecture that there are those in the Justice Department and in AT&T who are still reliving those tumultuous days wondering whether it all would have happened if Charlie Brown had been the CEO in the early 1970s rather than John deButts, or if President Reagan's choice for the antitrust division had been someone other than Bill Baxter. Yet, even if the management of AT&T and the leadership of the FCC had been endowed with perfect vision and wisdom, I suspect that the result would have been similar. It would not have happened in exactly the same way or at the same time, but it would have happened anyway. The history of communications demonstrates that the impact of technology has always been too great to permit the provision of communications services to remain static.

But the story of the events leading up to divestiture does not end with the MFJ and its immediate aftermath. Nor will it end for many years to come. The years of turmoil and judicial strife that culminated in the MFJ did not end the question of monopoly versus competition. Rather, it narrowed the domain of the question to that part of the system that provides local service.

But to what extent is even local telephone service a natural monopoly, and, even if it is, to what extent should the local operating companies be permitted to engage in competitive, nonregulated activities? How to answer these questions became an issue even before the MFJ could be consummated and has become only more complex as the years have passed since then.

Chapter

28

The End of Monopoly?

The term *Baby Bells* was more than a useful bit of slang to describe the regulated remnants of the old Bell system. It also reflected the fact that each of the new companies was going to be subjected to the play of the same technological and market forces that forced the split-up of the parent company. The only difference was the fact that the domain was local rather than nationwide. The settlement agreed to in 1982 reflected the state of the communications world at that time. But who could say how long it would last in a world of rapidly changing technology?

Agree with the MFJ or not, no one could say that its basis was arbitrary. It conformed to Baxter's theories of the essential incompatibility of regulated and unregulated businesses under a single roof. The MFJ created a wall between the two types of activity. The new AT&T was in a competitive arena and no longer had to be regulated. In contrast, the Baby Bells provided monopoly services and required regulation.

The MFJ was approved by Judge Greene with remarkably few changes considering the opposition to the decree on the part of so many people. Part of the reason for this was the fact that complex issues such as this one have so many interests on opposite sides of almost every one of its many facets, that there is a tendency for the voices to cancel one another out. It was this diversity of opinion that prevented even powerful cabinet members from stopping Baxter, and made years of attempts by the Congress to rewrite the communications act come to naught. Still, it would have been unreasonable to expect that the MFJ could escape completely the political processes that often fuzz the edges of theoretically sound plans. The FCC, for example, had some influence on the course of events. Its actions, of course, were responsible for many of the events that led up to the MFJ. Yet it played no role in the legal action and was not very enthusiastic about the outcome. After the MFJ was approved, the FCC flexed its muscles a bit when it ruled that even though long-distance service was theoretically competitive, AT&T had such a large share of the market—in regulationese it was a *dominant* carrier—that it required continued regulation by the FCC to protect the public. Certainly, no one could deny that AT&T was dominant in 1984 when the consent decree took effect, but since then, it has been losing market share steadily. There will undoubtedly come a day in which the company will no longer be considered sufficiently dominant to require regulation, but ten years after divestiture it has still not reached that point.

This action on the part of the FCC was a small perturbation to the consent decree. It did not strike at the fundamental basis for the divestiture. Somewhat more threatening was an action of Judge Greene himself during the Tunney Act proceedings in which he, while concurring with certain prohibitions that the MFJ placed on the Baby Bells, declined to make them permanent, permitting the companies, instead, to appeal to the court for relief when they felt so justified. While this action reflected the judge's feelings that regulatory changes might be necessary in a world of rapidly changing technology, it placed the court in the unusual role of regulator, one of the reasons that the FCC was not entirely enthusiastic about the MFJ. These prohibitions were all designed to keep the new companies on the regulated monopoly side of the wall, when everyone knew that their business instincts would impel them to attempt to breech the wall. The conventional wisdom held that breeches in the other direction, that is, competition by others in the Baby Bells' activity of providing universal telephone service, were extremely unlikely. To be sure, it was recognized from the start that there was nothing to prevent the longdistance carriers from bringing their services directly to their customers without going through the local carrier, a process known as *bypass*. Such services would only be economical for the very largest business customers, but there was fear from the inception of the MFJ that if enough of this occurred, the bypassed local companies would have to raise their rates to their other customers. Concerned about the prospect, some congressmen supported a temporary ban on such bypass for a limited number of years. But this as well as many other proposals came to naught as the members of Congress were unable to pass a bill in the aftermath of the MFJ.

But bypass, while of some concern to all the parties to the MFJ, was not head-to-head competition to a major portion of the customer base of the local area companies and was, therefore, not a broad-based threat to the new monopolies. Nor was there anything else on the horizon—or so the traditional thinking went. Thus, it is quite understandable that in 1982 everyone assumed that while long distance communication had become competitive, the local telephone companies had been placed in much the same position as the electric power companies. Who could possibly duplicate their vast web of wires and switches to offer competitive telephone service? Each Baby Bell was a powerful monopoly that might well be in an advantageous position to compete against other information media or even the former parent company and its competitors, but, aside from the bypass question, there was little anyone else could do to interfere with them in their domain. Some states went so far as to make such competition illegal in recognition of this fact of life. And yet, the parties to the MFJ might have seen signs of change even in the early 1980s, indicators of the fact that even local telephone service would be subject to technology-driven market forces.

Of course, everyone knows that technology never remains static. And yet how hard it is for most of us so much of the time to interpret the significance of technological change. It is only human nature to assume that the future will be a simple extrapolation of the present. How else can we explain the failure of the American automobile industry to react to the competition of their Japanese counterparts until they faced a dwindling market share and huge losses? Or, especially, the slow reaction of IBM to the enormous changes in the computer market brought about by the microprocessor?

This reluctance to understand change was responsible for the incredulity with which the FCC and others greeted MCI's audacity in challenging AT&T in the 1960s and 1970s, defying the conventional wisdom of the natural monopoly. There were not many who really appreciated how the availability of microwave radios had changed the economic rules of the game. But now it was another decade. An obvious question to ask was whether the microwave radio could impact the local area as it had the long-distance market. What was clear was that if it were going to happen, it would have to be in a very different way, because the local telephone companies used cable in preference to microwave relay for solid technical reasons. Anyone who wanted to compete with the Baby Bells on their own turf would face the same technical and economic facts of life.

Of course, the microwave relay that AT&T introduced into its network after the war to replace cables was not the only way in which wireless can compete with wirelines. Indeed, ever since Marconi arrived on the scene, there has been a tug of war between wire and wireless techniques competing in different ways, with now the one and now the other gaining the upper hand. Recall that the two competed head to head for transoceanic telegraph services from the start. Then once wireless telephony became possible, it had the transoceanic market all to itself for decades until the first undersea telephone cables finally made their appearance. Then, only a few years later, the advantage returned to the wireless in the form of satellite relay. And, most ironic of all, the microwave relays that ultimately led to divestiture were themselves superseded on high-density routes by optical cables. These same optical fibers subsequently began competing with satellites on the transoceanic routes. And, of course, during this same time frame, the electrical cable was making ever greater inroads into the television business. To imagine that the microwave relay was the only way in which wireless could compete with wires was to ignore history.

The new competitive turf turned out to be mobile radio, in a form called the *personal communications system*. It uses a highly-portable radio powered by lightweight batteries enticing its user to carry it along wherever he or she may go. It is digital and can support data and fax as well as voice. But the thing that makes it truly unique and the feature that gives it its name is the fact that when you make a call it is to a person and not to a telephone. A subscriber to this service carries the same number with him wherever he or she goes, at home, in the office, or in transit.

Clearly PCS, as the name of the system is abbreviated, has a special market in which it serves a unique role, that of people on the go who do not want to be out of touch wherever they are. In this arena, its most natural competitors are the existing mobile systems such as the pager and cellular radio. But the most revolutionary thing about PCS is the fact that it has the potential to compete head-to-head with local wire-based telephone service by bypassing substantial portions of the old fixed-plant local systems just as cable TV bypasses over-the-air television. The fascinating thing about PCS is not that it occurred at all, but that its occurrence threatens to undermine Baxter's theoretical underpinning of the Modification to the Final Judgment barely ten years after the fact.

Of course, the PCS did not spring out of thin air in the 1990s. The seeds of modern mobile radio were being sown at the Bell Laboratories even before divestiture in the form of cellular radio. Mobile telephone systems had long been used by special groups such as taxis and police, but they were a relative rarity elsewhere. Then the cellular concept added a new wrinkle that both improved the quality and, most important, allowed many more subscribers to be served. Within a few years, cellular was to gain such enormous popularity, that its price began to fall to the point where almost anyone who wanted one, even as a status symbol, could afford a cellular phone in his or her automobile.

Cellular systems depend heavily on computers for their operation. Their performance is much superior to that of the older mobile radio systems because they communicate over short distances to a fixed hub in the center of a small geographic area or *cell* where the problems with interference of all kinds are bound to be much less severe. The hub station switches the call to the hub of another cell if the call is to another automobile or to the local telephone plant if to a standard phone. As a mobile user travels from one cell to another, the computers handle the transition from one hub to the next smoothly. This superior performance is what contributes to the competition potential between an essentially mobile system and a traditional fixed one.

If one could communicate from one's car, why not while walking down the street? And if a radio system worked under those circumstances, would it not also work from your home or business and thereby be in a position to compete with the standard fixed telephone system? Might this not be a way in which a long-distance carrier and a mobile carrier could mount a joint venture to bypass the local telephone carrier not only for large companies but for everyone? Cellular, as we know it, is not in the best position to threaten the existing local telephone companies, because the cells are large enough in size to require more battery power than one would like for a truly portable system.

But improved portability is just where personal communications systems enter the picture. ARPA had introduced the notion in the early 1980s in the military context. Commercial efforts had their origins in Britain in 1989 in the attempt to develop an advanced cordless telephone that would permit subscribers to wander downtown from their homes and still remain in touch. The FCC, impressed by the British accomplishments, expressed the willingness to provide frequency spectrum for innovative mobile radio systems, and the PCS concept was the result. One motivation was surely the desire to introduce competition into mobile radio. The FCC had long felt that the prices of cellular service were higher than they should be, the result of the fact that only enough frequency spectrum was allocated for two competing systems in each location. To this end, late in 1993, the FCC allocated a substantial amount of microwave frequency spectrum for PCS services.

The PCS radio is more portable than is the cellular, because, for one reason, it operates in cells considerably smaller than those used in conventional cellular. These smaller cells assure that the user will always be near the cell's hub and thereby assure high-quality connectivity in all locations with very low-power highly portable equipment. Unlike conventional cellular, personal communication systems are digital, with all the quality and flexibility that the term implies. Thus, the PCS radio accepts fax and keyboard inputs as well as voice without the need for conventional modems—in short, any kind of input device that converts information into digital form. But with all these desirable properties, PCS becomes more than a superior mobile system. It has the potential to provide a wholly new competitive environment for local service.

First and most obvious, it introduces additional competition into the mobile market. It appears that the Baby Bells, which are heavily invested in the cellular market, will not be allowed into the PCS band. It is very unlikely that this exclusion will mean competition between the Bells using older technology with newcomers using new technology, since there will be nothing to stop the Bells or anyone else operating cellular radio systems to upgrade their technology, say, to digital, and to use their computers to change the character of the service from telephone-to-telephone to person-to-person. A likely result is the one hoped for by the FCC of widening the mobile market to the benefit of the consumer.

But that is only the most obvious of outcomes. If the PCS concept proves to be successful and popular in the marketplace, then it has the potential to introduce real competition into the local service area. There are even proposed versions in which satellites relay the digits over long distances bypassing not only the local telephone companies but the long-distance companies as well.

Congress, at the urging of the FCC, introduced the auction as a novel way of allocating spectrum for PCS services, and potential wireless entrepreneurs have paid enormous sums of money for the ability to compete in this domain. Despite this concrete expression of faith, the history of communications should make anyone wary of predicting how successful PCS will ultimately be in the marketplace or whether it will constitute meaningful competition to the old fixed telephone services. Yet its existence and potential demonstrate that the notion of a natural monopoly even in a restricted sense is an endangered species.

Chapter

29

Blurring Traditional Lines

In the roaring days of the Reagan administration, it was not unusual to see news headlines featuring mergers, takeovers, and leveraged buyouts throughout industry. By the late 1980s, as economic recession took hold and then receded ever so slowly, these ventures mostly died out—except for the communications industry. In the 1990s the business headlines featured continued mergers and acquisitions involving communications companies, cellular companies, and cable television and other entertainment interests. Prominent among these deals was one involving AT&T. But most prominent of all were those where the communications company was one of the Baby Bells and the proposed partner was a large cable television company with connections to the motion picture industry.

Deals such as these that defied the spirit, if not the letter, of the Modification to the Final Judgment would not have been possible a decade earlier. After all, the Baby Bells were to be established as regulated monopolies, barred from competitive unregulated activities. For this reason, the consent decree as approved by Judge Greene built in certain safeguards to prevent them from getting into competitive business areas that might be in conflict with their monopoly business. Among these were three specific restrictions: the companies could not furnish information services; they could not provide long-distance services beyond their own boundaries in competition with AT&T and the other long-distance companies; and they could not engage in manufacturing to prevent a potential Western Electric problem from developing.

Judge Greene was more flexible than Bill Baxter and, as we have already noted, established a mechanism within his court by which the

Baby Bells could appeal specific restrictions. Particularly annoying was the ban on information services. The information age was upon us, and the distinction between simple transport services and enhanced services of various kinds was becoming increasingly more difficult to sustain as time went on. The telephone companies, chafing under their inhibitions, took advantage of this appeal mechanism by petitioning the court for relief whenever the opportunity presented itself. The judge continued to resist in most instances until finally, in 1992, an appellate court reversed him on the information services prohibition.

The reaction to this decision was strong and immediate. Fearing the presence of powerful new competitors in this lucrative field, virtually all the other communications interests led by the newspapers sprang to the attack. Full page advertisements began appearing in the newspapers attacking the decision and the Baby Bells. And then the predictable happened: The newspapers and their allies attempted to undo the court's decision with legislation. Using their influence in Congress, they precipitated an effort in the House Judiciary Committee to make the information services prohibition a matter of law rather than a judge's ruling. Hearings were held in a flurry of publicity, but, as had happened so often in the past, no bill ever emerged from the committee. Once again, the pressure from so many competing constituencies made action impossible.

This reaction by the newspapers was a virtual replay of a powerful lobbying effort in 1982 when the Congress attempted, in vain, to undo the efforts of Baxter and Brown. At that time, there was no question of the Baby Bells participating in delivering information services, but a competitive AT&T was a threat. Fearing this, the ill-fated legislation would have banned AT&T from providing such services for a period of seven years. The reason for such aggressive lobbying by the newspapers was the fear that their advertising revenues could be significantly reduced if AT&T were to offer electronic versions of its yellow-page advertising. To be sure, the information is an electronic version of information already provided in paper form. But since the Yellow Pages are published annually, they pose little threat to the advertising revenue of the print dailies. However, information in electronic form can change more rapidly than daily, in fact, on a moment's notice, and this capability is what appeared to threaten the lifeblood of the newspaper industry. Judge Greene was persuaded to include this seven-year ban against AT&T. At the same time, he gave the Baby Bells the authority to publish the Yellow Pages, reversing the provisions of the agreement between Baxter and Brown that allowed the restructured AT&T to retain them.

While it was the newspapers who were reading the technological tea leaves with alarm, they were not to be the major players in the competition that was to come. In pressuring first the courts and later the Congress, the newspapers were joined by most of the other information industries who viewed the Baby Bells as a threat, but since the newspapers had the most to lose in the short run, they overshadowed all the other participants. Yet, anyone thinking about the longer term implications of the telephone system furnishing information services might have predicted that, eventually, the most formidable competition to the Baby Bells would come from the cable TV industry, which, after all, was in the business of delivering electronic information services of a particular kind to the public. There were other similarities, as well. They cover almost the same geographical turf, and they run wires from telephone pole to telephone pole or underground on this same turf. But the same thing can be said about the power companies. The conventional wisdom in the early 1980s was that there was about as much chance of a telephone company competing with a cable company, or vice versa, as there was of its competing with a power company.

Cable was not even much of a factor in television broadcasting in the early 1980s. This was perhaps why there was so little opposition when the regulation originally imposed upon the industry was removed in the deregulation fervor that began in the Carter administration and continued under President Reagan, this despite the fact that most areas could claim only a single cable company. But this situation was to change rapidly within only a few years as cable programming was greatly expanded. The cable industry grew in size and influence, and, in many cases, in arrogance fostered by unrestrained monopoly. Finally, when steadily increasing prices and indifferent service had precipitated an escalating level of complaints from subscribers, the Congress reacted by restoring the regulation in an uncommon burst of bipartisan unanimity that permitted them to override a presidential veto in the waning days of the Bush administration.

But even if cable had been widespread at the time of the MFJ, it would never have occurred to very many people that the telephone and television industries might be future competitors. A few technical planners might predict that future technology advances would allow the cables to become two-way or the telephone system to carry video, but to most people at that time this was an unlikely possibility. It would have taken very radical thinking in the early 1980s to suppose that the cleavage between broadcasting and point-to-point communication that occurred when AT&T left broadcasting sixty years earlier would close in the foreseeable future.

It is not that telephone and cable companies never had anything to do with one another. Almost from the inception of cable service in the late 1940s, petty feuding had developed between local cable and telephone companies forcing the FCC to bar the telephone companies from owning cable companies *in their own areas*, except by a special waiver procedure. The Congress confirmed this restriction shortly after the breakup of the Bell system, an action taken largely under pressure to liberalize the waiver process. But, at the same time, they chose not to undo the prohibition to prevent the stifling of competition within the area of local communications.

To most people the cleavage between telephone and television was and still is cultural, not technical. Broadcasting and telephony occupy different functions in our lives. The business of television is dissemination of news and entertainment to the masses. It is one-way and autocratic, from the few to the many. The broadcasters choose their material guided by their perception of the tastes of their audience and the objectives of their advertisers. Feedback from the audience is, at best, indirect, expressed largely by their choice of programming as indicated by the ratings, making the broadcasters responsive over the long run to the desires of their viewers. Should the broadcast audience wish to directly express an opinion about what it has viewed, it has to resort to other media—the telephone, telex, fax, or mail—to do so. People readily express their opinions when given the opportunity on call-in shows. But the audience response to the general range of programming is indirect, manifested only through its program choices. We may grumble about it, but most of us take what the broadcasters give us, like it or not.

If the one-way broadcasting systems can be called autocratic, then the two-way telephone system is the very essence of democracy. It is the vehicle for distributing information from one person to another. According to the principles of universality established by Bell and Theodore Vail, all network subscribers are inherently equal. The telephone system does not know the status in life of its users. Each participant in a conversation has the same opportunity to talk and listen, to interrupt or respond. If one party dominates a conversation, it is by force of personality and articulateness, not the network's doing.

The cultural differences between *democratic* and *autocratic* communication mask their technical similarity. Both newspapers and mail share the property of being print media delivered to your door using some form of transportation. Yet newspapers are autocratic, while mail may be either democratic or autocratic. Similarly, when seated in your car, you may receive autocratic communication via the conventional broadcast radio and participate in democratic communication with your cellular radio telephone. And both telephone and cable television services come into our homes by wires usually strung on the same telephone poles. But since the uses of the telephone and the television are so different, we place the two into different compartments in the way we think of them: The one is a mass medium available to all; the other is the vehicle for obtaining personal information. They exist, ostensibly, in two different worlds.

History is filled with examples of competition within either the democratic or autocratic category. Did not the early telephone compete with the telegraph, and the radio telegraph with its wireline predecessor? Similarly, the radio and television competed with first, the stage, then the movies, newspapers, and magazines. But the rules of engagement change when a two-way democratic system begins to compete with a one-way autocratic system. A democratic system distributing autocratic information blurs traditional boundaries. Some of the intensity of the fight between the newspapers and telephone companies had to have been due to the fear of the unknown.

For a while, the contentious issue of electronic advertising that stimulated this fight obscured the more important fact that the advance of technology was making it possible for telephone and cable TV networks to compete head to head. The protest, as phrased by the newspapers, was directed at the telephone companies as the *providers* of the information, not as the *carriers* of the information: The ability of a telephone company to use its network to interconnect any one subscriber to any other regardless of the nature of the information to be exchanged is incontestable. Interconnection has been the traditional role of telephone companies ever since Bell conceived the notion of universal service. This was the way in which AT&T thought of the *toll broadcasting* that it introduced in the early days of radio broadcasting as a way of supporting its network. Even after the telephone company retreated from its position in broadcasting, it maintained its exclusive role of providing the long-distance transport that made network radio possible. Then, when television came along, the telephone network played this same role to the extent that it could. There was never a question about the legitimacy of this kind of traffic within the telephone network. Consistent with this, the Baby Bells have always been free to provide the networks that *distribute* cable TV services in their areas, even though they were banned from *owning* the cable companies.

It was the computer that began to perturb this neatly compartmented world. It started innocently enough. When computers required communication among themselves—from the specialized networks that serve SABRE and similar communities, to the ARPANET, to the thousands of data networks that now constitute the Internet—it was the telephone companies here and abroad that provided the necessary connections. But there is a difference when the subscriber is a computer rather than an individual. A computer is much more likely to have information of interest to *many* others than is an individual telephone subscriber. The research networks that formed the initial core of the Internet contain various kinds of information available to anyone with a connection into this vast network of networks. Other networks are geared to subscribers of less computer sophistication than the research networks. For example, groups of libraries in some metropolitan areas have computerized their catalogues and made them available to subscribers through their own private computer networks. Anyone with a home computer can dial in to such a network to find which libraries have which titles and whether a title in a library's possession is on the shelves or checked out. Of course, a subscriber of any network connected to the Internet, can, with the proper permissions, obtain access to anything on any of the networks, although sometimes this is easier said than done for unsophisticated computer users. To fill this void, a new kind of information company— Prodigy, CompuServe, and America Online are well-known examples— has come into existence, one that integrates a large variety of databases and makes them available to subscribers in a very accessible way. This application of the computer is, therefore, converting the telephone networks into carriers of public information that has traditionally been delivered by the autocratic media.

It is not that using the telephone system to dispense information from a public source to anyone who wishes it is entirely new. There are a few areas in which the telephone has been used in that way for a long time. Obtaining weather information is a good example. A local call will give you a recording of the local weather forecast updated every hour. You can obtain the same for any location in the country at the cost of a long-distance call to the appropriate area. It is more current, if less detailed, than the weather report printed in the daily newspaper. Similarly, you can obtain stock quotes by telephone, subject again to the limitation of using the voice medium to convey the information and making only limited use of the feedback inherent in the two-way network.

But information services of this kind are primitive compared to those that can be delivered when there are computers at both ends of the line. Using this technology, the information-services companies are able to provide a large variety of offerings—news, financial data, weather reports, airline schedules, movie reviews, and advertising of all kinds of merchandise are a few of them—in competition with the autocratic media. These information companies charge their subscribers as do the cable TV companies, a fixed monthly fee of a few dollars for a set of basic services with others available at extra cost. A local phone call provides the connection. All the information is displayed on the computer monitor and the subscriber has the option of printing out anything or everything.

The most obvious of the advantages of obtaining information in this way—one shared with the older telephone information services—is the ability of the subscriber to obtain the information at the time of his or her choosing, not the vendor's. The subscriber sits at the computer and requests whatever information he or she wants almost at the spur of the moment. If the requested information is news, then the latest headlines are displayed and the subscriber can pursue the stories behind the headlines in whatever detail the vendor chooses to offer. Or else a few keystrokes will bring up specialized news topics such as investments, the arts, sports, weather or almost anything else. The format is analogous to that of a newspaper in which the headlines and lead stories are on the front page with a table of contents leading the reader to the more specialized information in the back pages.

It is also similar to a newspaper in that the presentation is in the form of text, charts, and cartoons —photographs would take too long to transmit. In fact, with the ability to print out selected items, the subscriber can create a customized newspaper. The service differs from the newspaper in that it tends to short articles rather than the more comprehensive stories that newspapers often print. Computer information sources could provide more in-depth stories if there were sufficient demand, although their ability to do much of this is limited by the transmission time. Thus it bears some resemblance to television news in its concentration on headlines rather than on long stories.

Radio and television attempt timeliness in news delivery in different ways. Of course, when important events occur, they interrupt their regular programming to bring their listeners and viewers flash reports, but most news does not merit this special attention. As television took over the bulk of the entertainment market, radio station owners began to seek specialized market niches, and one of the more common of these is the all-news station. While you cannot get your news on demand, the lead stories are broadcast often enough to provide what most people want with a minimal delay. Of course this frequency just applies to the headlines. The second-level stories have to be broadcast less often.

Ordinary over-the-air television does not have the luxury of being able to provide the video equivalent of the all-news radio station. Only cable television has sufficient capacity to do this: many dozens of channels as compared to ten at most. This capacity gives the cable vendor the flexibility to carry a wide variety of programming appealing to many tastes in addition to the standard network and local programming carried by the local TV stations. Some of these additional channels emulate the standard channel programming featuring reruns of old network programs and old movies. Some feature other entertainment material in the same spirit often at additional cost; Home Box Office and

Showtime being examples of this. Some are what is called *narrowcasting*: programming that caters to more specialized tastes, such as religious programs, courtroom trials, congressional hearings, foreign language programs, rock videos, and many others, all largely in the entertainment category with some bordering on the informational. Still other channels are devoted to programming more readily classifiable as informational as opposed to entertainment. By far the most prominent of these channels is CNN, the Cable News Network, that has achieved a high measure of prominence and respect during the few years of its existence. Other information channels specialize in weather, financial news, and shopping.

It is these information channels that parallel, in some degree, the products of the computer-based information companies. Like the radio stations, these specialized channels broadcast their information continuously and regularly. To compensate for their inability to provide information on demand, the cable information channels broadcast their information sufficiently often so that no subscriber has to wait very long for the information. Rather than selecting information from a menu, the cable subscriber makes a selection among different kinds of information by changing channels. While this mode of operation is reasonably convenient as far as it goes, the fact that the information has to be broadcast continuously rather than on demand severely limits the amount and variety of the information that can be presented in this way. Even the many cable channels soon run out of space for the less popular forms of information. A well-designed menu organized around the two-way nature of the telephone network can lead the subscriber of a computer information system to huge varieties and stores of information that are well beyond the capability of even the largest cable TV system.

Some forms of information demand a response. The cable TV shopping channel provides high-quality video representations of its wares, but to make the purchase, the subscriber has to go to the telephone and complete the purchase manually just as if he or she were responding to a newspaper advertisement or a catalog. The two-way telephone network allows the computer service company to complete a transaction with far greater convenience. All the subscriber needs to do is select the desired item, indicate that he or she wants to purchase the item, and the sale is completed using a previously stored credit card number.

Shopping is only one of the information commodities that benefits from this aspect of two-way service. The newspaper provides the stock market quotations of the previous day, and the financial channel broadcasts this information during the course of the day, but the computer service company provides quotations of any desired stock on demand

and, in addition, allows the subscriber to buy or sell on line. In similar fashion, the subscriber has access to an airline reservation system—EAASY SABRE, a scaled-down version of SABRE, is one of these—from which he or she can, if desired, make airline, hotel, and rental-car reservations on line, charging them to a credit card.

Television information compensates, in part, for its limitations in the information arena by using the video form in the most appealing of ways. Indeed, because of this, everything on television regardless of its purpose has an entertainment component that the other competing media cannot match. Television coverage gives glamor to news events that appear to be routine when reported in newspapers or via electronic information services. The fact that television shopping services have been so successful is a tribute to the attractive and realistic way in which merchandise is presented. As powerful as the video medium may be for the dissemination of information about the news or anything else, its principal strength lies in its ability to entertain.

Thus, when television first made its appearance on the scene, the established industry with the most to lose was the motion picture industry. As popular as the radio drama was, it never threatened the motion picture as the dominant way in which people were entertained by drama. The television drama was much more serious competition. I have already noted how at first the motion picture industry was devastated by the newcomer and how in time the two joined forces, with Hollywood becoming the principal provider of television drama. Then along came the videocassette recorder in the late 1970s and with it the video store to introduce competition at still another level for both the motion picture and network television. No matter how many channels of entertainment on the cable show dozens of movies in a given week, it is not quite the same as seeing the movie of your choice precisely when you want to see it, not when the cable channel wants to show it to you. The video store has thrived because enough people have developed the habit of turning their living rooms into movie theaters with a self-chosen schedule.

Now imagine a computer service company that, in addition to providing financial market reports, news, and weather, offers a complete schedule of movies as well. Or, alternatively, imagine a cable TV system that can transmit in both directions, allowing it to do the same thing. In either case, all you have to do is select the movie of your choice from a menu, and the movie is transmitted to your home on your schedule. It is the closest thing imaginable to instant gratification.

This capability is no different, in principle, from any other information service. But it cannot be provided very easily on telephone networks in which an enormous digital capacity is divided into narrowband analog circuits that are geared to the provision of voice service, but are hardly adequate for video. Nor is it within the capability of the one-way cable networks. But what is to stop the local telephone companies from increasing the capacity of their subscriber connections, say by replacing some of their existing wires with optical cable? Similarly, the cable companies could modify their networks both to increase their already substantial capacity and to provide some two-way capability. If both industries undertake these upgrades, then we would enjoy the benefits of two wire networks interconnecting homes and businesses competing to provide a whole spectrum of exciting new services.

The battle lines are being drawn for this potential competition between the telephone and cable companies. And it is this fact more than any other that creates excitement and/or dismay when one of the Baby Bells announces plans to merge with a cable vendor. On the face of it, this kind of alliance is quite logical: Massive upgrades to communications plants are expensive. So if a telephone company is allowed to own a cable company in its area, would it not make eminent sense to use the same upgraded network for all services? Besides, combining forces in this way might expedite the upgrade process. Of course, there is the potential problem that such an arrangement reduces competition. Even here, a little thought should convince one that whether or not there are competing distribution systems is not the important question. Much more significant is the question of what services will come over the wires and which vendors will provide them.

This is not simply a case of two distribution systems becoming more alike. It is, rather, a merging between an autocratic system and a democratic system and a change in the way we think about them. The owner of a traditional autocratic system is in the business of providing programming; the distribution system is almost incidental. In contrast, the owner of a democratic system is in the business of providing connectivity. When one company owns both, it is apt to become schizophrenic about its role. On the one hand, as the provider of a democratic network, it is a common carrier that is bound to make its facilities available to anyone who is willing to pay to use them. On the other hand, it is an information supplier in competition with those to whom it is providing common carriage.

This duality represents a very profound change that gives the question of monopoly, natural or otherwise, an entirely different cast. The AT&T divestiture had to do with distribution. The 1982 Consent Decree made the assumption that local telephone companies constituted distribution monopolies in local areas as the residuum of the old AT&T monopoly. Questions of wireless competition aside, even in this transformed world, a single network may still be the most efficient way of providing the delivery network, that is, the natural monopoly assumption may still be valid. In this regard, I conjecture that a single optical network in a local area has more than enough capacity to carry as much information and entertainment as any individual subscriber could desire.

But capacity is really beside the point if the competitive battlefield is in providing services rather than distributing them. Even within the category of traditional broadcasting, we have seen a slow but steady increase in competition. The free-for-all in the earliest days of radio soon gave way to the NBC monopoly. Then after CBS became a competitor and NBC was forced to spin off ABC, the industry settled down as a three-headed oligopoly. In the 1960s, the Public Broadcasting System joined the competition after the commercial networks limited their news reporting on controversial subjects so as not to offend advertisers. The rise of cable opened up this process still more. No longer are programmers required to own or franchise their radio or TV stations. They can, in principle, make arrangements with cable companies to carry their programming. This added diversity has diminished the influence of the major networks still more. It is hard to imagine the news restrictions of the 1960s with the kind and variety of news and public affairs coverage that cable TV gives us today. But even the current level of competition is as nothing when compared to the potential varieties that can be available when the distribution network is a common carrier with the capacity to serve any source of programming. In the extreme, the vast commercial network can become, like the Internet, a veritable marketplace of information.

The fact that this common carrier network is two-way is bound to affect the nature of home entertainment in fundamental ways. To be sure, there will always be a market for conventional broadcasting as we have known it for decades. But the ability to obtain feedback from the audience will almost surely lead to alternatives beyond the obvious ones of allowing subscribers to select the movie of their choice from a menu or to play video games with remote partners. Such alternatives will change the way we live and work in profound ways, some obvious, but others essentially as unpredictable as those brought about when wireless telegraphy evolved to radio broadcasting three quarters of a century ago.

Thus the mergers that might take place involving Baby Bells, cable companies, and Hollywood interests in the near or more distant future are eyebrow raisers because the resulting companies can be so large that they can inhibit the free access of potential program suppliers to the new networks. Attempting to dominate is certainly consistent with the history of both the communications and entertainment industries. To control such domination, some have advocated the complete separation of the networks and the information sources through the creation of regulated information distribution utilities that would provide the networks only, connecting to all program suppliers impartially. This treatment of the network providers as pure common carriers is certainly consistent with the history of the telephone industry but hardly of the television industry. I suspect that Bill Baxter would be delighted at such a prospect, but hardly the Baby Bells and the existing cable companies.

What will the situation be like as we enter the next century? It could be highly competitive with a combination of telephone companies, cable companies, and wireless companies vying for our information dollars for both local and long-distance services. Then again, the tendency to mergers could leave us with monopolies or oligopolies of one form or another. Whatever happens, the regulatory mechanism will need modification. Under the old Communications Act of 1934, telephone companies, cable companies, and broadcasters are all separate entities providing different services under different rules. Now technology is causing the services to merge whether or not the companies that provide them remain distinct or not. There appears to be general agreement that this changing technical environment demands a changed regulatory environment, but less agreement on what it should be. In one way it is reminiscent of the flurry of congressional activity in the 1970s and 1980s before and after the divestiture decision. Now as then the competing interests are struggling to place their own industries in the best competitive position for the future. But now there is no all-consuming issue comparable to the AT&T breakup dominating the discussion, which is all to the good.

To regulate or not is only one of the legal questions introduced by the merging technologies. Another one relates to the question of copyright protection. Until the electronic age hit us, it was easy for a composer to protect his or her work. The emergence of the tape recorder made it a little more difficult since now a single record could be copied and distributed in violation of the copyright laws. The emergence of the digital tape recorder exacerbated this problem. With this technology compact discs could be copied simply by transferring the digits from one medium to another with absolutely no degradation of quality. Digital technology made it so much more tempting to evade the copyright laws that a war between equipment manufacturers and record companies kept the digital tape recorders off the market until Congress found a way to modify the copyright laws to the satisfaction of all the parties. But now in a world in which so much information, entertainment, and other, is on the threshold of being supplied on line in digital form, how can this protection be extended? It would be a pity if the information explosion that seems to be in the offing is dampened by a problem such as this.

It would be surprising if the video, which is responsible for so much of the information transformation that is taking place, is not itself transformed in the process. In fact, the nature of the picture that we watch on our screens has been very slow to change. Aside from the color that was added in the 1950s, it is no different from the original introduced in the 1930s. Some of the changes that will come about will not make the picture in your home look any different, but are necessary adjuncts to all the systemic changes that are underway. But other changes will yield pictures of almost unbelievable quality, an achievement that constitutes another revolution in its own right.

Chapter

30

The Video Scene

The conventional wisdom about the ability of telephone companies to carry video was shattered in 1992 with the announcement, widely reported in the press, that certain of the Baby Bells would begin transmitting video on demand over their existing wires on an experimental basis. So as not to be outdone, the cable companies were announcing, at about the same time, that they would soon be carrying as many as 500 channels of video on their existing cables.

As seemingly remarkable as the cable companies' achievement of packing five channels in the space of one, the phone companies' announcement seemed like sheer magic. How could a narrowband circuit that can support only moderate-quality voice service possibly carry video? One of the answers to this question is that telephone lines are not always as constraining as would appear. Removing the old loading coils, introduced nearly 100 years ago to increase telephone range, and keeping the lines from the home to the central office short, say no longer than a mile or so, gives the telephone line a fighting chance. Then another technology called *bandwidth compression* enters the picture to do the job for both the telephone line and the TV cable.[108]

What bandwidth compression does is to squeeze some of the inherent redundancy out of audio or video signals so that less bandwidth is required to transmit them. This is a potentially dangerous thing to do, because most processes that compress a television signal remove information from the signal, and the quality of the picture is thus bound to be degraded. The trick is to find compression schemes that remove information to which the eye is not particularly sensitive. A good example of this approach goes back as far as 100 years ago when the motion picture pioneers observed that they could obtain the illusion of continuous motion with as few as fifty frames per second because of the phenomenon of persistence of vision. And since there is much that is not known about visual perception, research and development in compression includes psychology and art and, perhaps, a bit of intuition along with technology.

No one can deny that the results of this work have been impressive. The only question is how long the modest increases in the capacity of the existing copper wires and cables brought about by compression will satisfy our appetites for video. As long as it does, the enormous expense of converting these wires to optical fibers can be deferred.

But there is still another wrinkle to this problem that has maintained the pressure for creating a higher capacity network without diminishing the importance of compression: *high definition television*, or HDTV, for short. Many in the industry have felt, for a long time, that today's television will be replaced eventually by a higher quality standard, one commensurate with the improved definition of motion pictures. Of course, higher bandwidth requirements go along with the higher definition. This is a problem that cannot be solved solely by installing optical cable since any new standard must be suitable for through-the-air broadcasting with its highly constrained bandwidth as well as cable, placing a still greater reliance on compression technology.[109]

The Japanese have led the way in the development of HDTV technology. Since 1989 they have been broadcasting an experimental HDTV channel of such high quality that it has impressed virtually everyone who has seen it. The quality follows from the fact that the video picture has some six to eight times as many equivalent picture elements as the conventional broadcast television pictures. This spectacular accomplishment led many to the belief that the time for a new era in home entertainment had arrived, and, even more significantly, it has convinced many Americans that heroic efforts are needed to restore its entertainment industry manufacturing capability to allow this country to compete with the Japanese and perhaps with the Europeans for a share of this prospective business opportunity.[110]

The Japanese system is very expensive, but that doesn't mean that the inherent cost of HDTV will be beyond the means of most consumers. Rather, its cost will be determined largely by whether video consumers are as willing to pay some kind of a premium for a higher quality picture as were audio consumers when the compact disc hit the market. We have only to recall that the price of compact disc players dropped dramatically when large numbers of people began to become captivated by this new technology. Similarly, it is reasonable to suppose that the price of the HDTV receivers will decrease in the same way once brought out into the

American market, provided that the average viewer becomes similarly entranced by the higher quality television picture.

The quality that we perceive in any picture depends not only on its inherent resolution but also on how much it is magnified. For example, motion pictures use 35 mm and often 70 mm film to give them the very high resolution that permits us to enjoy them on enormous screens even when we sit near the front of the theater where the apparent magnification is the greatest. The resolution of standard television is much poorer, comparable to that of the 16 mm film that was once standard for home movies, but far better than the 8 mm that was the home standard when the TV format was first adopted. But this reduced definition as compared to the movies is less significant than one might think as long as most of us are content to watch television programs on small screens—the typical home TV set uses a screen twelve inches in height, called a 20-inch screen after the length of its diagonal. We typically sit some six to twelve feet from the screen, a comfortable distance in our living or family rooms. A viewer would have to sit closer than six feet from a screen of this size to notice any granularity in the TV picture.

Recorded video places even less of a demand on the TV set than does broadcast video, because the definition standard for the VHS video recording is somewhat lower than the broadcast standard. BETA, the former competitor of VHS, had somewhat greater definition and the optical laserdiscs have even better quality, almost up to the standard of broadcast video as received on cable or a high-quality home antenna. Thus, when you watch a movie from a videotape cassette on a small screen, you might observe the granularity in the picture at distances greater than the customary six feet.

The single factor that makes the current standard potentially unsatisfactory is the advent of the large screen display. As long as the viewing public is content with relatively small screens, the broadcast television granularity standard is as adequate today as it was in the early days of television when much larger screens were not technically feasible for home viewers. But the technology of large screen displays has advanced over the intervening years, and it is these larger screens that show up the limitations of the present standard. For example, the picture on a three-foot-high screen would begin to look granular to a viewer sitting within eighteen feet of the picture, three times farther than when a one-foot-high screen is used. And as the screen gets larger, the problem increases proportionally. A four-foot-high screen, not unusual for projecting home movies, would send the viewer back twenty-four feet, perhaps out of the room, to avoid the granularity. These facts of life constitute a fundamental limitation on the quality of today's large-screen systems. Some viewers might not be bothered at all by a coarser picture, but some might. An improvement in definition by two to three times in both the horizontal and vertical dimensions could bring the quality of these large screen displays up to that of the motion picture theater at a reasonable viewing distance. On the other hand, viewers who continued to use small screens would hardly notice the difference.

The shape of the screen is also important. Today's TV screens are wider than they are high by the ratio of four to three. This ratio was chosen in the early days of television broadcasting following the lead of the motion pictures of the World War II era. Later the cinematographers began to experiment with ways of creating the illusion of a three-dimensional image without resorting to the cumbersome stereoscopic technique in which two images are projected and the viewers are forced to wear polarized glasses to restrict each eye to see only one of the images. They found that a wide screen gave a viewer seated front and center something of the experience of being inside a three-dimensional image. So, when you miss a new film in theaters and wait for the video release a few months later, you may suffer much more than the delay. Especially for films in which broad expanses of scenery are an important part of the action, the viewing sensation is far different in the theater from what it is on the home screen.

Indeed, much of today's activity in HDTV has the goal of reducing this difference to make the sensation of home viewing more like that of the theater. It means developing large display screens that are economical enough for the mass market. Then it requires the higher definition format needed for the larger screens—preferably direct view but possibly projection—along with a higher ratio of width to height than currently used. While this larger ratio (16/9, or 1.78, vs. 4/3) is still a bit less than that used in the movies (1.85 or 2.25), it is large enough to capture some of the wide-screen effects.

Meeting all these requirements is a tall technical order. Television engineers have been working on different aspects of the problem for many years and will continue to do so even after the first designs are converted into commercial products. Building economical large-screen systems is not a simple problem. Even trickier was the problem of finding a standard for broadcasting the high-definition signal to meet an apparently inconsistent set of demands.

One of these demands goes by the name of *compatibility*. The market is now saturated with television sets meeting the current standards—in 1989 there were 605 million sets in the world, close to 30 percent of them in the United States. If a station begins broadcasting its programs in the high-definition format, what will be the affect on all the television sets now installed in people's homes?

Clearly, bandwidth is another severe problem. HDTV contains about six to eight times as much information in each frame as does conventional TV. Can this information be crammed into the currently defined channels without degrading the quality, or will more than a single channel be required? If the latter is the case, where will the additional bandwidth come from?

HDTV is not the first new technology to pose compatibility problems. Recall how, back in the 1930s, David Sarnoff rebuffed his erstwhile friend, Edwin Armstrong, over the issue of replacing AM with FM because doing so would have rendered all the radio sets in the nation obsolete. When color TV was first introduced, there were millions of black and white receivers in homes, and the FCC demanded that these old sets be able to receive the color transmissions in black and white. However, color TV did not pose the bandwidth problem of HDTV. While some additional bandwidth was needed to carry the additional color information, the prescribed six-megahertz channels that were carrying the older black and white TV were sufficiently wide to carry the color signals.

Stereo audio recordings were introduced at about the same time as color broadcasting. The millions of existing monaural phonographs created a similar compatibility problem. And, as in the television situation, the technique for impressing stereo signals on records was one that permitted the existing monaural phonographs to extract monaural sound from the new stereo records. The television standard required the approval of the FCC, which was adamant on the subject of compatibility. There is no such regulation in the recording industry. But since radio broadcasting is so important to the recording industry, it was essential that the stereo broadcasting format meet the FCC compatibility demands, and the format chosen permitted the large number of existing monaural FM receivers to receive the FM stereo broadcasts.

The demands of HDTV are so substantial that there is no relatively simple solution such as was found for color TV or FM stereo. Convinced of this fact, the FCC stipulated in 1990 that rather than demanding compatibility in the conventional sense on a single channel, a station broadcasting a program in the HDTV format would be required to broadcast the same program in the older format simultaneously, using separate channels for each broadcast. This approach makes the assumption that the older format will wither away in time as the older TV sets wear out and the bandwidth reserved for serving them can gradually be turned over to the newer format. Initially the FCC left open the question of how much bandwidth would be allowed for the HDTV channel. Later it ruled that the existing channel structure would have to be maintained and that a single six-megahertz channel was all that would be allowed. Since the amount of information in a HDTV frame is six to eight times that in a conventional TV frame, the FCC's ruling demanded that some kind of video compression be used. And, at the same time, it made a digital transmission format all but essential.

The experimental Japanese system bypasses many of these problems. For one thing, it is analog and makes no attempt to be compatible with the existing television format in Japan. It avoids the issue of spectrum limitations by having its own distribution system independent of the standard broadcast stations and cable facilities, one that uses a dedicated satellite broadcasting directly to the home receivers. Its bandwidth is limited only by the limitations of the satellite system. Even then, a small amount of compression is needed to squeeze the HDTV signal into that bandwidth, but far less than would be needed for a system meeting the FCC's bandwidth requirements.

The FCC did more than encourage a digital HDTV standard through its rulings on spectrum utilization and compatibility. It has also been quite explicit in its encouragement of digital schemes in contention for the standard. Many such have been proposed. To select the best scheme among the many contenders, the FCC established a formal technical evaluation. By the time the evaluation was nearing a conclusion in the spring of 1993, all the analog contenders, including one that was a variant of the Japanese system had dropped out. The competition concluded with a Grand Alliance of the residual competitors, combining the best features of each into a hybrid design with all the contending companies receiving a piece of the action.

It is not that compression technology was only introduced in the 1990s as a way of increasing the capacity of existing cables or of making HDTV feasible. Forms of audio compression have been in use since before World War II. And, beginning in the late 1970s, private video conferencing systems were being installed by AT&T and the domestic satellite communications carriers. The conference format inherently limits the amount of motion that can take place. Consequently it is reasonable to expect that more compression is achievable than for motion pictures where rapid motion is the rule. At the extreme is the video telephone where the amount of motion is even more restricted, and where still greater bandwidth reduction can be expected. AT&T introduced its Picturephone on an experimental basis in the late 1960s and discontinued it shortly thereafter. Viewed decades later, it was clearly an idea ahead of its time and technology. Modern technology now makes it feasible at rather nominal costs, which will surely continue decreasing if consumer demand warrants.

There is still another motivation for this emphasis on video compression. Its source is from neither broadcast nor person-to-person communication but, rather, from the recording and computer industries in their desire to store video in digital form on compact discs or other recording media. The use of an optical disc for storing video is not new at all. The laserdisc made its appearance in the late 1970s and was hardly noticed, because it had the misfortune of hitting the market at about the same time as the videotape cassette. Both were analog storage schemes, and while the disc provided somewhat better quality video, its inability to record put it at a severe disadvantage. The laserdisc acquired a new lease on life in the mid 1980s when its sound track was converted from analog to digital. One could now obtain a recording of, say, an opera or Broadway musical with the audio quality of a CD, a significant advantage over the mediocre sound on VCRs. This digital sound rescued the optical medium from complete oblivion.

But there were many other advantages to be derived if the video could be digitized along with the audio. Such digitized video began to appear in the early 1990s with the emergence of more versatile forms of compact discs and associated equipment, known as *multimedia*. In each case, the CD stores graphics, text, and small segments of video as well as audio. This capability is only natural because the disc stores digits, without regard for the source of the digits. They can represent audio as does the CD, but they can also represent text, pictures, and video; it is all the same to the storage medium. One example is called the interactive compact disc, known as CD-I, a proprietary product of Philips. The CD-I player, hooked up to a television set, allows its user to select a variety of entertainment and educational material by interacting with the disc. It is the recording equivalent of the on-line interaction common on computer networks and to which the cable industry aspires.

Another more general approach takes advantage of the fact that the compact disc is a handy way of storing very large amounts of data on a computer. In this form, the CD is customarily called a CD-ROM where the acronym ROM is an old bit of computer terminology standing for *read-only memory*, that is, a memory containing permanent information that cannot be changed. All the computer requires is a drive similar to the audio compact disc player that extracts the digits from the CD-ROM and sends them to the computer. The CD-ROM, like the CD, stores digits. The first CD-ROMs were used for encyclopedic information, largely text but including graphics as well. It was only a matter of time before applications were found for mixes of all sorts of data including audio and video as on the CD-I.

Just as HDTV is dependent on compression to squeeze video signals in the space of a single TV channel, so these storage media based on the compact disc are dependent on compression to squeeze large amounts of video on a single disc. Without compression the CD cannot hold more than a few minutes worth of video. With compression CDs can store from several minutes to two hours depending on the amount of compression and the definition being sought.

Whether it be TV broadcasting or video storage, the same kinds of techniques are used to reduce the amount of information required to represent the moving image. The most intuitive compression techniques are those that compare successive frames and send only those elements of the picture that change. This is the area in which the video conference and especially the video telephone have the most to gain because of the limited amount of motion in these formats. After all, how much can the picture of a single person or a group around a conference table change in the small fraction of a second between frames? But there is also a significant amount to be gained by first examining each frame for redundancies that can be removed without degrading the picture excessively. It should also be noted that some of these compression techniques are reversible, in that the stream of digits can be compressed and then decompressed to recover the original digits without loss of information. Schemes with this property can work on any stream of digits regardless of their source and are often used as a way of expanding the capacity of a computer memory. The thing that almost all the techniques have in common is the ability to be implemented without too much complexity in a digital computer, the factor that appears to make a digital standard inevitable for HDTV.

When new inventions hit the scene, it cannot always be taken for granted that standards will be adopted throughout industry. We have only to recall the warfare between the LP and 45-rpm record formats in the 1940s and between the VHS and BETA video formats thirty years later. Both battles slowed the market penetration of these products as consumers waited to see how it would all come out. In contrast, the rapidity with which the compact disc dominated the audio recording market is a graphic demonstration of the power of standardization. Fortunately, it appears that the digital video industry will be standardized. However, the range of video applications running the gamut from the video telephone at one end to HDTV at the other make it unreasonable to expect that a single standard will suffice for all. Consequently, the industry is establishing two standards, one for full-motion video and a less demanding standard for what is euphemistically called *near-full-motion* video. The full-motion standard includes a range of data rates suitable for conventional and high-definition television. The near-full-motion category covers a range of lower data rates, adequate for the video telephone on one end to high-quality video conferencing on the other.

Still another standard is under development, this one suitable for the transmission of extremely high definition still pictures such as X-ray and magnetic resonance imaging (MRI) photographs. If a very high definition copy of an X-ray photograph could be sent electronically to an expert in a particular medical area regardless of where he or she happened to be, then a patient could have the benefit of a diagnosis by a world-class expert regardless of his or her location. Just as facsimile has revolutionized the office, so this kind of video fax could revolutionize other fields.

Thus, the video medium that began to take the world by storm in the days following World War II continues on its revolutionary path in many new forms. It has transformed the way we are entertained and promises to continue that transformation into the foreseeable future. We have also seen how it is now in the process of fomenting radical change in the structure of the whole communications industry, forcing us to look at both the broadcast and telephone networks in unaccustomed ways. But there is more to communication than video and more to video than entertainment. Above all, the communications media have the ability to inform. Thus, while most of this evolution of our networks is driven by our almost insatiable appetite for entertainment, it would be surprising if these developments did not also have a sizable impact upon the way in which we satisfy our information needs as we approach a new century.

Chapter

31

An Information Infrastructure for the Twenty-First Century

Is the ability to call up movies on demand the modern-day counterpart of Morse's great achievement of substituting communication for transportation? How about the ability to go shopping from the privacy of your living room, or to play a video game with someone half-way around the world, or to talk and view on the videophone? While the answer to each of these questions has to be in the affirmative, there are many who suggest that an example of a significantly more important counterpart is the *virtual library*.

A virtual library is not the library as we have known it for centuries. Gone are the stack after stack filled with books and magazines. In their place are electronic versions stored in the memory of a computer with electronic connections to its subscribers. This library has an elaborate electronic index that you can scan to help you find suggestions of appropriate places to look for the information you are seeking. Select something and the book or article appears on your screen. You can do the equivalent of skimming through the pages to find the text, photographs, tables or diagrams that are of interest to you. In some cases, you can watch the video and listen to the audio included with the text.

An example of such a virtual library is an experimental capability at Cornell University that goes by the name of the Chemistry Online Retrieval Experiment, or CORE.[111] Twenty journals published by the American Chemical Society, including photographs, diagrams, and other figures and tables, are stored in a computer and made available to chemists. When the program first came on-line in 1993, it contained two years worth of the journals with the intent of going back another ten years or so. An important ingredient of CORE is an indexing capability that allows a chemistry researcher to find the information he or she wants by typing in certain key words of the subject of interest, and then retrieving the referenced articles.

CORE is not the only virtual library of this degree of sophistication. There are several others in different subject areas, all oriented toward academic disciplines. Their builders cite many reasons for their desirability. One is convenience; it is just easier to stay in one place rather than roaming around the library stacks. Another is completeness; someone else may have checked out the book or magazine that you need desperately. Also important is the fact that each individual no longer has to subscribe to the journals. The library can serve all.

An even more ambitious concept is the collaborative laboratory, which some have called the *collaboratory*. It carries the virtual library one step further by including data from ongoing experiments. An article in the magazine *Science* describes an example of it in this way:

> Robert Weller has a dream. The Woods Hole Oceanographic Institution oceanographer dreams that one day he will be able to turn on his computer in the morning and transform his office into a global oceanography institute. In his dream, he can bring up data on water temperature, air temperature, wind speeds, currents, air pressure, humidity, salinity, and solar radiation from ocean monitoring devices all across the world— all there at his fingertips and all as fresh as today's catch. Then, without leaving the keyboard, he can analyze this data, borrowing time on a supercomputer that may be halfway across the country. If he wishes, he can link up with colleagues from other institutions to look for patterns in the data and compare the details with predictions from ocean models. Results in hand, he can then instruct the monitoring devices to modify their observations to answer new questions or improve later data.[112]

The collaboratory represents the zenith of scientific collaboration. It links together everything required to carry out an experimental and theoretical program of research by collaborators who may be located anywhere in the world. It may exist only as a dream for many years. Nevertheless, the National Academy of Sciences is of the position that the concept is one that deserves serious consideration. While it sounds extremely ambitious, there is nothing in the concept that does not follow directly from communication and computing capabilities that are either in existence or close to it. I would imagine that one of the main impediments to the widespread implementation of such collaboratories is the perversity of people who might not be so ready to allow others to share their research data.

In one sense, virtual libraries and collaboratories are extensions of electronic databases that already exist on private networks, through the

Internet, or via information service integration companies. However, the level of sophistication of the newer experimental systems, including their ability to provide video, high-resolution photographs, and high-quality graphics, adds another dimension to their potential usefulness and impact. They are, to be sure, academic research projects. Yet it is not difficult to extrapolate from them to generalizations that might be more widely applicable. One rather straightforward application of the collaboratory is to remote medical diagnosis. Just imagine the sensors as devices for taking pulse, blood pressure, electrocardiograms, and temperature and we have the mechanism for doctors at major medical centers to monitor emergency situations quickly and efficiently and then make judgments for the steps to be taken.

The potential for education is also very great. Centralized repositories of educational materials, in the form of text, graphics, audio, and video, can be made available to school districts regardless of their location and regardless of their affluence. No less is the potential impact upon business. If information is not easy to obtain, most of us will continue to be forced to make decisions without it rather than to spend the time and resources to track something down. By bringing information wherever it happens to be to people wherever they happen to be, the virtual library has the potential to boost our productivity and increase our effectiveness in everything we do at work or at home. Morse's telegraph may have made specific pieces of information quickly available, but this generations's communications capabilities have the potential of making everything ever written from literature to lists of products available to all comers. It carries the replacement of transportation by communication to the extreme. It is truly the mountain coming to Mohammed.

The virtual libraries share one thing in common with the entertainment applications: both require two-way communications networks similar to today's telephone systems but with much higher bandwidths from end to end (at least in one direction), or, to use the transportation metaphor, *information superhighways*. Surprisingly enough, this term began to enter the vernacular beginning with the Clinton/Gore presidential campaign of 1992 and then, with the help of the press, blossomed into a buzzword as the new administration began to take over the reins of government. The reason for this political connection had nothing to do with increasing entertainment opportunities. It was, rather, the contention of the candidates that such a capability was of economic importance to the nation's future, based on the impact that services such as virtual libraries might have on education and industrial productivity.

The phrase *information superhighways* might have been strange in a political context, but at least its intent was clear. However, the term was accompanied by another, the *national information infrastructure*, that was anything but clear. Early in the Clinton administration, Congressman Edward J. Markey, chairman of the Subcommittee on Telecommunications and Finance of the House Committee on Energy and Commerce, conceded as much when he began to introduce his speeches with a good news/bad news story. "The good news," he would say, "is that Congress is 100 percent behind the development of a national information infrastructure. The bad news is that nobody has the vaguest idea of what that means. We've got a bit of a dilemma."[113] It comes as hardly a surprise that such an esoteric technical term was not understandable to the average layperson. What is surprising, however, is the fact that the notion of an information infrastructure was so vague even to people in the information field that it was no wonder that Congressman Markey was led to his semiserious joke.

If the term used were *national communications infrastructure*, then there would have been less confusion. It is clear what we mean by communications, and the meaning of a communications infrastructure follows from that definition. It is the sum total of all the nation's communications assets, on which we depend in our business and personal lives. In the days before divestiture, the AT&T network would have been a good approximation to the greater part of this infrastructure. Even in the aftermath of divestiture, the infrastructure is still easy to describe in an understandable way. It includes the public telephone systems, both long-distance and local, and the cellular and other wireless systems, together with the thousands of data networks linked together in the Internet. It also includes the autocratic over-the-air and cable networks and all the private systems, both democratic and autocratic. The worldwide communications infrastructure would add the overseas equivalents.

The phrase *information superhighway* was quite clearly a popular way of describing high-data-rate upgrades to this communications infrastructure. But substituting *information* for *communications* in describing the infrastructure converts a rather clear expression into a vague one subject to a variety of interpretations. For while information includes communication, it also includes other things not nearly as well defined.

I first heard about information superhighways and information infrastructures in a conversation with Bob Kahn in 1985. He told me then that he was about to leave ARPA to start a new venture that had as its goal the fostering of the development of this infrastructure. This infrastructure, in Kahn's view, was as important to the well-being of the nation's economy at the tail end of the century as was the interstate highway system in the postwar decades, and the railroads in the last century. Just as improvements to the transportation infrastructure in previous generations fueled the nation's economy, so an upgrade of this kind to the nation's information infrastructure was essential to facilitating the exchange of information, this generation's counterpart to the goods and services of the past. This conversation was held many years before the CORE and other virtual library projects were conceived. Yet the virtual library was precisely what Kahn had in mind as the kind of application that ubiquitous high-performance computer networks would make possible.

One of Kahn's initial endeavors was the development of very high-speed computer networks. But, as the virtual libraries show, the wires and switches in the communications network are only part of what is needed to make remote information available speedily. Thus, Kahn also focused on all the other elements of an information system that had to accompany the distribution network. Obviously, the databases and other sources of information are part of this infrastructure, and another of his earliest efforts was on the technology of digital libraries. But that is far from all. Just imagine a huge virtual library containing information on not just one subject but many subjects, and not in one location but in hundreds or thousands of locations distributed throughout the network. How is a subscriber to find what he or she wants in this vast marketplace of information? This problem became evident in the Internet by the early 1990s as the number of users grew to the tens of millions. Indeed several systems have been developed—the best known are Gopher, WAIS, and Mosaic/WWW—that allow users to browse databases scattered throughout the world as if they were on a single computer.[114]

But Kahn imagined something more sophisticated: a knowledge robot or *Knowbot* that would function as a kind of automated peripatetic librarian to assist the user in locating the desired information by traveling from database to database.[115] If it's not a Knowbot, then something that does the equivalent is absolutely essential if the information is to be readily available. This "librarian" is probably the most graphic example of a whole class of network services—others include E-mail, protocols for transferring blocks of data from one place to another, and security—that together with the databases convert a communications infrastructure into an information infrastructure. It followed that to build an infrastructure in Kahn's image involved a series of initiatives addressing not only high-speed network technology, but its other elements as well—a formidable task.

Anyone who knows Bob Kahn would expect him to associate the future of communication with data networking, the field around which his world had rotated since the late 1960s, and not simply because of the central role he played in the origins of the ARPANET and all the other activities that stemmed from it. Rather, it is because of his conviction about the importance of computer networking, past, present, and future. To Kahn, computer networking is one of the great innovations in the history of communication.

It is hard to compare the significance of the many innovations that have occurred in this rich and varied history. They are so different in nature. On the one hand, there are the specific devices, such as the telegraph, the telephone, the automatic switch, the television, and the facsimile, the brilliant inventions that marked the course of history. Then there are the inventions in fundamental technology such as the vacuum tube and transistor that were so influential not only in communication but in everything electronic. But there is another kind of invention that has not been given the credit due it: the innovative system concepts. The contention of Morse and the other early telegraphers that if electricity could travel over wires, so could information was the brilliant insight that inspired the invention of the telegraph instruments. In this same category is Bell's concept of universal service, every bit as great a contribution as his telephone instrument. The same holds true for the simple notion that converted the wireless into radio broadcasting and paved the way for television. And when we observe the central role that the computer has assumed in the communications of the latter half of this century, one cannot help but recognize the validity of Kahn's contention about computer networking.

At the time of that conversation in 1985, Kahn had been at ARPA for about thirteen years. During that time he had made data networking into a significant new technology following its ARPANET origins, including getting the Internet underway. Now he was beginning the planning that would make his information infrastructure ideas become a reality.

It was his view that approaching this formidable problem required research and development that only the government would be willing to fund, analogous to the way in which the Defense Department supported the ARPANET. There were many unknowns both in the communications technology required for the high-speed network and in the computer technology relevant to the use of the network. But it was also clear to him that the government should not become involved in building the operational switches and circuits, if only because of the enormous cost. Besides, this activity was properly the entrepreneurship role of the communications industry that would have to bear the great expense of the network upgrades in order to reap its rewards.

Directing research of this nature was not appropriate for an agency such as ARPA. The cold war was still very much with us, and ARPA's mission was to develop cutting-edge technology for defense application. This national infrastructure, while ultimately beneficial to the national defense, was primarily aimed at the nation's economy. Since there was no agency comparable to ARPA in any of the government departments concerned with the civil world, Kahn came to the conclusion that the best place for him to work for his goals was in the private sector. Had these events transpired in 1993 rather than 1985, the answer might have been different, because the Clinton administration modified the agency's mission (and name) to include the development of technology of pertinence to both defense and nondefense needs.

And so Kahn and his longtime colleague Vinton Cerf went ahead to form a not-for-profit company called the Corporation for National Research Initiatives, CNRI for short. From this base, they would attempt to coordinate a research program similar to the way in which they and their colleagues had coordinated the research that led to the ARPANET and its aftermath. Their initial funding came in the form of modest grants from major corporations with a stake in the ultimate value of an information infrastructure. These corporations might disagree with one another on every topic but the utility of a common infrastructure data highway that could serve them all in contributing to the growth of the information industry.

That Kahn achieved some notable success in the next five years is evidenced by the appearance of the unusual jargon in the Clinton/Gore campaign. The prime mover behind this nontraditional political language was Senator Gore, who in his congressional career had championed the cause of science and technology, and who had made the issues associated with upgrading the nation's information infrastructure a personal goal. And, consistent with the campaign rhetoric, the Clinton administration made this project one of its key proposals for long-term economic revival of the nation. Is it not reasonable, they argued, that in the closing years of the century, the ability to move information around rather than people and things should fuel the growth of our information society? And is this ability not one of the keys to prosperity in the next century? The Council on Competitiveness, a nonprofit, nonpartisan organization of chief executives from business, higher education, and organized labor, put it this way: "he information infrastructure of the 21st century will enable all Americans to access information and communicate with each other easily, reliably, securely and cost-effectively in any medium—voice, data, image or video—anytime, anywhere. This capability will enhance the productivity of work and lead to dramatic improvements in social services, education and entertainment."[116] Statements such as these are as much gut feelings as anything else. No one can demonstrate with facts and figures the true dimensions of the effects of this information infrastructure because it is just as unknowable today as were the dimensions of the impact of radio broadcasting when Marconi first broadcast his Morse code signals across the Atlantic. As history has shown, a new capability has to have time to settle in and stimulate ideas.

Kahn and CNRI had achieved some success not only in their interactions with private industry and with Senator Gore but also, to some extent, with the Bush administration. In fact, the first concrete steps toward a national infrastructure was the administration's response to Senator Gore in its proposal for the idea of a *national research and engineering network* (NREN), the research precursor of what later come to be known as an information superhighway. The notion made its formal debut in a report submitted to the Congress by the president's science advisor, D. Allan Bromley, in 1991.[117] Considering President Bush's well-known antipathy toward industrial policy in which the government lends its support to particular areas of the economy, his espousal of this program is indicative of its bipartisan support.

According to the report, "The NREN . . . dramatically expands and enhances the U.S. portion of the worldwide infrastructure of interconnected computer networks called the Internet." The bill making the NREN into law, known familiarly as *Gore-I*, was passed in that same year, with the goal of 1996 for completing its first phase. In sponsoring this bill, Senator Gore was following in the footsteps of his father, a former senator, whose name was prominently associated with an older manifestation of national infrastructure in the interstate highway bill in the 1950s.

The Internet was a natural vehicle for this research program. It was already in a period of rapid expansion throughout the world, now incorporating commercial as well as government and not-for-profit networks. But it still remained a relatively low-speed network. While it might be able to manage a bit of compressed video, supporting any significant amount of video was well beyond its capacity. The expansion and enhancement referred to in the report is to make the existing network into one that can support the transfer of huge amounts of data of all sorts including video and audio, that is, a flexible multimedia network, precisely the vision of Bob Kahn had when he started CNRI.

The Clinton/Gore campaign in 1992, focused as it was on the economy, seized the ideas embodied in the NREN and made it one of its centerpieces for long-term economic growth and competitiveness with a proposal for a five-year, $2-billion program to extend the network to schools, hospitals, and homes. It was then that the national information infrastructure became capitalized into National Information Infrastructure and acquired the acronym NII. And it was then that the major communications carriers began to have second thoughts about the idea. In the days between the election and inauguration, the chairman of AT&T expressed his reservations about government involvement, and, a few months later, when a bill known as Boucher-I (after Congressman Rick Boucher, chairman of the Subcommittee on Science of the House Committee on Science, Space and Technology), based on the administration proposal, was in committee, the CEOs of all the major carriers made a statement that indicated, among other things, their concern that the non-commercial components of the Internet would siphon off revenue that rightly belonged to the carriers.

It was not that they had any disagreement about the eventual emergence of a high-speed multimedia network. Nor had they been reluctant to participate with the other researchers in the experimental high-speed network test beds established under the NREN program. It seemed that when the program gained its new prominence as part of the economic program of a new administration, they were concerned about excessive government involvement in what they regarded as a strictly commercial undertaking. In a commonly held view, the government's role should be limited to issues of national policy such as network security, safeguarding of intellectual property, and, above all, seeing to it that the communications regulators assist and not hinder the efforts of industry.

It is noteworthy that the carriers funded their own participation in these test beds, in contrast to the other participants who were mainly funded by the government. Such self-funding could be interpreted as a demonstration of the fact the carriers were firmly behind the program, but it also could be interpreted as a statement of their special and unique role in the American tradition of private rather than governmental ownership and control of the nation's communications systems. The new administration, in taking a more prominent role, made them uncomfortable.

We have seen how the very few exceptions to this tradition occurred during the Civil War and World War I, times of unquestioned national emergency. Even in the immediate aftermath of the First World War, the Wilson administration was rebuffed by the Congress when it cited national security as the rationale for retaining control of the fledgling wireless industry. It had to revert to a brilliant maneuver involving the private sector to attain its objectives.

Establishment of the ARPANET as a government network was also an exception to the rule, but one with, at best, a tenuous connection to national defense. This time there were no objections from Congress or industry. It was research in brand-new technology, and there was no threat to any existing revenue stream. Had AT&T built such a data network for commercial purposes, there would have been no need for the Defense Department to do so. It was simply the case where Defense Department computer science researchers had a vision lacking in the world of commercial communications. They viewed networking as the next research frontier in their field, and the government's desire to share expensive computer resources provided a convenient funding vehicle. Most significant of all was the fact that it was these computer scientists and not the successors of Alexander Graham Bell and Theodore Vail who had a vision of universal computer connectivity.

Undoubtedly, data networks would have been developed even if the Defense Department had not taken the initiative, but no one can say at what pace it would have happened. There was no demand for the service on the part of the Bell system subscribers, but neither was there in the Defense research community, any more than there was a demand for the telegraph, telephone, or wireless in their time. These things all came about because innovative people had the hunch that the demand would exist once the novel capability was demonstrated. But even if the lack of demand made the management of the Bell system uninterested, it would not have stopped the Bell Laboratories, which, before divestiture, had the freedom to investigate advanced technologies of all kinds.

Once the ARPANET showed the way, nearly all the computer research community, including the Bell Laboratories, got on the bandwagon. But the operating carriers participated only minimally, largely with electronic mail services. The explosion in computer connectivity marked by the initial expansion of the Internet occurred without the efforts of these carriers. It took the computer proliferation induced by the low-cost personal computer to create enough potential customers for the carriers to become interested, and it was this interest that has sparked the even greater recent growth of the Internet. Despite their participation, some carriers view the Internet with an ambivalence that reflects the unortho-dox nature of the network and the culture from which it sprang. Part of this ambivalence stems from a suspicion that much of the E-mail traffic on the government-sponsored networks such as first ARPANET and later NSFNET was due not only to its convenience but to the fact that it was free to its subscribers. These same carrier communicators also have the uneasy feeling that much of the use of E-mail, especially the bulletin boards, is frivolous and bound to decrease if individual users were assessed for the cost of the session as they are for telephone calls. The NSF policy, in fact, changed early in 1993 to require all but the extremely high data-rate users to use commercial networks and pay the regular fees. The NSFNET users greeted this change with a coolness that must have warmed the cockles of the carriers' hearts.[118]

It was his experience with the ARPANET that originally led Kahn to the conclusion that building this infrastructure was too important to the national welfare to be left to the normal processes in which the carriers provide services for which they see sufficient demand. A coordinated program embracing the entire research community as well as the carriers would stimulate this demand. Of course, only the carriers would build the operational networks that would capitalize on this increased demand and derive its revenues. Yet, with this kind of history, it is not surprising that the carriers became suspicious of increased government activity in this area, despite all the protestations that the government has no desire to infringe upon the prerogatives and revenue sources of the carriers. An activist government policy after a century and one-half in which the government's role was limited to regulation was not something to which the industry could adjust very easily. Yet an impartial examination of the issues involved would indicate that the government and industry have roles that are mutually supporting.

Chapter

32

The Way to the New Infrastructure

In all the discussion between the carriers and the government, there was no disagreement about the fact that the information superhighway was to be a multimedia vehicle for transporting both information and entertainment. Although never stated explicitly, it was perhaps the novelty of a single network or set of networks playing the role of today's autocratic and democratic networks that led to some of the suspicion surrounding the government's intentions. The government's interest in the superhighway lay in its informational possibilities. The carriers were, of course, interested in both information and entertainment. But the cost of the superhighway upgrade, estimated to be in the hundreds of billions of dollars, was not only beyond the government but also out of the reach of the carriers unless they were reasonably sure of a market for the services that the superhighway could supply. While in the long term one might expect a demand for broadband information services, in the near term it was clear that only the entertainment possibilities could hope to provide the guaranteed market that could justify such expenditures. Information services, especially high-bandwidth ones, are much more speculative and will have to ride the coattails of entertainment.

Entertainment has two very large advantages over information services in capitalizing on the new superhighway. For one thing, ever since radio broadcasting made its appearance in 1920, there has been a love affair between broadcasting and the public that shows no sign of diminishing. While nobody can predict how well any particular new video product will be accepted, it is reasonably clear that the vendors will find some expansions and variations that meet the public's approval. Just as important is the fact that very little more of the infrastructure than the superhighway itself will be needed to supply all the advanced entertainment services.

Information services lack both of these advantages. The earlier discussion makes it clear that providing information services requires much more of the infrastructure than the communications paths. Then, we do not know how popular these services will become. The numbers of people who now obtain information services through the Internet or the information service companies is much smaller than the number of TV viewers. To be sure, there are some very popular cable services such as home shopping that will become even more popular once they become interactive. However, it is not clear how rapidly the public will respond to other forms of information services, and this is something that will not be known until more of these services—such as virtual libraries that are sophisticated in their own right—are available. There is clearly something of the proverbial chicken and egg situation in which information services must be developed for unknown demands.

Even the most passionate advocates of new information services will have to agree to the reality of this disparity between entertainment and information and to the necessary consequence that the large-scale entry of information onto the superhighway must necessarily lag that of the entertainment services. For example, Bob Kahn likens the scenario of "entertainment first" to the way many people were first introduced to the home computer by the allure of games, but turned to more productive applications once they were able to leap the initial hurdle of learning how to use computers. According to this theory, once consumers become comfortable with using the high-speed multimedia networks in the pursuit of entertainment, they will be more likely to explore information opportunities. Recognition of these facts of life by both industry and government provides the background for understanding the kind of role the government can play. Thus, while it is not appropriate for the government to involve itself in facilitating the building of the superhighway, it can be a powerful advocate for speeding up the information side. And if these information opportunities are as significant as many people think they are, government expenditures to develop them and make them easy to use are of the utmost importance. That is why the high-speed test-bed efforts and the newer applications efforts started under the Clinton administration have so much leverage. Concerted government efforts in these areas do not infringe on the prerogatives of the carriers and should receive their support.

Much of the great expense in evolving toward the superhighway lies in constructing the on- and off-ramps to the information superhighway, the popular metaphoric way of describing the process of upgrading today's local area communications to two-way broadband digital service so that the large bandwidths now available in the heart of the networks can be extended to any subscriber. Probably the greatest contributor to this expense is the formidable job of converting the local telephone and/or cable television plants from copper to optical fibers. Most challenging technically is the task of furnishing the networks—long distance as well as local—with switches appropriate for multimedia data sources. There are some proponents of switches made out of optical components that, therefore, eliminate the problems inherent in converting signals back and forth from optical to electrical forms. Most observers agree, however, that while such switches may be promising in the long term, in the near term the new switches will be electrical following a systems approach known as *asynchronous transfer mode* (ATM), a form of packet switching with parameters making it suitable for the continuous data streams produced by voice and video transmissions as well as for bursty computer data, the application for which packet switching was originally invented.

Enough research and development has been done to assure that the technology necessary for the upgrade will be in hand. Nevertheless, the great expense of this upgrade will prevent it from happening overnight. In the meantime, many favor the widespread adoption of an intermediate approach known as the Integrated Services Digital Network (ISDN), which gains some of the advantages of the superhighway at a much lower cost. The concept of the ISDN has been around since the early 1980s, along with predictions that it would be widely implemented in the 1990s. Its name is a well-chosen one that indicates some of its advantages over the analog state of affairs that has existed for decades. It is *digital* from end to end. In addition, it *integrates* various kinds of services through a single digital connection that does the whole job in place of separate analog phone lines for each computer, telephone and fax machine. Finally—and this is probably the most important in the near term—it provides considerably higher data speeds than ordinarily obtainable over the analog network. It is this latter feature that makes the ISDN a halting first step on the way to the superhighway of the future.

The pace of ISDN implementation has, in fact, been much slower than anticipated, and it is easy to see why. The fact of the matter is that neither digitization nor integration provides a spectacular enough advance over today's digital networks with analog tails to warrant much additional cost to the subscriber. It is only when one gets to new services that can take advantage of the higher data speed of the service that the subscriber becomes really interested. For example, today's computer-based information services could provide their subscribers with much more graphical information and a moderate amount of compressed video with the additional capacity. This same additional capacity could be crucial in the marketing of the video telephone. According to John

Seazholtz of Bell Atlantic (the Baby Bell serving the middle-Atlantic seaboard region), there is a spectacular difference between the quality obtainable over analog circuits and over ISDN, enough to make the difference between acceptability and enthusiasm for the service.

There are some, largely in the computer industry, who are urging the government and industry to adopt an *ISDN first* approach to providing information services on a high speed network. They argue that ISDN can offer, in a more modest way, many of the innovations that the high-speed networks promise, and at a small fraction of the cost because there is no need for optical transmission and the current generation of circuit and packet switches are quite adequate. It provides a vehicle for attacking the chicken- and-egg problem of building information services even while cultivating demand for their use, much of which can be done without the full-blown superhighway.

There are many formidable problems, some of them conceptual, that will take many years to understand and toward the solution of which early experimentation on the ISDN could be very useful. I have already mentioned the problem, exemplified by Kahn's Knowbot, of locating what you want in a network filled with huge amounts of information in unknown locations. Then there is the even more difficult problem of gaining access to what you want and ignoring what you do not want in a vast sea of information. Daily papers are published with a set of features designed to appeal to a variety of tastes. A subscriber could obtain a customized newspaper by diligently selecting from categories of information of interest to him or her. But would it not be helpful if the network could do this for the subscriber based on a knowledge of his or her preferences?

This customized newspaper is one example of the problem of "delegation" as stated by Nicholas Negroponte of MIT.[119] One of his favorite examples of this property is how to set one's alarm clock at the right time to catch an early morning airplane. Today, we have no choice but to do this manually based on the scheduled flight time. But a network full of information should be able to follow changes in the weather and the flight schedules to ring the alarm at precisely the correct time without human intervention. Of course, there is the down side of this kind of capability that will enable on-line advertisers to target specific homes for particular products, the modern equivalent of the earlier quotation from John Brooks that the telephone ". . . impartially disseminates the useful knowledge of scientists and the babble of bores, the affection of the affectionate and the malice of the malicious."[120]

There are hosts of such problems involved in using the huge volumes of information that the superhighway will be able to deliver, some of which the ISDN can provide in a limited way. But the ISDN is only one of many paths to the future, some of which have already been noted. On the cable television side, efforts are underway to provide a limited amount of feedback capability. The telephone companies are beginning to offer video on demand along with both ISDN and conventional analog telephone service. Some carriers would rely on video compression to increase their capacities, while others are beginning to install optical links in a limited way. Thus, while there is the possibility of a straight evolutionary path from ISDN to *broadband ISDN*, as the wideband network is called, it is not likely that the industry will follow any single straight path without many detours.

But regardless of the path or paths ultimately taken to the new information infrastructure, an important thing to keep in mind is the fact that all its potential benefits are for all the people, for the socially and economically disadvantaged as well as for the affluent and intellectual elite. Just as it is appropriate for the government to add its support to the development of information applications, so the government, at the national or local level, may deem it proper to underwrite some of the cost of bringing information to all similar to its support to public schools and libraries. Still another function of government, often underestimated, is to find a legal mechanism to protect the investments of the creators of the virtual libraries and similar information banks, the problem closely related to protecting the creators of music recorded on compact discs that I referred to earlier. Without such protection the information infrastructure will never achieve its potential.

As long as human society has existed there have been divisions based on social and economic considerations. The modern world has introduced still another division, this one based on technical sophistication, knowledge, and aptitude. And it is just as important that the accessibility of the new information infrastructure should not be impeded by this kind of barrier as by social and economic barriers. Computer literacy is one aspect of a technical barrier. While many citizens have joined the computer age, more have not. For the new infrastructure to achieve its potential, the use of computers and computer networks has to complete the transition from being a tool of computer buffs to a tool of Everyman.

With the proper planning, the "entertainment first" approach can assist in this transition. Note that the CD-I player attaches to a television set, not a computer. Similarly, in taking its first halting steps to interactive TV, the cable company supplies a little box to be attached to the television set with computerlike functions but much simpler to use. The same computers that will be incorporated into the new television sets to take advantage of the new entertainment possibilities should be the interface to the information services that will follow. Almost everyone regardless of his or her station in life somehow manages to bring a television set into the house even when its cost runs to hundreds of dollars. For many, the digital television set will be their first use of computers, and hopefully it will be a salutary one. But just because the software has entertainment at its origin is not a guarantee of user-friendly design. We have only to note how the videocassette recorder has become the metaphor for difficult-to-use technology. Millions of people own VCRs but shy away from programming them, not so much because it is so difficult for anyone to read the operating manual and follow the necessary steps, but because the sequence of steps is more complex than it has to be, and the instructions in the operating manual are less clear than they might be. One has the feeling that if the designers of the VCRs really cared whether their customers were able to program them, they could have devised a simpler system. The VCR experience points out how important software is. It proves that even an industry such as the entertainment industry whose products are geared to appeal to the masses does not always pay enough attention to the needs of its users.

The NII and, of course, its global counterpart will live up to their potential only if software is given appropriate emphasis in the years to come. Unquestionably, the major technological influence on communication in the latter half of this century has been the computer, more accurately, computer hardware, where the revolutionary advances from vacuum tubes to transistors to integrated circuits to microprocessors has turned the economics of information handling on its head. Software, too, has advanced over this time period. After all, millions of people are using such sophisticated programs as word processors and spreadsheets without having to understand very much about how they work. Yet, when viewed in comparison to the hardware advances, these software advances are more properly characterized as evolutionary than revolutionary.

The situation today with computers is perhaps comparable to the state of radio in the early 1920s. Now, as then, in addition to the professional users we have a sizable group of hobbyists. Only now their passion is the personal computer instead of the amateur radio. Recall how commercial broadcasting grew out of the casual broadcasting habits of the amateurs, but that before it could really catch on with the masses, certain technological changes were necessary. To the amateurs, the act of communicating was only part of the objective. They were just as interested in tweaking their crystal sets to obtain the best possible reception as they were in the contents of what they were receiving. Once broadcasting went commercial, the amateurs were joined by average people who were interested in the content, not in the technology. The crystal sets that the amateurs built for themselves were completely unsuitable for the listeners interested in *Amos and Andy* or the *Cliquot*

Club Eskimos. These nonhobbyists had to have the reliability of vacuum tube radios.

In similar fashion, the Internet started out as a tool of computer science researchers, but over the years began admitting other communities to the club, reaching the point in the late 1980s where commercial networks were allowed to join. A great deal of information is available over the Internet, but the majority of its subscribers use only the E-mail services. Indeed, some of the commercial connections are for E-mail only. Since the other services are so difficult to use and since there was no particular attempt to help users surmount the hurdles, few other than professionals and dedicated hobbyists were able to take advantage of them. Today's equivalent of converting radios from crystals to vacuum tubes lies in building new generations of computer software that make the sophisticated capabilities inherent in the information infrastructure truly accessible to everyone. Even though people joke about and sometimes curse at the difficulty of using VCRs, they still use them. In view of our almost insatiable desire for entertainment, it seems inevitable that the entertainment part of the new communications world is almost sure to generate popularity even if it is not as easy to use as it might be. But whether the informational and educational promise in the new infrastructure lives up to its potential depends on how convenient the capabilities are to use. We can only hope that the entertainment industry has learned a lesson from the VCR.

Robert Lucky, a senior research executive at Bellcore, the organization that performs research and development for the Baby Bells, adds a different perspective to the software issue.[121] He points out that the world is moving toward information systems meeting standards that are common throughout the world. Every nation will have the same hardware and its underlying systems software. As we move into the next century, the single thing that will distinguish one nation's information systems from another's will be the applications that make use of these systems, the things that we call applications software. It is the applications software in VCRs that make programming them so complex. And it is applications software that will make virtual libraries and other things like them easy or cumbersome to use.

The history of communications has demonstrated time and again how each technological advance has brought about unexpected applications, perhaps not immediately, but eventually, as the users became accustomed to the potentialities of the new technology. As sophisticated as these hardware advances might have been, their conceptual simplicity made them easy to apply and use. Our ability to continue in this tradition will depend, in large measure, on how successful we are in developing sophisticated software that will allow ordinary people to take maximum advantage of the information infrastructure of the next century.

The potential is there. Whether or not it leads to societal change comparable to that resulting from the development of the telegraph, the telephone, and the wireless in their days remains to be seen.

Notes

[1]   Robert Luther Thompson, *Wiring a Continent: The History of the Telegraph Industry in the United States 1832-1836*, Princeton University Press, Princeton, N.J., 1947. This book was the principal source for much of the early history of the telegraph in this chapter.

[2]   Quoted by Thompson, ibid.

[3]   Daniel J. Czitrom describes the use of this term in *Media and the American Mind: From Morse to McLuhan*, University of North Carolina Press, Chapel Hill, 1982.

[4]   Thompson, *Wiring a Continent*.

[5]   For a the history of the American postal system, see, for example, Wayne E. Fuller, *The American Mail*, University of Chicago Press, Chicago, 1972.

[6]   For the interesting story of the attempts to lay a cable across the Atlantic, see Harry Field, *The Story of the Atlantic Telegraph*, Charles Scribner's Sons, New York, 1893.

[7]   Ibid.

[8]   Quoted by Thompson, *Wiring a Continent*.

[9]   Daniel R. Headrick, *The Tools of Empire*, Oxford University Press, New York, 1981.

[10]   For a more detailed discussion of the influence of the telegraph and the railroad upon each other see Alfred Dupont Chandler, *The Visible Hand: The Managerial Revolution in American Business*, Belknap Press, Cambridge, Mass., 1977.

[11]   Thompson, *Wiring a Continent*.

[12]   Alexander James Field, "The Magnetic Telegraph, Price and Quantity Data, and the New Management of Capital," *Journal of Economic History*, June 1992, pp. 401-13.

[13]   Ibid.

[14]   Kenneth D. Garbade and William L. Silber, "Technology, Communication and the Performance of Financial Markets: 1840-1975," *The Journal of Finance*, vol. 33, no. 3, June 1978.

[15]   This brief account of the origins of the modern newspaper was derived largely from the *Encyclopedia Brittanica*, William Benton, Publisher, Chicago, 1965.

[16]   E. D. Peek, "The Necessity and Use of Electrical Communications on the Battlefield," *Journal of the Military Service Institution of*

the United States, vol. 49, Dec. 1911. (Reprinted in *Military Signal Communications*, vol. 2, edited and with an introduction by Paul J. Scheips, Arno Press, New York, 1980.)

[17] Adolphus W. Greely, "The Military Telegraph Service," *Journal of the Military Service Institution of the United States*, vol. 12, Nov. 1891. (Reprinted in *Military Signal Communications*, vol. 1, edited and with an introduction by Paul J. Scheips, Arno Press, New York, 1980.)

[18] Ibid.

[19] Max Marshall, editor, *The Story of the U.S. Army Signal Corps*, F. Watts, New York, 1965.

[20] C. F. C. Beresford, "The Field Telegraph, Its Use in War and Its Employment in the Late Expeditions in the Soudan and South Africa," *Journal of the Royal United Service Institution*, vol. 30, no. 135, 1936. (Reprinted in *Military Signal Communications*, vol. 2, edited and with an introduction by Paul J. Scheips, Arno Press, New York, 1980.)

[21] Lonsdale A. Hale, "Tactics as Affected by Field Telegraphy," *Journal of the Royal United Service Institution*, vol. 313, no. 140, 1887. (Reprinted in *Military Signal Communications*, vol. 2, edited and with an introduction by Paul J. Scheips, Arno Press, New York, 1980.)

[22] Much of the early history of the telephone was derived from John Brooks, *The Telephone: The First Hundred Years*, Harper and Row, New York, 1975; and Robert V. Bruce, *Bell: Alexander Graham Bell and the Conquest of Solitude*, Little Brown & Co., Boston, 1973. For a good but elementary description of the history of the technology of communications systems with particular emphasis on telephone systems, see John R. Pierce and A. Michael Noll, *Signals: the Science of Telecommunications*, Scientific American Library, New York, 1990.

[23] Brooks, *The Telephone*.

[24] Bruce, *Bell*, and Ira Flatow, *They All Laughed*, HarperCollins, New York, 1992.

[25] Quoted by Ithiel de Sola Pool in *The Telephone's First Century— and Beyond*, Thomas J. Crowell Company, New York, 1977.

[26] Ithiel de Sola Pool, "Social Effects of the Telephone," and Asa Briggs, "The Pleasure Telephone," both in *The Social Aspect of the Telephone*, Ithiel De Sola Pool, editor, MIT Press, Cambridge, Mass., 1977.

[27] Ithiel de Sola Pool et al., "Foresight and Hindsight: The Case of the Telephone," in *The Social Impact of the Telephone*, Ithiel de Sola Pool, editor, MIT Press, Cambridge, Mass., 1977.

[28] Neil H. Wasserman tells the story of this invention and how it came to symbolize the distinction between the new mathematically oriented discipline of electrical engineering and empirical invention in *From Invention to Innovation*, The Johns Hopkins University Press, Baltimore, 1985.

[29] Karl L. Wildes and Nilo Lundgren, *A Century of Electrical Engineering and Computer Science at MIT, 1882-1982*, MIT Press, Cambridge, Mass. and London, England, 1985.

[30] de Sola Pool et al., "Foresight and Hindsight".

[31] Charles R. Perry, "The British Experience 1876-1912: The Impact of the Telephone during the Years of Delay," in *The Social Impact of the Telephone*, Ithiel de Sola Pool, MIT Press, Cambridge, Mass., 1977.

[32] Ibid.

[33] Jacques Attali and Yves Stourdze, "The Birth of the Telephone and Economic Crisis: The Slow Death of Monologue in French Society," in *The Social Impact of the Telephone*, Ithiel de Sola Pool, MIT Press, Cambridge, Mass., 1977.

[34] Quoted by de Sola Pool in *The Telephone's First Century*.

[35] Sidney H. Aronson, "Bell's Electrical Toy: What's the Use? The Sociology of Early Telephone Usage," in *The Social Impact of the Telephone*, Ithiel de Sola Pool, editor, MIT Press, Cambridge, Mass., 1977.

[36] Brooks, *The Telephone*.

[37] Claude S. Fischer, *America Calling: A Social History of the Telephone to 1940*, University of California Press, Berkeley, 1992.

[38] Ibid.

[39] Ibid.

[40] Brooks, *The Telephone*.

[41] Fischer, *America Calling*.

[42] Ibid.

[43] Quoted by de Sola Pool in *The Telephone's First Century*.

[44] Information on the early history of the wireless was derived from Degna Marconi, *My Father, Marconi*, McGraw Hill Book Company, New York, 1962; and from Susan J. Douglas, *Inventing American Broadcasting 1899-1922*, The Johns Hopkins University Press, Baltimore, 1987.

[45] Quoted in the *IEEE Spectrum*, December 1974, p. 50.

[46] Marconi, *My Father*.

[47] Thomas S. W. Lewis, *Empire of the Air*, HarperCollins, New York, 1991, provides good insight into the personality and work of De Forest.

[48] James E. Brittain, *Alexanderson. Pioneer in American Electrical Engineering*, The Johns Hopkins University Press, Baltimore, 1992, is a recent biography.

[49] Feeling that the American Institute of Electrical Engineers (AIEE) was insufficiently receptive to the new radio technology, the early radio professionals founded the Institute of Radio Engineeers (IRE) in 1912. The two professional societies merged in 1963 to form the Institute of Electrical and Electronic Engineers (IEEE).

[50] John H. Davis, Neil F. Dinn, and Warren E. Falconer in "Technologies for Global Communications," *IEEE Communications Magazine*, Oct. 1992, note that the cost of a three-minute transatlantic phone call started out at $75 in 1927 dropping to $30 by 1930. With the installation of the first transatlantic cable, the price dropped to $12 as the quality improved. Today's prices are well under $10, less than 10 percent of the 1956 price when inflation is taken into account.

[51] Lucien Capone Jr., "C3 Challenges in the 1980s," address delivered to the Fort Monmouth, N. J. chapter of the Armed Forces Communications and Electronics Association, November, 1980.

[52] A rather complete discussion of the role of communications in World War I is given in *The Story of the U.S. Army Signal Corps*, Max Marshall, editor, F. Watts, New York, 1965; and a somewhat briefer account in the *Historical Sketch of the Signal Corps (1860–1941)*, Eastern Signal Corps School, Fort Monmouth, N.J., 1942.

[53] Douglas, *Inventing American Broadcasting*. Her story ends in 1922 when radio broadcasting was about to take off. Good accounts of the events that followed are given in George H. Douglas, *The Early Days of Radio Broadcasting*, McFarland, Jefferson, N.C., 1987; and Eric Barnouw, *Tube of Plenty: The Evolution of American TV*, Oxford University Press, Oxford and New York, 1975.

[54] Lewis, in *Empire*, provides a detailed account of the events to follow.

[55] Lewis, in *Empire,* treats Sarnoff's career in detail.

[56] Douglas, *Inventing American Broadcasting*.

[57] Douglas, *Inventing American Broadcasting*.

[58] Douglas, *The Early Days of Radio Broadcasting*.

[59] Lewis, *Empire*.

[60] *The International World of Electronic Media*, by Lynne Schafer Gross, McGraw-Hill Book Company, New York, 1995, describes broadcasting in several countries. An excellent description of the

evolution of broadcasting in the United Kingdom is found in Chapter 4 by Brian T. Evans.

[61] The early struggles between Zworykin and Farnsworth are described in Christopher H. Sterling and John M. Kitross, *Stay Tuned*, Wadsworth Publishing Company, Belmont, Calif., 1990.

[62] Lewis, in *Empire*, describes Armstrong's life and career.

[63] Barnouw, in *Early Days*, gives a good description of these and other events in the history of television broadcasting.

[64] Quoted by Herbert I. Schiller in *Mass Communications and American Empire*, Beacon Press, Boston, 1969.

[65] Gross, *International World*.

[66] Alex S. Jones, "Rethinking Newpapers," *The New York Times*, Jan. 6, 1991.

[67] For a detailed exposition of the arguments against the video telephone, see A. Michael Noll, "Anatomy of a Failure: Picturephone Revisited," *Telecommunications Policy*, vol. 16, no. 4, May/June 1992.

[68] Robert Watson-Watt, *Pulse of Radar*, Dial Press, New York, 1959.

[69] Arthur C. Clarke, "Extra-Terrestrial Relays," *Wireless World*, vol. 51, no. 10, Oct. 1945. (Reprinted in *Progress in Astronautics and Aeronautics*, vol. 19: *Communications Satellite Systems and Technology*, R.B. Marsten, editor, 1966.)

[70] For more detail on the key events in the early history of the communications satellite, see John R. Bittner, *Broadcasting and Telecommunication, An Introduction*, Prentice-Hall, Englewood Cliffs, N.J., 1985.

[71] The contest over the invention of the first computer is described in detail in Alice Burks and Arthur Burks, *The First Electronic Computer: The Atanasoff Story*, University of Michigan Press, Ann Arbor, 1988.

[72] For a nontechnical discussion of digital and analog concepts see Irwin Lebow, *The Digital Connection: A Layman's Guide to the Information Age*, W. H. Freeman and Co., New York, 1990.

[73] Gloria B. Lubkin, "John Bardeen," *Physics Today*, vol. 45, No. 4, April 1992, the introductory article in a special issue devoted to Bardeen shortly after his death.

[74] Quoted by T. R. Reid in *The Chip*, Simon and Schuster, New York, 1984.

[75] Conyers Herring, "Reflections from the Early Years of Solid-State Physics," *Physics Today*, vol. 45, no. 4, April 1992, pp. 26–33.

[76] Ira Flatow tells this story in *They All Laughed*, HarperCollins, New York, 1992.

[77] From "Three Men Who Changed Our World—25 Years Later," *Bell Laboratories Record*, Dec. 1972.

[78] Reid, *The Chip*.

[79] The detailed story of the invention of the integrated circuit is given in Fred Warshofsky, *The Chip War: The Battle for the World of Tomorrow*, Charles Scribner's Sons, New York, 1989.

[80] Ibid.

[81] John Naisbitt, *Megatrends*, Warner Books, Inc., New York, 1982.

[82] A. W. Burks, H. Goldstine, and J. von Neumann, "Preliminary Discussion of the Logical Design of an Electronic Computing Instrument," The Institute for Advanced Study, Princeton, N.J., 1947.

[83] The story is told in detail by Reid, *The Chip*.

[84] Max D. Hopper, "Rattling SABRE—New Ways to Compete on Information," *Harvard Business Review*, May-June 1990, pp. 118–125.

[85] For a survey of airline reservation systems, see the report by the U.S. Department of Transportation, "Study of Airline Computer Reservations Systems," DOT-P-37-88-2, May 1988.

[86] The name of this organization has varied over the time of its existence. It started out as ARPA, whence the name of the network. Later, the Defense Department added the word "Defense" to the name and the letter "D" to the acronym to remind the world who controlled the agency. Then, once the cold war was over, when the Clinton administration wanted DARPA to stress technology of importance to both defense and civil applications, the "D" was dropped and the original name restored.

[87] The beginnings of the ARPANET and of packet communications are described in L. G. Roberts, "The Evolution of Packet Switching," *Proceedings of the IEEE*, vol. 66, no. 11, Nov. 1978, pp. 1307–1313, (special issue on packet communication networks).

[88] Paul Baran et al., "On Distributed Communications, Vol. I–XI," RAND Corporation Research Documents, Aug. 1964.

[89] D. W. Davies et al., "A Digital Communications Network for Computers Giving Rapid Response at Remote Terminals," ACM Symposium on Operating Systems Principles, Oct. 1967.

[90] L. G. Roberts, "Multiple Computer Networks and Intercomputer Communication," ACM Symposium Operating System Principles, Oct. 1967.

[91] For a brief history of the facsimile, see Jonathan Coopersmith, "Facsimile's False Starts," *IEEE Spectrum*, vol. 30, no. 2, Feb. 1993, pp. 46–49.

[92] For a discussion of digital transmission and its implications, see Lebow, *The Digital Connection*.

[93] Claude E. Shannon and Warren Weaver, *The Mathematical Theory of Communication*, University of Illinois Press, Urbana, 1949.

[94] Jeremy Campbell, *Grammatical Man: Information, Entropy, Language, and Life*, Simon and Schuster, New York, 1982.

[95] Claude E. Shannon, "The Bandwagon," *IEEE Transactions on Information Theory*, vol. IT-2, no. 3, 1956, p. 3.

[96] For a technical discussion of the compact disc, see Ken C. Pohlmann, *Principles of Digital Audio*, Howard W. Sams & Co., Indianapolis, 1985. See Lebow, *Digital Connection*, for a more popular discussion.

[97] For a readable treatment of lightwave technology, see A. Michael Noll, *Introduction to Telephones & Telephone Systems*, Artech House, Boston, 1991.

[98] For a detailed discussion of the history of fiber optics, see C. David Chaffee, *The Rewiring of America: The Fiber Optics Revolution*, Academic Press, Harcourt Brace Jovanovich, Boston, 1988.

[99] For a history of switching in the Bell system, see A. E. Joel, Jr., et al., *A History of Engineering and Science in the Bell System: Switching Technology (1925–1975)*, Bell Telephone Laboratories, 1982. A good discussion of switching that is less technical and more suited to lay readers can be found in Pierce and Noll, *Signals*.

[100] Quoted in Fred W. Henck and Bernard Strassburg, *A Slippery Slope: The Long Road to the Breakup of AT&T*, Greenwood Press, New York, 1988.

[101] Peter Temin with Louis Galambos, *The Fall of the Bell System: A Study in Prices and Politics*, Cambridge University Press, Cambridge, UK, 1987.

[102] For greater detail on the events leading up to this decision and its aftermath from the FCC's point of view, see Henck and Strassbourg, *A Slippery Slope*; from AT&T's point of view, see *The Deal of the Century: The Breakup of AT&T*, Steve Coll, Atheneum, New York, 1986; from MCI's point of view, see *On The Line: The Men of MCI—Who Took on AT&T, Risked Everything, And Won!* Larry Kahaner, Warner Books, New York, 1986. Temin, *The Fall*, provides the scholarly analysis of an economic historian.

[103] Henck and Strassburg, *A Slippery Slope*.

[104] Coll, *Deal of the Century*.

[105] Henck and Strassburg, *A Slippery Slope*.

[106] Ibid.

[107] Temin, *The Fall*.

[108] For a semitechnical discussion of video compression technology, see: "Video compression Makes Big Gains," *IEEE Spectrum*, Oct. 1991; and Ronald K. Jurgen, "Digital Video," *IEEE Spectrum*, March 1992.

[109] For a detailed discussion, see K. Blair Benson and Donald G. Fink, *HDTV: Advanced Television for the 1990s*, Intertext Publications, McGraw-Hill Book Co., New York, 1991.

[110] For a discussion of the pros and cons of government intervention in this field, see Cynthia Beltz, *High-Tech Maneuvers: Industrial Policy Lessons of HDTV*, The AEI Press, Washington, D.C., 1991.

[111] Larry Krumenaker, "Virtual Libraries, Complete with Journals, Get Real," *Science*, vol. 260, May 21, 1993, pp. 1066–1067.

[112] William A. Wulf, "The Collaboratory Opportunity," *Science*, vol. 261, Aug. 13, 1993. See also Robert Pool, "Beyond Data Bases and E-Mail," *Science*, vol. 261, August 13, 1993.

[113] *New Technology Week*, Washington, D.C., Monday, May 17, 1993.

[114] Gopher was developed at the University of Minnesota Computing Center. The Wide-Area Information Server (WAIS) was developed by a consortium led by Brewster Kahle from Thinking Machines, Inc. Mosiac is from the National Center for Supercomputing Applications at the University of Illinois and is based on the World Wide Web (WWW) developed at the European Particle Physics Laboratory CERN in Geneva by a team led by Tim Berners-Lee. The functionality of these systems is described by Bruce R. Schatz and Joseph B. Hardin in "NCSA Mosaic and the World Wide Web: Global Hypermedia Protocols for the Internet," *Science*, vol. 265, Aug. 12, 1994, pp. 895–901.

[115] The term *Knowbot* is copyrighted by the Corporation for National Research Initiatives (CNRI).

[116] The Council on Competitiveness, "Vision of a 21st Century Information Infrastructure," Washington, D.C., May 1993.

[117] "Grand Challenges: High Performance Computing and Communications," A Report by the Committee on Physical, Mathematical, and Engineering Sciences to Supplement the President's Fiscal Year 1992 Budget.

[118] Christopher Anderson, "The Rocky Road to a Data Highway," *Science*, vol. 260, May 21, 1993, pp. 1064 ff.

[119] Nicholas Negroponte, "The Present and Future of Multimedia Applications," MIT Seminar Series, Washington, D.C., Nov. 16, 1993.

[120] Brooks, *The Telephone*.

[121] Keynote address at the Defense Information Systems Agency Systems Engineering Conference, Fairfax, Virginia, June 1, 1993.

Index

and drama, 121; and music, 120; and opera, 122; beginning of commercial broadcasting, 116; cable, see Cable Television; first transatlantic broadcast, 135; influence on motion pictures, 122; influence on news, 117, 118; influence on newspapers, 119; influence on society, 117ff; influence on sports, 121; near-full-motion, 270; shopping services, 258; transition from radio, 108

Telex, 196
Teller, Edward, 167
TELPAK, 229
Telstar, 135
Tesla, Nikola, 74
Tesla coil, 74
Texas Instruments Company, 159, 160, 162, 163, 170
Thoreau, Henry David, 15, 56
Time-sharing, 179
Titanic, 83, 99, 101
Tizard, Henry, 131
Toll broadcasting, 105, 254
Toscanini, Arturo, 104
Transatlantic telephone cable, 156
Transatlantic radio service, 80
Transconductance, 158
Transistor, 154, 155–64, 222, 277; junction, 158; point-contact, 158
Transistor radio, 159
Transmission Control Protocol/Internet Protocol (TCP/IP), 190, 197
Transoceanic fiberoptic cable, 220
Transportation Command, 188
Transresistance, 158
Treasury Department, 9, 10
Treaty of Ghent, 25
Triode, 86, 87, 98, 103, 114
Truman, President Harry, 146, 227
Tunney Law, 240, 241
Two-way broadband digital service, 284
Tymnet, 189
Tyranny of numbers, 161

U

U.S. Centennial Exposition, 39
U.S. v. AT&T, 236–40
Underwater telephone cable, 133
Unisys Corporation, 146
United Kingdom, 44, 68, 78,; and broadcasting, 104, 119, 121; and radar, 127ff
United States and imperialism, 80
United States Central Command, 188
UNIVAC, 146, 147, 152
Universal connectivity, 39, 40
Universal service, 37, 233, 277

University of Bologna, 68
University of Pennsylvania, Moore School, 147–49, 151, 167
USA Today, 200

V

Vacuum tube, 45, 65, 85, 86, 87, 98, 153, 157, 160, 277; influence on the computer, 145; oscillator, 77; triode, 86, 87, 98,103, 114
Vail, Alfred, 9, 10, 37
Vail, Theodore, 37, 38, 40, 46, 49, 229, 230, 233, 242, 253, 281, Plate 7
Value Added Networks, 189
Valve, 149
Van Buren, President Martin, 10
Variable resistance microphone, 35, 36
Very-large-scale integration, 164, 166
VHS, 265, 270
Victor Emmanuel, 25
Video cassette recorder (VCR), 258, 265, 269, 288, 289
Video compression, 268, 287
Video conferencing, 123, 270
Video store, 258
Video telephone, 61, 123, 124, 268, 270
Vietnam War, 29, 118
Virtual library, 272, 273, 274, 276, 289
Visible speech, 33
Voice of America, 20
Volta, Alessandro, 8
von Neumann, John, 167, 168, 169, Plate 21; machine, 168, 169, 170

W

Waddy, Judge Joseph, 236
WAIS, 276
Walden, 15
Wall Street Journal, 200
War of 1812, 25
Watergate, 117, 118, 148, 237
Waterloo, Battle of, 18
Watson, Thomas, 45
Watson-Watt, Robert, 129ff
WEAF, 105, 106
Weather bureau, 200
Weinberger, Caspar, 238
Western Electric Co., 41, 219, 220, 227, 230, 236–39, 250
Western Union, 3, 14, 23, 26, 32, 34ff, 48, 201
Westinghouse, 98, 99, 101, 102
Wheeler, William, 218
White, Abraham, 75
Whiteman, Paul, 104
Wide-area networks, 191
Wilson, President Woodrow, 49, 95

Wireless, 65ff, 94ff, 105, 106, 109, 114, 126, 127
Wireless Telegraph and Signal Ltd., 73
WJZ, 106
World radio conference in 1906, 83
World War I, 49, 57, 74, 84, 85ff, 280; influence of radio, 88
World War II, 14, 59; influence of radar, 126ff
Worldwide Military Command and Control System (WMMCCS), 186, 187; Intercomputer Network (WIN), 187, 188

X

X-ray, 271

Y

Yellow Pages, 251
Young, Owen D., 97–99, 105

Z

Zapmail, 199
Zworykin, Vladimir, 109, Plate 17